# Yorkshire's 30 Championships

## 1893 - 2001

Paul E. Dyson

ADELPHI
CRICKET
PRESS

*Yorkshire's 30 Championships*

First Published in Great Britain 2002

© Paul E. Dyson, 2002

British Library Cataloguing-in-Publication Data.
A catalogue record for this book is available from the British Library.

ISBN 0 9522771 3 1

**Front cover**: *Darren Lehmann holds the Lord's Taverners Trophy as Yorkshire are crowned Cricinfo County Champions for 2001 at Scarborough. Photo: David Williams/Photogenic.*

**Back cover**: *The Yorkshire Championship-winning team of 1968: From left: back row – J.H.Hampshire, A.G.Nicholson, R.A.Hutton, D.Wilson, D.E.V.Padgett, P.J.Sharpe; front row – J.G.Binks, F.S.Trueman, D.B.Close (capt.), R.Illingworth, K.Taylor. It marked the end of an era.*

# Contents       Page

*Yorkshire captain David Byas holds the Lord's Taverners Trophy at Scarborough, after winning the 2001 Cricinfo County Chamoionship, with Peter Griffiths (Cricinfo Managing Director) and Andrew Hall (Head of Marketing) on the left and right, respectively. Photo courtesy: Paul McGregor/Cricinfo.*

# Foreword

By David Byas

I first played for Yorkshire in 1986 and it was soon made obvious to me, especially by members and senior players, that 18 years without winning the Championship was too long a period. The weight of hope and expectation was overwhelming, even more so that the Club had just been through the most controversial period in its history. The 1970s had thrown up not a single trophy from the four on offer in most seasons and winning the John Player League in 1983 had been little compensation for finishing in bottom place in the Championship for the only time since the competition's formation in 1890.

Fortunately, under the leadership of new captain Phil Carrick, a corner was turned in 1987, although I was not to play a part in it. We won the Benson & Hedges Cup and finished eighth in the Championship – our best position for six years. I returned to the side in the following season and started to establish myself in a team more optimistic than for several years. Unfortunately, because of the Yorkshire-born ruling, we were usually competing against counties with overseas players of quality and that put us at a permanent disadvantage. Phil tried to change this but lost the captaincy and this was passed on to Martyn Moxon.

Martyn led us for six years and for his final season we had Michael Bevan from Australia to bolster our line-up. I had gained my coveted county cap in 1991, the season before our first overseas signing, but 1995 was the first time we had a foreign player to make a valuable contribution. We reached the quarter-finals of the Benson & Hedges Cup, the semi-finals of the NatWest Trophy and our Championship position (eighth) was the best for eight years. Even so Martyn felt that, having won nothing in six years, it was time to hand over the reins and he resigned after the end of that promising season.

So the leadership of our county team was offered to me and I accepted immediately. There was no doubt that it would be a challenge but no one would turn down the opportunity to captain the best of all counties. However

I believed that the foundation of success had been laid and that it would not be too long in coming.

It was longer than I thought, and my first five seasons in charge were riddled with near-misses and dramatic failures when a trophy was just in sight. 1996 was a case in point; it was my first campaign at the helm and we improved on our Championship position by two places, our Sunday League position by nine places but lost two semi-finals – both to Lancashire at Old Trafford.

Frustratingly, it continued in the same way; we reached four more semi-finals, but when we actually won one, in the Benson & Hedges Cup in 1999, we played so abysmally at Lord's that not only did Gloucestershire romp home by 124 runs but we allowed them to score faster than any team in any final before, or since.

Another runners-up spot came our way in the following year when we finished second in the new National League and that would also have been our final position in the Championship had we not been ridiculously fined for a 'poor' pitch for our game against Surrey on my home ground at Scarborough. Still no trophies but consistency was coming.

2001 dawned with a new coach – Australian Wayne Clark. None of us knew much about him but we were soon won over by his method and approach. Within a month we were top of the Championship table – nothing new in that, even in recent times – but this time we stayed there. The momentum seemed unstoppable as we continually piled on the runs and bowled out most of the opposition that came our way. The eventual clinching moment, towards the end of August, was a swirling catch that came in my direction; after it hung in the air for what seemed like an eternity I gratefully clung on to it and was immediately surrounded by my ecstatic team-mates.

In the post-match aftermath I thought how it would be satisfying to win even more titles. However, since that time I have reflected further and decided that the 2001 season would be my last. I, along with the rest of the squad, had given our supporters a season to remember and it seemed right that that would be the final memory of my career. We are Champions once again.

# Introduction

The inspiration for this volume was a book with a similar title – *Yorkshire's 22 Championships* – by E.L.Roberts, published in 1949. In many ways this book is an updated version but also differs in certain respects.

The main aims of this book are to provide a history of the County Championship and detail on how Yorkshire won the title outright on the thirty occasions on which they have achieved this. As most readers will surely be aware, this figure of thirty is easily a record, Surrey being the current runners-up with a mere 17 outright Championships.

The statistical details provided on Yorkshire's first 29 Championships are kept to a minimum. Only the top five counties for each season are tabulated and merely the bare essentials of these are given. The various points systems in operation are not given in full detail as these were often very cumbersome. The numbers of matches won, lost and drawn as well as the final total of points and (if relevant) average are felt to be the only essential items in order to gain a meaningful comparison between the performance of Yorkshire and the other leading counties.

The qualification for the averages tables are 750 runs, 50 wickets and 20 catches with the proviso that other players are included if these totals were not achieved by at least three players in each category. Details on the matches themselves include all century-makers and all instances of bowlers taking five wickets in an innings. References in the text to national averages and best performances of the season apply to Championship matches only.

As will be noted, fuller details on the 2001 season are given. This follows on from an attempt to place, possibly for the first time, the barren years of 1969-2000 into some sort of historical perspective. Also, by way of scene-setting, the pre-official Championship years are covered as well as the years of frustration and Surrey dominance after the 1939-45 War.

The County Championship continues to be a much-maligned and under-valued competition. Its present format, with two divisions and each county playing every other county in its division twice per season, on a home and away basis, is surely equal and perfect. When compared with seasons when counties played different numbers of matches from each other or when all counties played the same number of matches but some counties once and others twice, the current system is highly satisfactory.

Others criticize the competition for its lack of quality and state that its main aim is to provide a training ground for Test players. Nonsense – its only aim should be to provide a first-class (in both senses of the term) competition between teams of professional cricketers. Although crowds may be, on some occasions, relatively small, huge numbers of fans do follow the competition's progress through the various types of media.

The Championship has become more evenly competitive in recent years with several 'unfashionable' counties, such as Glamorgan and Leicestershire, winning the title. There is no doubt that this is a good thing and that healthy jousting between teams of relatively similar strength makes for compelling viewing, especially when spread out over four days, even from the distance of Ceefax or Cricinfo. Anyone who states, as did Eric Roberts in the *Yorkshire Post* the day after Yorkshire clinched their 30th title that, "…once again God's in his (sic.) heaven and the county in its rightful place." is dealing in arrogant, even if tongue-in-cheek, nonsense. Yorkshire have no more right to win the Championship than anyone else and nothing would be better for the game than if Durham, Gloucestershire, Northamptonshire, Somerset or Sussex were to soon win their first title.

I am greatly indebted to Mick Pope, my colleague at Adelphi Cricket Press, for his contributions of pictures that enhance this book so well. I also value his advice and encouragement. Thanks also to Paul Kelly for his unstinting type-setting service provided for this project, from my own disks.

I am also grateful to David Byas for agreeing to write the foreword, in a conversation that took place just a couple of hours before the title was clinched, as well as all the players, past and present, who made it all possible.

Paul E. Dyson
Knaresborough
March 2002

# Yorkshire's 30 Championships

## 1893 - 2001

Paul E. Dyson

**ADELPHI**
**CRICKET**
**PRESS**

# Early Days

*Hyde Park Cricket Ground, Sheffield, scene of the first inter-county game in Yorkshire – against Norfolk in 1833.*

# 1833-1889

# Early Days

Cricket during the early part of the nineteenth century was organised very much on an *ad hoc* basis. Sheffield was the centre of what cricket there was in the county and when Norfolk visited in 1833 eleven players from that city decided to call themselves 'Yorkshire' in response to the status of their opponents. A further 28 matches were played by teams using that name before the formation of the official Yorkshire County Cricket Club.

This momentous event took place at a meeting at the Adelphi Hotel in Sheffield on January 8th 1863 and the team took the field for the first time against Surrey on June 4th of the same year at The Oval. The three-day fixture was a rain-affected draw but the three other games that were arranged for that season all concluded positively, there being victory over Surrey in the return match and a win and a defeat against Nottinghamshire.

Teams purporting to represent Kent and Surrey had been playing each other for much longer, however. One source gives a date as early as 1709 and with the official formation of Sussex CCC in 1839 inter-county matches in the south of England became populous enough for Peter-Wynne Thomas to have retrospectively compiled a list of champion counties from 1826 until 1863. This list includes Nottinghamshire, as well as the three southern counties, and teams known as Cambridgeshire, Hampshire and Middlesex had also become involved in what was a very informal fixture list.

Yorkshire was the fourth county to be officially constituted and a spate of similar bodies followed in the remainder of the decade and in the 1870s also. The 1860s were an exciting time in the development of cricket and *Wisden Cricketers' Almanack* was published for the first time in 1864. Although it remains unrivalled today, in the latter part of the nineteenth century it came under competition from James Lillywhite's *Cricketers' Annual*.

Both publications intermittently produced their own version of the champion counties as did a magazine simply known as *Cricket* as well as John Lillywhite's *Cricketers' Companion*. Three other authorities later produced lists from a retrospective viewpoint. The most widely accepted of these is that produced by the historian Rowland Bowen in 1959. His list began in 1864 (which is why Wynne-Thomas's list ends the year previously) as did that of W.G.Grace (published in *Cricket* in 1903). A final list runs from 1873 having been put together by Rev R.S.Holmes, a noted Yorkshire historian, and was published in the same magazine as Grace's compilation.

Thus, for some of the years between 1864 and 1889 there are as many as seven different versions of who the champion county was. Fortunately, for 15 of these 26 seasons, there is unanimous agreement. For the remainder, as the championship was completely unofficial, dispute will always remain.

There can be no denying that Yorkshire would have been the champion team in 1867 even though their fixtures were against only three of the other eight 'first-class' counties (another term used retrospectively for this era). They won all of their seven matches, these being against Cambridgeshire and Surrey (two each) and Lancashire (three). As with so many later campaigns the leading players were bowlers and in George Freeman and Tom Emmett the county had as good an opening attack as any in its history. The side was led by Roger Iddison who was the captain of the county for its first ten seasons. Three of the victories were by an innings and Surrey were dismissed for less than 100 in all four of their innings.

For each of the following five seasons both Nottinghamshire and Yorkshire appear in at least one of the lists, sometimes even as joint champions. The best of these seasons, from a White Rose point of view, was 1870 when the team won five and drew one of its six games. They did the double over Kent and Surrey, winning all four games convincingly but the two matches against their closest rivals were entirely different affairs. At Trent Bridge J.C.Shaw had match figures of 11-99 for the home side who dismissed the visitors for 108 and 122. Having disposed of Nottinghamshire for 56 in their first innings Yorkshire must have been confident that they would dismiss the midland county for fewer than the 174 required for victory. At 65-0 Nottinghamshire must have been confident of victory but collapsed mainly against Iddison (4-55) and fell just two runs short. In the return game at Bramall Lane the visitors were dismissed for 146 (Freeman six for 55) and Yorkshire beat that score by one run. Nottinghamshire were then all out for 142 and the game, which was ruined by time-wasting tactics, concluded as a draw with Yorkshire tantalisingly placed on 107-6 but having taken 92 overs to score the runs.

Joseph Robotham, Ephraim Lockwood and Andrew Greenwood all contributed effectively with the bat at various times during this era, as Iddison continued to do so also. The emergence of George Pinder as a first-rate wicket-keeper was also a factor in pressure being maintained on Yorkshire's opponents. He claimed to be the first 'keeper to stand up to the wicket when taking fast bowling.

The only other year when Yorkshire appeared in any of the seven lists as unofficial county champions was 1883. The fixture list was by now much more extensive and the county played two games against each of eight other teams winning nine, drawing five and losing only two. Most versions have Nottinghamshire as champions, however. Lockwood and Emmett remained from the previous successful team and to these were added, amongst others, Louis Hall to open the batting, all-rounders Willie Bates and George Ulyett, as well as the left-arm spin of Edmund Peate and Robert Peel, the pace of Allen Hill and the wicket-keeping skills of Joseph Hunter.

The most significant change was that of captain, however. 1883 was the first season in which the team was led, after he had come down from Cambridge, by Hon. Martin Bladen Hawke, better known (officially, later) as Lord Hawke. He was to contribute more to the county's development than any other player before or since. It was a successful season that marked a new era in more ways than one.

In December 1889, after a season which ended with Lancashire, Nottinghamshire and Surrey being joint champions in everyone's eyes, the Secretaries of these three counties, plus those from Gloucestershire, Kent, Middlesex, Sussex and Yorkshire met at Lord's. They agreed the fixture list for the following season, but, far more importantly, decided upon the method to produce an order of merit between them. Thus 1890 was to become the first season which would produce not only an official champion county but also a full table.

# First Successes

*Yorkshire's Championship-winning team of 1893. From left: back row –
E.Wainwright, J. Tunnicliffe, H.Turner (scorer), D.Hunter, R.Moorhouse; middle
row – G.Ulyett, F.S.Jackson, Lord Hawke (capt.), A.Sellers, R.Peel; front row –
J.T.Brown, E.Smith, G.H.Hirst. It was the county's first victory since the official
Championship had begun in 1890.*

# 1890-1899

# First Successes

## 1890-1892

Surrey were champions for each of these three seasons, Yorkshire finishing third equal, eighth and sixth, respectively. Somerset was added to the schedule in 1891. Counties were awarded one point for a win and a minus point for a defeat.

## 1893

### TOP FIVE COUNTIES

|            | Pld | W  | L | D | Pts |
|------------|-----|----|---|---|-----|
| Yorkshire  | 16  | 12 | 3 | 1 | 9   |
| Lancashire | 16  | 9  | 5 | 2 | 4   |
| Middlesex  | 16  | 9  | 6 | 1 | 3   |
| Kent       | 16  | 6  | 4 | 6 | 2   |
| Surrey     | 16  | 7  | 8 | 1 | -1  |

### LEADING YORKSHIRE AVERAGES

#### BATTING

|              | M  | I  | NO | Runs | HS  | Avge  | 100 | 50 |
|--------------|----|----|----|------|-----|-------|-----|----|
| J.T.Brown    | 16 | 26 | 1  | 712  | 84  | 28.48 | -   | 6  |
| J.Tunnicliffe| 16 | 26 | 3  | 653  | 77  | 28.39 | -   | 3  |
| A.Sellers    | 15 | 25 | 0  | 678  | 105 | 27.12 | 2   | 3  |
| G.H.Hirst    | 16 | 23 | 9  | 287  | 43  | 20.50 | -   | -  |

#### BOWLING

|              | O     | M   | R    | W  | Avge  | 5WI | 10WM | BB   |
|--------------|-------|-----|------|----|-------|-----|------|------|
| E.Wainwright | 600.1 | 208 | 1130 | 90 | 12.55 | 6   | 1    | 6-16 |
| R.Peel       | 627.2 | 276 | 922  | 65 | 14.18 | 6   | 2    | 7-55 |
| G.H.Hirst    | 568.2 | 244 | 963  | 59 | 16.32 | 2   | -    | 5-20 |

## FIELDING and WICKET-KEEPING

38 (29 ct, 9 st) D.Hunter
31 J.Tunnicliffe
19 E.Wainwright
12 G.Ulyett

# RESULTS

**Gloucester**, May 11, 12, 13: Gloucestershire 235 & 152 (E.Wainwright 6-56), Yorkshire 385 & 3-1. *Won by nine wickets*

**Headingley**, May 29, 30, 31: Sussex 125 (R.Peel 7-55) & 61 (E.Wainwright 6-16), Yorkshire 111 (A.W.Hilton 7-47) & 76-6. *Won by four wickets*

**Lord's**, June 1, 2, 3: Middlesex 169 & 279, Yorkshire 304 (A.Sellers 105) & 145-7. *Won by three wickets*

**Sheffield**, June 12, 13: Yorkshire 98 (T.Richardson 9-47) & 91 (W.Lockwood 8-39), Surrey 72 & 59 (T.Wardall 5-13, G.H.Hirst 5-28). *Won by 58 runs*

**Taunton**, June 15, 16, 17: Somerset 227 & 191 (J.T.Brown 5-41), Yorkshire 469. *Won by an innings and 51 runs*

**Headingley**, June 19,20: Yorkshire 107 (A.W.Mold 6-40) & 53 (J.Briggs 8-19), Lancashire 169 (R.Peel 5-28). *Lost by an innings and 9 runs*

**The Oval**, June 29, 30: Surrey 356 (K.J.Key 100) & 10-0, Yorkshire 125 (W.Lockwood 5-56) & 238 (W.Lockwood 6-64). *Lost by ten wickets*

**Bradford**, July 3, 4, 5: Yorkshire 220 (F.J.Shacklock 8-55) & 120-3, Nottinghamshire 321-8dec (W.Gunn 150). *Match drawn*

**Sheffield**, July 6, 7: Somerset 161 & 126 (E.Wainwright 5-38), Yorkshire 300 (A.Sellers 103). *Won by an innings and 13 runs*

**Trent Bridge**, July 13, 14: Nottinghamshire 124 (F.S.Jackson 5-42, E.Wainwright 5-62) & 38, Yorkshire 182 (W.Attewell 6-73). *Won by an innings and 20 runs*

**Huddersfield**, July 27, 28: Yorkshire 162 (F.G.Roberts 6-59) & 4-0, Gloucestershire 74 (R.Peel 6-27) & 91. *Won by ten wickets*

**Blackheath**, July 31, August 1: Kent 77 (E.Wainwright 5-32) & 132 (G.H.Hirst 5-20), Yorkshire 220. *Won by an innings and 11 runs*

**Old Trafford**, August 7, 8: Lancashire 64 & 50 (R.Peel 6-24), Yorkshire 58 (J.Briggs 6-35) & 51 (J.Briggs 5-25). *Lost by 5 runs*
**Bradford**, August 14, 15, 16: Yorkshire 234 (J.T.Hearne 5-80) & 184 (J.T.Hearne 5-62), Middlesex 191 (R.Peel 5-43) & 82. *Won by 145 runs*
**Sheffield**, August 21, 22, 23: Kent 161 (R.Peel 7-60) & 127, Yorkshire 211 (W.Wright 5-73) & 80-2. *Won by eight wickets*
**Hove**, August 24, 25, 26: Sussex 192 (E.Wainwright 6-23) & 194, Yorkshire 203 (W.A.Humphreys 8-98) & 185-2. *Won by eight wickets*

## NOTES and HIGHLIGHTS

Yorkshire's first Championship title, achieved thirty years since the Club's formation and ten years since Lord Hawke took over the captaincy, was probably one of the easiest they have gained. Five of the twelve victories were by an innings and in five of the remaining seven the team lost no more than two wickets in its second innings. The beginning and end of the season were Yorkshire's best spells as they won all of their first five games and seven of the last eight. On ten occasions Yorkshire's opponents were dismissed for totals fewer than 100 but Lancashire (three times) and Surrey (twice) also achieved the same feat against them.

The only blot on the landscape was the two defeats by second-placed Lancashire. One of these was a remarkable game at Old Trafford in which a total of 64 was the highest of the four innings. Yorkshire required only 57 to win but, after overnight rain and under a drying sun, Johnny Briggs was virtually unplayable and the last four wickets fell after lunch on the second day for a mere nine runs to leave the visitors six runs short of the target. The last wicket fell to a boundary catch from a shot by George Ulyett that looked destined to be a winning six. Briggs finished with match figures of 11-70 making a total of 23-135 over the two games against the White Rose county.

No batsman came in the top ten of the national averages but Ted Wainwright (second), Bobby Peel and George Hirst were all in the top ten of the national bowling averages. Particularly good innings figures were achieved by Hirst (28-20-20-5 against Kent at Blackheath), Peel (43.2-24-43-5 against Middlesex at Bradford) and Wainwirght (20.3-13-16-6 against Sussex at Headingley). A total of six players played throughout the season – Jack Brown, Hirst, David Hunter, John Tunnicliffe and Wainwright.

Ulyett bowed out at the end of the season, twenty years after his debut. He was considered the county's best batsman in the nineteenth century and scored over 14,000 runs for Yorkshire as well as taking over 400 wickets. As far as Test cricket is concerned, he played, uniquely, in England's, Australia's and South Africa's first matches and shared, with R.G.Barlow, the first century opening partnership as well as scoring the first century for England in Australia.

## PLAYER of the SEASON

*Ted Wainwright, one of Yorkshire's leading all-rounders of the 1890s.*

The leading bowler, both in terms of wicket aggregate and average was Ted Wainwright. He was to have the distinction of playing in all of the first six of the title-winning seasons. An effective all-rounder, he eventually scored over 11,000 runs in the middle order and took more than 1000 wickets at medium pace or with off-spin for Yorkshire. Not content with these contributions, he took his place in the slips alongside Tunnicliffe and held over 300 catches for the county. Born in Tinsley, Sheffield, in 1865, he played for the county from 1888 to 1902. Bowling was his forte and his off-breaks showed appreciable turn although his command of length meant that he was never placed in the top bracket of bowlers. He played in only five Test matches, not taking a single wicket.

His batting was sound rather than spectacular and his highest score, 228, came later at The Oval in 1899 when he and Hirst added 340 in three-and-a-half hours. 1894 would be his best season with the ball (166 wickets at 12.73) and this included career-best figures of 9-66 against Middlesex at Bramall Lane. On this occasion he took the last five wickets in seven balls, including the hat-trick. He performed the 'double' in 1897 and later became coach at Shrewsbury School. He died in Sheffield in 1919.

## 1894 and 1895

Surrey was the champion county for both seasons, Yorkshire finishing second and third, respectively. In 1894 the champions finished only one point ahead of Yorkshire but had done the double over them. A further five counties were introduced in 1895, namely Derbyshire, Essex, Hampshire, Leicestershire and Warwickshire.

For the 1896 season the system for allocating final placings was changed due to the considerable variation in the numbers of games being played by each county. A percentage was calculated, this being arrived at by dividing the number of points obtained by the number of finished games.

## 1896

## TOP FIVE COUNTIES

|  | Pld | W | L | D | Pts | % |
|---|---|---|---|---|---|---|
| Yorkshire | 26 | 16 | 3 | 7 | 13 | 68.42 |
| Lancashire | 22 | 11 | 4 | 7 | 7 | 46.66 |
| Middlesex | 16 | 8 | 3 | 5 | 5 | 45.45 |
| Surrey | 26 | 17 | 7 | 2 | 10 | 38.46 |
| Essex | 12 | 5 | 4 | 3 | 1 | 11.11 |

## LEADING YORKSHIRE AVERAGES

### BATTING

|               | M   | I   | NO  | Runs | HS   | Avge  | 100 | 50  |
|---------------|-----|-----|-----|------|------|-------|-----|-----|
| J.T.Brown     | 24  | 41  | 7   | 1556 | 203  | 45.76 | 4   | 7   |
| F.S.Jackson   | 16  | 25  | 1   | 1030 | 117  | 42.91 | 3   | 5   |
| R.Peel        | 24  | 35  | 3   | 1135 | 210* | 35.46 | 3   | 3   |
| G.H.Hirst     | 25  | 34  | 3   | 1018 | 107  | 32.83 | 1   | 10  |
| J.Tuinnicliffe| 26  | 45  | 4   | 1223 | 99   | 29.82 | -   | 9   |
| E.Wainwright  | 25  | 37  | 5   | 817  | 145  | 25.53 | 2   | 2   |
| D.Denton      | 23  | 34  | 0   | 853  | 113  | 25.09 | 1   | 3   |

### BOWLING

|              | O      | M   | R    | W   | Avge  | 5WI | 10WM | BB    |
|--------------|--------|-----|------|-----|-------|-----|------|-------|
| S.Haigh      | 485.3  | 164 | 1085 | 71  | 15.28 | 7   | 2    | 8-35  |
| E.Wainwright | 769.2  | 249 | 1685 | 90  | 18.72 | 6   | 2    | 8-34  |
| R.Peel       | 1080.4 | 418 | 1850 | 97  | 19.07 | 6   | 3    | 6-19  |
| G.H.Hirst    | 860.4  | 300 | 1913 | 80  | 23.91 | 3   | -    | 8-59  |

### FIELDING and WICKET-KEEPING

61 (48 ct, 13 st) D.Hunter
46 J.Tunnicliffe
22 E.Wainwright
16 J.T.Brown, G.H.Hirst

## RESULTS

**Old Trafford**, May 4, 5, 6: Lancashire 150 & 139, Yorkshire 123 (J.Briggs 5-44) & 168-8. *Won by two wickets*

**Edgbaston**, May 7, 8, 9: Yorkshire 887 (R.Peel 210*, Lord Hawke 166, E.Wainwright 126, F.S.Jackson 117), Warwickshire 203 (G.H.Hirst 8-59) & 48-1. *Match drawn*

**Taunton**, May 11, 12, 13: Somerset 323 (L.C.H.Palairet 113) & 208 (E.Wainwright 6-49), Yorkshire 400 (R.Moorhouse 113, E.J.Tyler 7-196) & 132-5. *Won by five wickets*

**Sheffield**, July 27, 28: Yorkshire 141 (C.L.Townsend 5-70) & 296, Gloucestershire 79 (R.Peel 6-43) & 92. *Won by 266 runs*
**The Oval**, July 30, 31, August 1: Surrey 439 (T.W.Hayward 164, R.Peel 5-94), Yorkshire 172 & 206. *Lost by an innings and 61 runs*
**Harrogate**, August 6, 7, 8: Hampshire 176 (E.Wainwright 7-55) & 121 (S.Haigh 8-35), Yorkshire 266 (J.T.Brown 120) & 32-0. *Won by ten wickets*
**Scarborough**, August 13, 14, 15: Yorkshire 184 & 130-8dec (F.Geeson 6-48), Leicestershire 93 (E.Wainwright 7-43) & 59 (R.Peel 6-19). *Won by 162 runs*
**Bradford**, August 17, 18, 19: Middlesex 263 (E.Wainwright 6-45) & 332 (G.H.Hirst 5-109), Yorkshire 363 (F.S.Jackson 115, C.M.Wells 5-87) & 143-1. *Match drawn*
**Hove**, August 20, 21, 22: Yorkshire 407 (R.Peel 106, F.S.Jackson 102), Sussex 191 (K.S.Ranjitsinhji 100, E.Smith 5-42) & 260-2 (K.S.Ranjitsinhji 125*). *Match drawn*
**Tonbridge**, August 24, 25, 26: Yorkshire 184 (W.Wright 5-69) & 124-7dec, Kent 98 & 103 (E.Smith 5-26). *Won by 107 runs*

## NOTES and HIGHLIGHTS

Yorkshire were unbeaten in their first 14 matches and although Surrey kept in touch and eventually won more games than the champions, the final margin of victory was convincing. The first game of the season, against Lancashire at Old Trafford, was one of the most exciting of the campaign and the final day of a low-scoring match began with Yorkshire needing 18 runs for victory with only two wickets remaining. Fortunately, the visitors had no further alarms.

The second game, against Warwickshire, broke several records: Yorkshire's total remains the highest county score of all-time; it was the first occasion four centuries had been scored in the same innings; Peel and Lord Hawke both made the highest scores of their careers and established the current record of 292 for Yorkshire's eighth wicket. As may be noted from the batting averages there was a considerable weight of runs scored. Robert Moorhouse (675 at 28.13) and Hawke (577 at 27.48) also contributed at various times.

Batting at numbers 6, 7 and 8 Frank Milligan, John Mounsey and Hirst each scored two half-centuries in the match against Hampshire at Southampton and, remarkably, these were the only such scores for Yorkshire in the game. For Sussex at Hove K.S.Ranjitsinhji scored two centuries on the final day of the match, having also scored a century against Yorkshire earlier in the season. William Storer also scored three centuries against Yorkshire – in the space of just nine days.

As in 1893, Hirst, Peel and Wainwright took most wickets but F.S.Jackson (37 at 21.03) and Milligan (33 at 22.58) also made telling contributions. Only Tunnicliffe, who had an outstanding season in the slips, played in every match throughout the campaign.

## PLAYER of the SEASON

1896 was the best season of Jack Brown's career and one of the outstanding opening batsmen in the county's history was at the peak of his powers. Born in Driffield in 1869, he first played for the county in 1889 and was to score over 15,000 runs for Yorkshire forming a formidable partnership with Tunnicliffe. He passed 1000 runs in each of ten successive seasons from 1894 with his neat and stylish play. His best innings came in 1897 and he broke the world record for any wicket in the following season in a first wicket stand of 554 with Tunnicliffe.

Brown's leg-breaks often came in useful and he took 190 first-class wickets, including a hat-trick. He played in eight Tests, topping the averages in the 1894/95 series in Australia, making his only Test century at Melbourne – an innings which began with a 28-minute half-century. He dropped out of the game during the early part of the 1904 season due to ill-health and died in London in the same year.

### 1897

Lancashire won the County Championship for the first time with Yorkshire finishing fourth. Brown scored the first triple-century for Yorkshire – an innings of 311 against Sussex at Sheffield.

# 1898

## TOP FIVE COUNTIES

|  | Pld | W | L | D | Pts | % |
|---|---|---|---|---|---|---|
| Yorkshire | 26 | 16 | 3 | 7 | 13 | 68.42 |
| Middlesex | 18 | 10 | 3 | 5 | 7 | 53.84 |
| Gloucestershire | 20 | 9 | 3 | 8 | 6 | 50.00 |
| Surrey | 24 | 11 | 4 | 9 | 7 | 46.66 |
| Essex | 20 | 10 | 6 | 4 | 4 | 25.00 |

## LEADING YORKSHIRE AVERAGES

### BATTING

|  | M | I | NO | Runs | HS | Avge | 100 | 50 |
|---|---|---|---|---|---|---|---|---|
| J.Tunnicliffe | 24 | 38 | 5 | 1538 | 243 | 46.60 | 4 | 8 |
| F.S.Jackson | 23 | 32 | 3 | 1326 | 160 | 45.72 | 5 | 2 |
| J.T.Brown | 26 | 40 | 2 | 1389 | 300 | 36.55 | 3 | 2 |
| Lord Hawke | 25 | 30 | 6 | 797 | 134 | 33.20 | 2 | 4 |
| D.Denton | 26 | 38 | 1 | 819 | 99 | 22.14 | - | 4 |

### BOWLING

|  | O | M | R | W | Avge | 5WI | 10WM | BB |
|---|---|---|---|---|---|---|---|---|
| W.Rhodes | 990 | 393 | 1745 | 126 | 13.84 | 11 | 3 | 7-24 |
| E.Wainwright | 432.1 | 161 | 802 | 56 | 14.32 | 4 | 1 | 7-24 |
| F.S.Jackson | 697.3 | 285 | 1217 | 80 | 15.21 | 4 | - | 7-42 |
| S.Haigh | 747 | 260 | 1618 | 88 | 18.38 | 4 | 1 | 8-21 |

### FIELDING and WICKET-KEEPING

46 (29 ct, 17 st) D.Hunter
28 J.Tunnicliffe
20 F.S.Jackson
19 G.H.Hirst

# RESULTS

**Bath**, May 16, 17, 18: Yorkshire 163 (G.Fowler 5-65, E.J.Tyler 5-68) & 174-7dec, Somerset 104 (W.Rhodes 7-24) & 35 (W.Rhodes 6-21). *Won by 198 runs*

**Bristol**, May 19, 20, 21: Yorkshire 263-3 (J.Tunnicliffe 107*) v Gloucestershire. *Match drawn*

**Southampton**, May 26, 27: Hampshire 42 (S.Haigh 8-21) & 36 (S.Haigh 6-22), Yorkshire 157. *Won by an innings and 79 runs*

**Headingley**, May 30, 31, June 1: Warwickshire 218 (W.Rhodes 5-69) & 50-5dec, Yorkshire 112 (S.Santall 5-39) & 85-0. *Match drawn*

**Leyton**, June 2, 3, 4: Essex 78 (F.S.Jackson 5-46) & 168, Yorkshire 118 (W.Mead 5-51, F.G.Bull 5-62) & 129-7. *Won by three wickets*

**Bradford**, June 6, 7, 8: Surrey 139 (E.Wainwright 5-43, W.Rhodes 5-46) & 37 (W.Rhodes 7-24), Yorkshire 297-9dec (G.H.Hirst 130*). *Won by an innings and 121 runs*

**Huddersfield**, June 9, 10, 11: Yorkshire 226 (E.Tate 5-83), Hampshire 45 (E.Wainwright 7-24) & 83. *Won by an innings and 98 runs*

**Sheffield**, June 13, 14, 15: Yorkshire 289 (Lord Hawke 107*) & 229-3dec (J.Tunnicliffe 108*), Kent 218 & 171. *Won by 129 runs*

**Lord's**, June 16, 17, 18: Yorkshire 445 (F.S.Jackson 133), Middlesex 118 (S.Haigh 7-60) & 318 (F.G.J.Ford 127). *Won by an innings and 9 runs*

**Headingley**, June 20, 21, 22: Nottinghamshire 215 (F.S.Jackson 5-59) & 105-4dec, Yorkshire 143 & 56-6. *Match drawn*

**Leicester**, June 23, 24: Yorkshire 449 (F.S.Jackson 147), Leicestershire 57 (F.S.Jackson 5-20, W.Rhodes 5-33) & 126. *Won by an innings and 226 runs*

**Bradford**, June 27, 28, 29: Essex 64 (W.Rhodes 6-24) & 176 (W.Rhodes 5-68), Yorkshire 278 (F.G.Bull 5-90). *Won by an innings and 38 runs*

**Dewsbury**, June 30, July 1: Leicestershire 56 (W.Rhodes 5-25, E.Wainwright 5-31) & 98 (E.Wainwright 7-54), Yorkshire 178 (A.D.Pougher 6-53). *Won by an innings and 24 runs*

**Bradford**, July 4, 5, 6: Sussex 189 (S.Haigh 5-50) & 218 (J.T.Brown 6-52), Yorkshire 282 & 126-3. *Won by seven wickets*

**Sheffield**, July 11, 12, 13: Yorkshire 316 (J.T.Brown 144) & 253-2dec (F.S.Jackson 134*, J.Tunnicliffe 102), Lancashire 288 & 140-5. *Match drawn*

**Maidstone**, July 14, 15, 16: Yorkshire 199 & 124 (W.Wright 5-43), Kent 199 & 127-4. *Lost by six wickets*

**Scarborough**, July 21, 22, 23: Somerset 208 & 242, Yorkshire 397 (F.S.Jackson 139) & 54-4. *Won by six wickets*

**Sheffield**, July 25, 26: Yorkshire 331 (F.S.Jackson 160), Gloucestershire 192 (W.Rhodes 6-71) & 127. *Won by an innings and 12 runs*

**Harrogate**, July 28, 29, 30: Yorkshire 252 (J.W.Hancock 5-61) & 321-9dec, Derbyshire 238 & 219-3 (H.Bagshaw 100*). *Match drawn*

**Edgbaston**, August 1, 2, 3: Warwickshire 406 (W.G.Quaife 157*) & 102-4, Yorkshire 448 (Lord Hawke 134). *Match drawn*

**The Oval**, August 4, 5, 6: Surrey 536 (R.Abel 114), Yorkshire 78 (W.Lockwood 5-30) & 186 (W.Lockwood 6-96). *Lost by an innings and 272 runs*

**Trent Bridge**, August 8, 9, 10: Yorkshire 277 (J.R.Gunn 8-108), Nottinghamshire 90 (W.Rhodes 6-32) & 90-1. *Match drawn*

**Old Trafford**, August 11, 12: Lancashire 112 & 64, Yorkshire 114 & 63-0. *Won by ten wickets*

**Headingley**, August 15, 16: Yorkshire 142 & 45 (A.E.Trott 7-13), Middlesex 128 (F.S.Jackson 7-42) & 62-2. *Lost by eight wickets*

**Chesterfield**, August 18, 19, 20: Yorkshire 662 (J.T.Brown 300, J.Tunnicliffe 243), Derbyshire 118 & 157. *Won by an innings and 387 runs*

**Hove**, August 22, 23, 24: Yorkshire 428 (J.T.Brown 150) & 166-7dec, Sussex 311 (C.B.Fry 179*) & 91. *Won by 192 runs*

## NOTES and HIGHLIGHTS

This was another convincing performance by Yorkshire who won five games more than any of their opponents and nine of the 16 victories necessitated the county batting only once. A good start was obtained, as in 1896, with none of the first 15 games resulting in defeats. Yorkshire's opponents were dismissed for fewer than 100 runs on 14 occasions but the White Rose county suffered the same indignity only twice.

The most dramatic match of the season was the home game with Surrey, at Bradford. After a blank first day Surrey scored 139 and Yorkshire replied with 142-8. Hirst and Schofield Haigh (85) took their partnership to 192 and, after a declaration, the visitors were skittled out for a mere 37 in 39.1 overs by Wilfred Rhodes and Wainwright (3-10) who bowled unchanged. The last five batsmen were all dismissed by the Hunter/Rhodes combination, three being stumped and two caught.

Hampshire had suffered a similar fate just 12 days earlier, at Southampton, except that their game lasted a mere six hours, again after a blank first day (unfortunately for H.Baldwin's benefit). Haigh and Rhodes dismissed the home side in 30.4 overs, Yorkshire gained a lead of over 100 and Haigh got to work again, Hampshire lasting only 26.2 overs at the second attempt. Haigh finished with match figures of 14-43 and the home side's two innings contained no less than nine ducks. In the return match Hampshire were dismissed for 45 and 83, this meaning that they averaged 5.12 runs per wicket over the two games.

In complete contrast to these two games was the match at Chesterfield that began with a world record partnership of 554 runs between Brown and Tunnicliffe. It was the first stand to exceed 500 in any first-class game and, as a world first-wicket record, stood for 34 years before being beaten by two more Yorkshiremen! The pair batted for only 305 minutes together, the runs being scored at a rate of 105 per hour and both players hit 48 fours. Tunnicliffe's innings was the highest of his career and, in tenth position, he was the highest-placed Yorkshireman in the national averages.

*Jack Brown and John Tunnicliffe in front of the Chesterfield scoreboard showing their world-record partnership total achieved against Derbyshire in 1898.*

The bowling averages, however, were dominated by Yorkshire players. They were led by Rhodes and Wainwright with Jackson in fourth place. Rhodes had excellent innings figures of 30-16-25-5 against Leicestershire at Dewsbury. Jackson had his best season with Yorkshire and it contained his best career performances with both bat and ball, these being in the home matches against Gloucestershire and Middlesex, respectively. Wainwright also had a good all-round season scoring 603 runs at 23.19 in addition to his feats with the ball. Brown's figures against Sussex at Bradford were the best of his career.

One of the main reasons for the successful season was the side's stability. Eleven men each played in over twenty matches and only 21 of the total of 286 appearances were by players outside this first-choice team. Brown, David Denton, Haigh and Rhodes did not miss any games at all.

Rhodes' season was all the more remarkable when it is considered that it was his first in county cricket. His debut performance of 13-45 against Somerset at Bath in the first game of the season remains a Yorkshire record.

Milligan's short county career ended with the 1898 season. As an amateur, he could afford a carefree approach, but was an effective all-rounder and played for England in South Africa. He remained in the area to fight for Rhodesia but sadly lost his life at the tender age of thirty.

## PLAYER of the SEASON

In 1898 John Tunnicliffe produced the best season of his career, scoring 1804 runs in all matches, the obvious highlight being the only double century of his career that contributed to the world record partnership for any wicket. He was probably the best Yorkshire player never to appear for England. He was the first of Yorkshire's Pudsey lineage, being born there in 1866, and made his debut for the county in 1891. He scored his first century in 1895, passing 1000 runs for the first time and had by now formed his formidable partnership with Brown. With his height and long reach, Tunnicliffe was also a very fine slip fielder eventually taking more catches per match (1.41) than any other non-wicket-keeper in Yorkshire's history, ending his career with 667 catches.

Tunnicliffe's batting was never colourful but always dependable. He learnt to acquire a solid defence and this was the backbone of his game. He scored over 19,000 runs for the county, including over 1000 in his last season, 1907, when he retired at the age of 41 to become the coach at Clifton College. He died in Bristol in 1948.

## 1899

Yorkshire ended the season in third place as Surrey made the Championship title their sixth victory in its tenth year. Worcestershire became the fifteenth county to take part.

# The First Great Team

*Yorkshire's Championship-winning team of 1900. From left: back row - T.Mycroft (umpire), J.B.Wolstinholme (sec.), W.Rhodes, J.Tunnicliffe, D.Hunter, L.Whitehead, J.Hoyland (scorer), A.Shaw (umpire); middle row – E.Wainwright, T.L.Taylor, Lord Hawke (capt.), S.Haigh, G.H.Hirst; front row – J.T.Brown, D.Denton. The county remained undefeated and began a hat-trick of titles.*

# 1900-1914

# The First Great Team

## 1900

### TOP FIVE COUNTIES

| | Pld | W | L | D | Pts | % |
|---|---|---|---|---|---|---|
| Yorkshire | 28 | 16 | 0 | 12 | 16 | 100.00 |
| Lancashire | 28 | 15 | 2 | 11 | 13 | 76.47 |
| Kent | 22 | 8 | 4 | 10 | 4 | 33.33 |
| Sussex | 24 | 4 | 2 | 18 | 2 | 33.33 |
| Nottinghamshire | 18 | 7 | 4 | 7 | 3 | 27.27 |

## LEADING YORKSHIRE AVERAGES

### BATTING

| | M | I | NO | Runs | HS | Avge | 100 | 50 |
|---|---|---|---|---|---|---|---|---|
| G.H.Hirst | 28 | 42 | 6 | 1573 | 155 | 43.69 | 4 | 11 |
| J.Tunnicliffe | 27 | 43 | 4 | 1428 | 158 | 36.61 | 4 | 6 |
| D.Denton | 28 | 44 | 4 | 1111 | 96 | 27.77 | - | 8 |
| J.T.Brown (Driffield) | 23 | 37 | 3 | 812 | 128 | 23.88 | 1 | 3 |

### BOWLING

| | O | M | R | W | Avge | 5WI | 10WM | BB |
|---|---|---|---|---|---|---|---|---|
| W.Rhodes | 1165.1 | 359 | 2532 | 206 | 12.29 | 21 | 6 | 8-23 |
| S.Haigh | 825.4 | 217 | 2054 | 145 | 14.16 | 10 | 1 | 7-33 |
| J.T.Brown (Darfield) | 204.1 | 41 | 529 | 23 | 23.00 | 2 | - | 6-34 |

## FIELDING and WICKET-KEEPING

60 (35 ct, 25 st) D.Hunter
46 J.Tunnicliffe
33 E.Wainwright
20 G.H.Hirst

# RESULTS

**Bradford**, May 7: Worcestershire 43 & 51 (W.Rhodes 7-20), Yorkshire 99 (A.F.Bannister 5-30). *Won by an innings and 5 runs*
**Catford**, May 10, 11, 12: Yorkshire 163 & 260 (E.Wainwright 116), Kent 112 (J.T.Brown 6-34) & 180. *Won by 131 runs*
**Sheffield**, May 21, 22, 23: Derbyshire 175 (W.Rhodes 7-72) & 9-1, Yorkshire 259-8dec. *Match drawn*
**Huddersfield**, May 24, 25, 26: Leicestershire 262 (E.Smith 5-77) & 100 (W.Rhodes 6-52), Yorkshire 302 (J.T.Brown 128, J.H.King 7-91) & 61-0. *Won by ten wickets*
**Headingley**, May 28, 29, 30: Warwickshire 228 & 294 (W.Rhodes 6-49), Yorkshire 359 & 86-3. *Match drawn*
**Lord's**, May 31, June 1, 2: Middlesex 202 (E.Smith 5-42) & 202 (S.Haigh 6-57), Yorkshire 307 (A.E.Trott 6-118) & 98-4. *Won by six wickets*
**Leicester**, June 7, 8, 9: Leicestershire 162 & 93 (S.Haigh 5-52), Yorkshire 241 & 15-0. *Won by ten wickets*
**Bradford**, June 11, 12, 13: Yorkshire 230 (W.R.Cuttell 5-115) & 64-6, Lancashire 96 (W.Rhodes 8-43). *Match drawn*
**Leyton**, June 14, 15, 16: Essex 132 (J.T.Brown 6-57) & 120 (W.Rhodes 7-46), Yorkshire 152 & 102-4. *Won by six wickets*
**Sheffield**, June 18, 19, 20: Surrey 242 (D.L.A.Jephson 109) & 146 (W.Rhodes 6-58), Yorkshire 195 (W.Brockwell 7-78) & 31-1. *Match drawn*
**Hull**, June 21, 22, 23: Hampshire 128 (W.Rhodes 6-43) & 61 (W.Rhodes 8-23), Yorkshire 460. *Won by an innings and 271 runs*
**Derby**, June 25, 26: Derbyshire 69 (W.Rhodes 7-32) & 102 (S.Haigh 6-54), Yorkshire 195. *Won by an innings and 24 runs*
**Dewsbury**, June 28, 29: Yorkshire 137 (B.Cranfield 6-64) & 191 (G.H.Hirst 106, B.Cranfield 7-95), Somerset 140 & 48 (S.Haigh 5-25). *Won by 140 runs*

**Headingley**, July 2, 3, 4: Kent 230 (S.Haigh 5-70) & 42-3dec, Yorkshire 132 (C.Blythe 5-41) & 51-3. *Match drawn*

**Scarborough,** July 5, 6, 7: Nottinghamshire 279 (W.B.Goodacre 104*) & 72-6, Yorkshire 311 (G.H.Hirst 155). *Match drawn*

**Sheffield**, July 9, 10, 11: Sussex 232 (G.H.Hirst 6-49) & 164 (W.Rhodes 7-59), Yorkshire 489-9dec (E.Smith 116*, C.H.G.Bland 6-151). *Won by an innings and 93 runs*

**Portsmouth**, July 12, 13, 14: Hampshire 202 & 299 (S.Haigh 5-57), Yorkshire 372 (J.Tunnicliffe 138, H.Baldwin 6-87) & 133-4. *Won by six wickets*

**Worcester**, July 16, 17, 18: Yorkshire 189 & 349-8dec (J.Tunnicliffe 158, G.A.Wilson 5-116), Worcestershire 237 (S.Haigh 5-81) & 143-5. *Match drawn*

**Old Trafford**, July 19, 20, 21: Yorkshire 235 & 146 (W.R.Cuttell 5-51), Lancashire 228 (S.Haigh 5-59) & 20-1. *Match drawn*

**Bradford**, July 23, 24, 25: Yorkshire 409 (G.H.Hirst 111) & 187, Gloucestershire 269 (G.L.Jessop 104, W.Rhodes 8-72) & 287 (G.L.Jessop 139, W.Rhodes 6-120). *Won by 40 runs*

**The Oval**, July 26, 27, 28: Surrey 360 (D.L.A.Jephson 121) & 52 (S.Haigh 6-21), Yorkshire 380 (T.L.Taylor 147, J.Tunnicliffe 101, T.Richardson 6-119). *Match drawn*

**Trent Bridge**, July 30, 31, August 1: Yorkshire 270 (T.G.Wass 6-108) & 197-3 (J.Tunnicliffe 100*), Nottinghamshire 335 (A.Shrewsbury 128). *Match drawn*

**Harrogate** August 2, 3, 4: Yorkshire 171 (W.Mead 6-65) & 42-1dec, Essex 65 (W.Rhodes 6-40) & 52 (W.Rhodes 8-28). *Won by 96 runs*

**Edgbaston**, August 9, 10, 11: Warwickshire 84 (W.Rhodes 6-47) & 43-7, Yorkshire 158-2dec. *Match drawn*

**Headingley**, August 13, 14, 15: Yorkshire 235 (C.M.Wells 5-33) & 96 (C.M.Wells 8-35), Middlesex 192 (S.Haigh 6-61) & 76 (S.Haigh 7-33). *Won by 63 runs*

**Cheltenham**, August 16, 17, 18: Gloucestershire 101 (W.Rhodes 6-36) & 160 (W.Rhodes 7-67), Yorkshire 305 (G.H.Hirst 108, G.L.Jessop 5-67). *Won by an innings and 44 runs*

**Taunton**, August 20, 21, 22: Somerset 250 (W.Rhodes 6-59) & 148, Yorkshire 518-8dec (E.Wainwright 109). *Won by an innings and 120 runs*

**Hove**, August 23, 24, 25: Yorkshire 214 (F.W.Tate 6-43) & 199-8 (J.Vine 5-97), Sussex 268 (W.Rhodes 7-115). *Match drawn*

# NOTES and HIGHLIGHTS

1900's race for the title was a re-enactment of the 'Wars of the Roses' with neither Yorkshire nor Lancashire losing a single game for almost the first three months of the campaign. The turning point was when the Red Rose county lost to Gloucestershire, a mid-table side, at the end of July, as well as a second game later but Yorkshire remained unbeaten and were thus worthy winners. The champions were never dismissed for fewer than 95 but their opponents managed it on ten occasions. They also showed their domination by allowing their opponents to pass 300 only twice but achieved the feat twelve times themselves.

The first game of the season, at Bradford, lasted only one day! Despite being dismissed for fewer than 100 Yorkshire won by an innings, Rhodes (11-36) and Haigh (7-49) bowling unchanged throughout both of Worcestershire's innings. After the visitors had been dismissed for 43, Yorkshire collapsed to 11-4 but Wainwright (34) and Hirst (24) gave the score some respectability before the final denoument.

The same venue witnessed a completely different game over two months later when a match was dominated by the performances of three players. The eventual difference between the two sides came down to the fact that Hirst (111 and 92) was well-supported in the first innings whereas Gloucestershire's Gilbert Jessop (104 and 139) fought a lone battle until it was too late. Rhodes (14-192) came under heavy punishment from Jessop whose second innings (in which he hit the left-arm spinner for seven sixes) lasted only 88 minutes.

Three games later and Rhodes took another 14 wickets, but this time for only 68 runs and in more dramatic circumstances. On the first day at Harrogate, Yorkshire scored 159-9 but the second day was blank. A further 12 runs were added on the final morning before Essex were summarily dismissed for a mere 65. The home side then compiled a brief second innings and a declaration set Essex 149 to win. 25 overs and 65 minutes later the game was over and Yorkshire had won by the very convincing margin, for a low-scoring match, of 96 runs.

Rhodes also took 14 wickets (for 66) in the match against Hampshire at Hull and this was the best match return by any bowler for the whole season. Naturally enough, he topped the national averages - with Haigh in fourth place – achieving an aggregate of 68 wickets (average 9.29) in the month of June alone.

Tom Taylor, in scoring 740 runs at 49.33, was the only Yorkshire batsman (in eighth place) in the top ten of the national averages but Hunter was the leading wicket-keeper. Denton, Haigh and Hirst played in every match. Ernest Smith (553 runs at 29.10 and 29 wickets at 25.89) contributed well. In addition to his 1500 runs, Hirst also took 49 wickets at 25.04.

Lord Hawke, as a captain, was now at the height of his powers. His fourth title was the most convincing of all thus far and the pressure that the team exerted in the field ensured that their opponents only rarely felt in control of the situation.

## PLAYER of the SEASON

The first bowler to take 200 wickets in a Championship season with Yorkshire, Wilfred Rhodes would become one of the most effective all-rounders of all-time. His slow left-arm bowling in particular would eventually create the world record for most first-class wickets (a staggering 4187). He also compiled the longest Test career (over 30 years), became the oldest Test cricketer (at 52) and made most appearances in the Championship (763). He proved a wise and reliable ally for the amateur captains of his time, virtually leading Yorkshire by default, and could read a game probably better than any other player in the entire history of cricket.

Rhodes was born in Kirkheaton in 1877 and made his county debut in 1898. He soon learnt to spin the ball powerfully as well as deceive batsmen with flight and length. His best performance came in 1899 when he took nine for 28 against Essex at Leyton. He eventually took five wickets in an innings on over 250 occasions for Yorkshire alone. His record of taking 100 wickets in a season on 23 occasions remains unbeaten as does the feat of achieving 16 'doubles'.

Rhodes' batting was very much his second string at the start of his career but he eventually opened the innings for England and remains the only England player to bat in all eleven positions in the order. He played in a total of 58 Tests scoring over 2000 runs and taking over 100 wickets. His first-wicket stand of 323 with Jack Hobbs at Melbourne in 1911/12 remains the England record against Australia. He had a sound technique and this served him well on all types of pitch. His best score for Yorkshire was an innings of 267 not out made against Leicestershire at Headingley in 1921.

Rhodes always remained an undemonstrative player, efficient and workmanlike. Cricket was his job, not an activity done in the name of fun. After retirement he coached at Harrow School, and, despite later becoming blind, always retained a keen interest in the game. He died in Dorset in 1973 at the age of 95.

## 1901

## TOP FIVE COUNTIES

|  | Pld | W | L | D | Pts | % |
|---|---|---|---|---|---|---|
| Yorkshire | 27 | 20 | 1 | 6 | 19 | 90.47 |
| Middlesex | 18 | 6 | 2 | 10 | 4 | 50.00 |
| Lancashire | 28 | 11 | 5 | 12 | 6 | 37.50 |
| Sussex | 24 | 8 | 4 | 12 | 4 | 33.33 |
| Warwickshire | 16 | 7 | 4 | 5 | 3 | 27.27 |

## LEADING YORKSHIRE AVERAGES

### BATTING

|  | M | I | NO | Runs | HS | Avge | 100 | 50 |
|---|---|---|---|---|---|---|---|---|
| F.Mitchell | 27 | 38 | 4 | 1674 | 162* | 49.23 | 7 | 6 |
| G.H.Hirst | 27 | 36 | 1 | 1174 | 214 | 33.54 | 2 | 6 |
| J.T.Brown | 27 | 42 | 4 | 1263 | 134* | 33.23 | 3 | 5 |
| T.L.Taylor | 20 | 27 | 1 | 783 | 156 | 30.11 | 2 | 3 |
| J.Tunnicliffe | 27 | 42 | 4 | 1075 | 145 | 28.28 | 1 | 6 |
| D.Denton | 25 | 36 | 1 | 967 | 86 | 27.62 | - | 6 |

## BOWLING

|            | O      | M   | R    | W   | Avge  | 5WI | 10WM | BB   |
|------------|--------|-----|------|-----|-------|-----|------|------|
| W.Rhodes   | 1155.4 | 390 | 2664 | 196 | 13.59 | 20  | 8    | 8-53 |
| G.H.Hirst  | 848.5  | 200 | 2262 | 135 | 16.75 | 12  | 4    | 7-21 |
| S.Haigh    | 361.3  | 73  | 1082 | 49  | 22.08 | 3   | -    | 5-23 |

## FIELDING and WICKET-KEEPING

62 J.Tunnicliffe
61 (34 ct, 27 st) D.Hunter
21 E.Wainwright
20 W.Rhodes

# RESULTS

**Bristol**, May 9, 10, 11: Gloucestershire 150 (W.Rhodes 7-78) & 89 (W.Rhodes 7-63), Yorkshire 224 (F.G.Roberts 6-95) & 16-0. *Won by ten wickets*

**Taunton**, May 13, 14, 15: Somerset 349 (L.C.H.Palairet 103, W.Rhodes 6-115) & 281 (W.Rhodes 6-67), Yorkshire 391 & 241-9 (L.C.Braund 6-113). *Won by one wicket*

**Dewsbury**, May 16, 17, 18: Yorkshire 205 (G.A.Wilson 5-99) & 245, Worcestershire 218 (W.H.Wilkes 109) & 141. *Won by 90 runs*

**Huddersfield**, May 20, 21: Yorkshire 481-8dec (J.Tunnicliffe 145), Derbyshire 106 (J.T.Brown 5-33) & 93 (G.H.Hirst 7-43). *Won by an innings and 282 runs*

**Old Trafford**, May 27, 28: Lancashire 133 (G.H.Hirst 5-54, W.Rhodes 5-67) & 44 (G.H.Hirst 7-23), Yorkshire 134 & 44-1. *Won by nine wickets*

**Leicester,** May 30, 31: Yorkshire 348, Leicestershire 84 (W.Rhodes 6-41) & 136 (W.Rhodes 7-55). *Won by an innings and 128 runs*

**Bournemouth**, June 3, 4: Yorkshire 365 (F.Mitchell 100, C.B.Llewellyn 5-137), Hampshire 75 (G.H.Hirst 6-42) & 208. *Won by an innings and 82 runs*

**Lord's**, June 6, 7, 8: Yorkshire 398 (F.Mitchell 100) & 54-3, Middlesex 168 (W.Rhodes 8-53) & 282 (S.Haigh 5-106). *Won by seven wickets*

**Bradford**, June 10, 11, 12: Surrey 172 (G.H.Hirst 7-78) & 431 (R.Abel 125, V.F.S.Crawford 110), Yorkshire 290 (A.Mitchell 106*, T.Richardson 7-105) & 157-7. *Match drawn*

**Edgbaston**, June 13, 14, 15: Yorkshire 401-5dec (F.Mitchell 162*, J.T.Brown 121), Warwickshire 320 (W.G.Quaife 118*). *Match drawn*
**Headingley**, June 17, 18: Yorkshire 252 (W.Mead 5-78), Essex 97 (S.Haigh 5-23) & 95 (W.Rhodes 6-45). *Won by an innings and 60 runs*
**Trent Bridge**, June 20, 21: Yorkshire 204 (J.R.Gunn 5-49), Nottinghamshire 13 (W.Rhodes 6-4) & 173 (G.H.Hirst 6-26). *Won by an innings and 18 runs*
**Sheffield**, June 24, 25, 26: Yorkshire 201 (J.R.Mason 7-90) & 309, Kent 218 (F.Marchant 111) & 80 (W.Rhodes 5-34). *Won by 212 runs*
**Glossop**, June 27, 28, 29: Yorkshire 213 (W.Bestwick 7-70) & 359-5dec (E.Wainwright 108*), Derbyshire 141 (S.Haigh 5-55) & 186. *Won by 245 runs*
**Bradford**, July 1, 2, 3: Sussex 52 (G.H.Hirst 5-11, W.Rhodes 5-36) & 155 (E.Wainwright 5-19), Yorkshire 158 & 50-0. *Won by ten wickets*
**Scarborough**, July 4, 5, 6: Yorkshire 562 (F.Mitchell 122, T.L.Taylor 113, J.H.King 5-112), Leicestershire 103 (G.H.Hirst 7-21) & 212 (W.Rhodes 6-46). *Won by an innings and 247 runs*
**Worcester,** July 11, 12, 13: Worcestershire 156 & 162, Yorkshire 530 (G.H.Hirst 214). *Won by an innings and 212 runs*
**Headingley**, July 15, 16, 17: Somerset 87 (W.Rhodes 5-39) & 630 (L.C.H.Palairet 173, F.A.Phillips 122, L.C.Braund 107, Rhodes 6-145), Yorkshire 325 & 113. *Lost by 279 runs*
**Bradford**, July 18, 19, 20: Warwickshire 401 (S.Kinneir 123), Yorkshire 237 (F.E.Field 6-92) & 281-2 (J.T.Brown 134*, F.Mitchell 116*). *Match drawn*
**Sheffield**, July 22, 23: Yorkshire 528 (S.Haigh 159, G.H.Hirst 125), Nottinghamshire 151 (J.T.Brown (Darfield) 7-54) & 151. *Won by an innings and 226 runs*
**The Oval**, July 25, 26, 27: Surrey v Yorkshire. *Match abandoned*
**Hull**, July 29, 30: Yorkshire 186 (F.G.Roberts 5-62) & 123, Gloucestershire 70 (W.Rhodes 7-20) & 184 (W.Rhodes 5-66). *Won by 55 runs*
**Headingley**, August 5, 6, 7: Yorkshire 319 (F.Mitchell 106, J.Sharp 6-109) & 175-5, Lancashire 413 (A.C.MacLaren 117, A.Ward 100). *Match drawn*
**Harrogate**, August 8, 9: Hampshire 204 (G.H.Hirst 6-85) & 154 (W.Rhodes 5-51), Yorkshire 439 (T.L.Taylor 156, J.T.Brown 110). *Won by an innings and 81 runs*
**Sheffield**, August 12, 13, 14: Yorkshire 363, Middlesex 62-3. *Match drawn*

**Leyton**, August 15, 16: Essex 30 (G.H.Hirst 7-12) & 41 (G.H.Hirst 5-17),
Yorkshire 104 (W.Mead 6-40). *Won by an innings and 33 runs*
**Hove**, August 19, 20, 21: Sussex 560-5dec (C.B.Fry 209, E.H.Killick 200),
Yorkshire 92 & 107-0. *Match drawn*
**Canterbury**, August 22, 23, 24: Yorkshire 251 & 265, Kent 206 (W.Rhodes
8-55) & 63 (G.H.Hirst 7-24). *Won by 247 runs*

## NOTES and HIGHLIGHTS

This was probably the most convincing win of Yorkshire's 30
Championships. The side won 20 of its 27 games and even a sensational
and totally unexpected defeat to Somerset had no real effect on the title's
destiny. Half of the victories were by an innings and most of the remainder
were by very convincing margins. All of the first eight games were won,
including four consecutive victories each of which were completed in two
days. Yorkshire were never dismissed for fewer than 90 but their opponents
were similarly dealt with no less than twelve times.

Both games against Somerset were excellent matches. In the first encounter,
at Taunton, Yorkshire, batting second, gained a first innings lead of 42 but,
facing an eventual target of 240, looked in trouble at 119-6. Wainwright
and Lord Hawke pulled the situation round and victory came almost at the
last gasp with three minutes and one wicket to spare.

The return fixture at Headingley saw a difference of 543 runs between
Somerset's two innings – a Championship record that stood for 82 years.
Hirst, Haigh and Rhodes dismissed the visitors for 87 then made the three
top scores (61, 37 and 44, respectively) to give Yorkshire a comfortable
lead of 238. This was almost wiped out by Somerset's opening stand alone
the pair, both having made ducks in the first innings, each replying with
centuries and leading the way to a massive 630. Yorkshire's target was
392 but they got nowhere near and collapsed to an ignominious defeat to a
county that was to finish no higher than twelfth.

A few weeks earlier, in complete contrast, Nottinghamshire had been
dismissed for a paltry 13 at Trent Bridge. The highest score was 4 and
there were three ducks. The whole process lasted 55 minutes, during which

there were precisely seven scoring strokes. The bowling was led by Rhodes whose full figures were 7.5-4-4-6. The home side scored 160 more at the second attempt but only three batsmen made double figures and they still lost by an innings.

A remarkable first day took place in the match at Leyton when 27 wickets fell. Essex were all out for 30 in 16.1 overs and this took less than an hour. Yorkshire also struggled but Taylor (44) ensured some relative respectability. The home side were all out, for a second time, before noon on the second day but their 41 was not much of an improvement and Hirst (12-29) and Rhodes (6-37) had bowled unchanged throughout the match to bring the visitors an innings victory. Other than Taylor, only four batsmen on either side passed double figures, Essex's top score being 12.

No batsman came in the top ten of the national averages but the batting was extremely consistent. Each of the eleven men who played in at least 20 games averaged over 20, except for Hunter, and only one scored fewer than 500 runs. Seven batsmen each scored at least one century. Haigh made the highest score of his career in the game against Nottinghamshire at Sheffield.

The real architects of the title were Rhodes and Hirst who were the top two bowlers in the national averages. They bowled 64% of Yorkshire's overs and took 71% of the wickets. They both achieved particularly economical figures at various times, Hirst with 15-9-11-5 against Sussex at Bradford and Rhodes with 20.2-12-20-7 against Gloucestershire at Hull.

Brown, Hirst, Mitchell, Rhodes and Tunnicliffe each played in every match. One of the main reasons for the successful season was the side's stability, as in 1898. Only 23 of the total of 297 appearances were by players outside the first-choice team. Hirst became the first Yorkshire player to complete the double of 1000 runs and 100 wickets in a season of Championship cricket. Brown, in addition to his 1263 runs, took 43 wickets at 24.98, his leg-breaks adding another dimension to the team's skills.

## PLAYER of the SEASON

1901 was Frank Mitchell's best season for Yorkshire and his achievement included four centuries in six innings in four consecutive matches at the start of June making a total of 484 runs at 161.33. A double international in two senses of the term, Frank Mitchell represented England at both rugby and cricket and would also play Test cricket for South Africa. Born in Market Weighton in 1872, Mitchell first played for Yorkshire in 1894 and captained Cambridge University two years later. He played in only two full seasons for the county but was a hard-hitting, aggressive batsman who scored at a good rate and could adapt his game for different types of pitch. In 1899 he scored seven half-centuries in twelve days as well as his career best score of 194 against Leicestershire at Grace Road.

Mitchell's two Tests for England were both in South Africa towards the end of the 1890s and he settled there after fighting in the Boer War. In 1912 he led his adopted country in three Tests in England. He later followed a distinguished career as a sports journalist and died at Blackheath in 1935.

### 1902

### TOP FIVE COUNTIES

|                  | Pld | W  | L | D  | Pts | %     |
|------------------|-----|----|---|----|-----|-------|
| Yorkshire        | 25  | 13 | 1 | 11 | 12  | 85.71 |
| Sussex           | 24  | 7  | 3 | 14 | 4   | 40.00 |
| Nottinghamshire  | 20  | 6  | 3 | 11 | 3   | 33.33 |
| Surrey           | 28  | 8  | 5 | 15 | 3   | 23.07 |
| Lancashire       | 23  | 7  | 5 | 11 | 2   | 16.16 |

## LEADING YORKSHIRE AVERAGES

### BATTING

|              | M  | I  | NO | Runs | HS   | Avge  | 100 | 50 |
|--------------|----|----|----|------|------|-------|-----|----|
| T.L.Taylor   | 22 | 31 | 3  | 1276 | 142* | 45.57 | 4   | 8  |
| G.H.Hirst    | 21 | 28 | 3  | 1025 | 134  | 41.00 | 2   | 6  |
| D.Denton     | 25 | 34 | 4  | 934  | 127  | 31.13 | 2   | 3  |
| I.Washington | 23 | 35 | 5  | 906  | 100* | 30.20 | 1   | 5  |
| J.Tunnicliffe| 25 | 37 | 0  | 1079 | 127  | 29.16 | 3   | 5  |
| J.T.Brown    | 24 | 36 | 2  | 868  | 91   | 25.52 | -   | 6  |

### BOWLING

|            | O     | M   | R    | W   | Avge  | 5WI | 10WM | BB   |
|------------|-------|-----|------|-----|-------|-----|------|------|
| S.Haigh    | 608.4 | 173 | 1475 | 123 | 11.99 | 12  | 3    | 7-38 |
| W.Rhodes   | 876.4 | 291 | 1748 | 140 | 12.48 | 12  | 5    | 8-26 |
| G.H.Hirst  | 475   | 135 | 1089 | 53  | 20.54 | 2   | 1    | 7-68 |

### FIELDING and WICKET-KEEPING

45 (29 ct, 16 st) D.Hunter
32 J.Tunnicliffe
10 J.T.Brown (Driffield), D.Denton

## RESULTS

**Leyton**, May 8, 9, 10: Essex 89 (S.Haigh 5-32), Yorkshire 171-3 (F.S.Jackson 101*). *Match drawn*

**Headingley**, May 12, 13, 14: Yorkshire 302 (F.W.Tate 5-81) & 182-5dec, Sussex 232 & 126-3. *Match drawn*

**Huddersfield**, May 15, 16, 17: Leicestershire 228 & 10-1, Yorkshire 323-6dec (T.L.Taylor 114). *Match drawn*

**Sheffield**, May 19, 20: Lancashire 72 & 54 (F.S.Jackson 5-8), Yorkshire 148 (S.F.Barnes 6-39). *Won by an innings and 22 runs*

**Bradford**, May 26, 27: Yorkshire 337 (J.Tunnicliffe 127), Kent 100 (W.Rhodes 6-42) & 129 (F.S.Jackson 6-30). *Won by an innings and 108 runs*

**Dewsbury**, May 29, 30, 31: Yorkshire 393 (T.L.Taylor 106), Derbyshire 23-2. *Match drawn*

**Chesterfield**, June 5, 6, 7: Yorkshire 150 (J.J.Hulme 5-68) & 309 (T.L.Taylor 142*), Derbyshire 64 (S.Haigh 5-31, G.H.Hirst 5-32) & 24-3. *Match drawn*

**Bradford**, June 9, 10: Middlesex 73 (W.Rhodes 7-24) & 80 (S.Haigh 7-47), Yorkshire 175 (A.E.Trott 6-69). *Won by an innings and 22 runs*

**Sheffield**, June 16, 17, 18: Somerset 86 (F.S.Jackson 6-29) & 106 (S.Haigh 6-19), Yorkshire 74 (L.C.Braund 6-30) & 84 (L.C.Braund 9-41). *Lost by 34 runs*

**Edgbaston**, June 19, 20, 21: Warwickshire 100 (S.Haigh 6-48) & 45 (S.Haigh 5-18), Yorkshire 208 (S.Hargreave 6-51). *Won by an innings and 63 runs*

**Hull,** June 26, 27, 28: Yorkshire 184 (G.Anthony 5-22) & 346 (J.Tunnicliffe 105, J.R.Gunn 6-128), Nottinghamshire 155 (G.H.Hirst 7-68) & 148. ***Won by 227 runs***

**Headingley**, June 30, July 1, 2: Surrey 188 (W.Rhodes 5-76) & 72, Yorkshire 362-8dec (I.Washington 100*). *Won by an innings and 102 runs*

**Hove**, July 10, 11, 12: Yorkshire 372 & 84-6, Sussex 455 (W.Newham 109, G.Brann 108). *Match drawn*

**Bradford**, July 14, 15, 16: Yorkshire 504 (G.H.Hirst 134, D.Denton 127), Essex 281 (F.L.Fane 106, W.Rhodes 7-123) & 193 (W.Rhodes 5-72). *Won by an innings and 30 runs*

**Trent Bridge**, July 17, 18, 19: Nottinghamshire 328 (J.A.Dixon 123, W.Rhodes 5-91) & 255-2 (J.Iremonger 128*), Yorkshire 497 (T.L.Taylor 120, J.Tunnicliffe 104). *Match drawn*

**Headingley**, July 21, 22, 23: Yorkshire 253 (E.J.Spry 8-83), Gloucestershire 46 (W.Rhodes 5-22) & 116 (W.Rhodes 7-36). *Won by an innings and 91 runs*

**Worcester**, July 24, 25, 26: Yorkshire 257 & 248 (G.T.Simpson-Hayward 5-75), Worcestershire 230 (S.Haigh 5-90). *Match drawn*

**Sheffield**, July 28, 29, 30: Yorkshire 135 & 270, Warwickshire 207 (S.Haigh 5-29) & 98 (W.Rhodes 6-33). *Won by 100 runs*

**The Oval**, July 31, August 1, 2: Yorkshire 470 (Lord Hawke 126, W.Lockwood 7-159) & 363-3, Surrey 359. *Match drawn*

**Old Trafford**, August 4, 5, 6: Lancashire 243 (S.Haigh 5-62), Yorkshire 499-5 (G.H.Hirst 112*, D.Denton 108*). *Match drawn*

**Leicester**, August 7, 8, 9: Leicestershire v Yorkshire *Match abandoned*

**Harrogate**, August 11, 12: Worcestershire 82 (S.Haigh 7-38) & 130, Yorkshire 79 (E.G.Arnold 7-35) & 134-4. *Won by six wickets*

**Cheltenham**, August 14, 15: Gloucestershire 104 & 55 (W.Rhodes 6-34), Yorkshire 261. *Won by an innings and 102 runs*
**Taunton**, August 18, 19, 20: Yorkshire 129 & 63-1, Somerset 104 (W.Rhodes 6-32). *Match drawn*
**Lord's**, August 21, 22: Middlesex 99 (S.Haigh 5-39) & 93 (S.Haigh 7-40), Yorkshire 125 (B.J.T.Bosanquet 6-28) & 68-6. *Won by four wickets*
**Catford**, August 25, 26: Kent 71 (W.Rhodes 8-26) & 100, Yorkshire 97 (A.Hearne 5-22) & 78-1. *Won by nine wickets*

## NOTES and HIGHLIGHTS

Although Yorkshire did not win as many games as in the previous season, the margin of victory in 1902 was just as convincing. Although the county won only three of its first nine matches, eight of the eventual 13 wins were by an innings. The campaign finished in style with victories in four of the last five games, each of these being concluded in two days. The only blot on the season was another defeat by Somerset, who thus became the only county to defeat Yorkshire in the first three years of the twentieth-century.

Lancashire came to Sheffield for the Whitsuntide match but were beaten in two days despite there being only 60 minutes play on day one. The visitors collapsed twice, mainly to Jackson who had match figures of eight for 13 in 10.3 overs. The same player (33) top-scored in a Yorkshire innings that contained eight double-figure scores. Lancashire could manage only two in both innings combined.

It was a similar story three weeks later at Bradford. Match figures of 10-56 and 9-53 by Rhodes and Haigh, respectively, ensured a stranglehold on Middlesex and in Yorkshire's solitary innings a score of 64 by Tunnicliffe with support from Hirst (46 not out) gave enough respectability to complete another innings victory. All of Haigh's seven victims in Middlesex's second innings were bowled.

Somerset's victory, at Taunton as in 1901, was due almost entirely to one man. Len Braund had outstanding match figures of 15-71 and made more runs (65 in total – 34% of his side's effort) than anyone else on either side. Somerset's first knock began with an opening stand of 44 but then all ten wickets fell for 42! The home side's second innings contained six ducks with Haigh bowling all of the last five batsmen and Yorkshire were set a target of 119. Beaumont Cranfield took the first wicket but Braund's leg-breaks accounted for the rest. He finished the match with the best innings and match analyses for the whole season.

The return fixture with Middlesex was another low-scoring affair and, yet again, the home county failed to reach 100 in either innings. Once more Haigh (12-79) and Rhodes (7-81) did the damage, thus taking 38 of the 40 wickets to fall in the two fixtures. Haigh bowled all of the first five batsmen in Middlesex's second innings and this ensured that Yorkshire, who were soon 24-4, did not have a large target to face.

Again, it was the bowling that played the major part in Yorkshire winning the title. Haigh led the national averages with Rhodes (third) and Jackson (36 wickets at 14.58 – fifth) also appearing in the top ten. 101 (82%) of Haigh's 123 wickets were bowled or lbw – a convincing testimony to his accuracy. Taylor (seventh) was the county's only representative in the top ten of the batting. In addition to his tally of wickets Jackson also scored 544 runs at 32.00.

Denton and Tunnicliffe played in every fixture and Lord Hawke had captained Yorkshire to its first hat-trick of titles. He was able to call on twelve England players at various times and an eleven consisting of Brown, Tunnicliffe, Denton, Jackson (or Mitchell), Taylor, Hirst, Rhodes, Wainwright (in his final season), Haigh, Hawke and Hunter was one of the strongest in the county's history.

## PLAYER of the SEASON

The batting averages for the 1902 season were led by Tom Taylor who was playing, sadly, in his last full season. But for business commitments - he played as an amateur - he could have had a most distinguished career and was even designated by Lord Hawke to be his eventual successor. Born in Leeds in 1878, he went up to Cambridge and led the University side in 1900, having made his county debut in the previous season. As a batsman, he possessed a strong defence but could also attack in brilliant style. His best score for Yorkshire was 156 against Hampshire at Harrogate in 1901.

*Lord Hawke (left) and T.L.Taylor. The former captained Yorkshire for 28 years and was President also for 28 years spanning 1883 to 1938. By contrast, Taylor played for eight years and was President for thirteen.*

His wicket-keeping skills received little opportunity but it was believed by at least one critic that he was a more nimble practitioner than the current incumbent, David Hunter. He became Yorkshire president in 1948 and served in that capacity until he died in his native city in 1960.

## 1903 and 1904

Middlesex lifted the title for the first time, in 1903, with Yorkshire in third place. 1904 saw The Roses as the top two counties, with Lancashire as convincing winners. For 1905 Northamptonshire were added to the first-class list and this brought the number of counties up to 16.

# 1905

## TOP FIVE COUNTIES

|  | Pld | W | L | D | Pts | % |
|---|---|---|---|---|---|---|
| Yorkshire | 28 | 18 | 3 | 7 | 15 | 71.42 |
| Lancashire | 25 | 12 | 3 | 10 | 9 | 60.00 |
| Sussex | 28 | 13 | 4 | 11 | 9 | 52.94 |
| Surrey | 27 | 14 | 6 | 7 | 8 | 40.00 |
| Leicestershire | 22 | 8 | 5 | 9 | 3 | 23.07 |

*NOTE: Surrey's total of drawn games includes one match that was tied.*

## LEADING YORKSHIRE AVERAGES

### BATTING

|  | M | I | NO | Runs | HS | Avge | 100 | 50 |
|---|---|---|---|---|---|---|---|---|
| G.H.Hirst | 24 | 35 | 7 | 1713 | 341 | 61.17 | 4 | 8 |
| D.Denton | 28 | 43 | 1 | 1963 | 172 | 46.73 | 7 | 8 |
| W.Rhodes | 25 | 35 | 4 | 1117 | 201 | 36.03 | 2 | 9 |
| J.Tunnicliffe | 21 | 38 | 5 | 913 | 102 | 27.66 | 1 | 5 |

### BOWLING

|  | O | M | R | W | Avge | 5WI | 10WM | BB |
|---|---|---|---|---|---|---|---|---|
| S.Haigh | 622 | 177 | 1429 | 97 | 14.73 | 8 | 2 | 6-21 |
| W.Rhodes | 842.5 | 232 | 1986 | 126 | 15.76 | 10 | 3 | 8-90 |
| G.H.Hirst | 599.3 | 124 | 1618 | 88 | 18.38 | 4 | 1 | 7-48 |
| H.Myers | 396.1 | 75 | 1209 | 62 | 19.50 | 3 | - | 7-15 |
| W.Ringrose | 384.3 | 72 | 1206 | 60 | 20.10 | 5 | - | 7-51 |

### FIELDING and WICKET-KEEPING

63 (47 ct, 16st) D.Hunter
35 W.Rhodes
30 D.Denton
22 J.Tunnicliffe

# RESULTS

**Taunton**, May 4, 5, 6: Yorkshire 549-9dec (W.Rhodes 201), Somerset 98 (G.H.Hirst 7-48) & 227. *Won by an innings and 244 runs*

**Bristol**, May 8, 9, 10: Yorkshire 338 (E.G.Dennett 7-158), Gloucestershire 96 (W.Rhodes 5-36) & 187. *Won by an innings and 55 runs*

**Worcester**, May 11, 12, 13: Yorkshire 225 (G.H.Hirst 108*, E.G.Arnold 5-70) & 232, Worcestershire 97 (H.Myers 6-50) & 295 (F.L.Bowley 151, W.Rhodes 6-87). *Won by 65 runs*

**Bradford**, May 15, 16: Yorkshire 289 (F.S.Jackson 111, W.Bestwick 5-91), Derbyshire 108 & 120. *Won by an innings and 61 runs*

**Leicester**, May 18, 19, 20: Leicestershire 419 (C.J.B.Wood 160*, S.Coe 100, W.Ringrose 5-104) & 121-7, Yorkshire 515 (G.H.Hirst 341, G.Gill 6-172). *Match drawn*

**Edgbaston**, May 25, 26, 27: Warwickshire 313 (J.H.G.Devey 125, W.Rhodes 8-90) & 238-4 (W.G.Quaife 109*), Yorkshire 361 (D.Denton 132, J.Tunnicliffe 102). *Match drawn*

**Headingley**, May 29, 30, 31: Yorkshire 323 & 157, Worcestershire 119 (S.Haigh 6-36) & 158 (S.Haigh 6-59). *Won by 203 runs*

**Lord's**, June 1, 2, 3: Middlesex 145 (S.Haigh 6-56) & 232, Yorkshire 275 (D.Denton 102) & 103-3. *Won by seven wickets*

**Old Trafford**, June 12, 13, 14: Lancashire 399 (J.T.Tyldesley 134, R.H.Spooner 109, S.Haigh 6-74), Yorkshire 133 (W.Brearley 5-31) & 214 (A.Kermode 6-70). *Lost by an innings and 52 runs*

**Derby,** June 15, 16: Yorkshire 123 (A.Warren 7-57) & 161 (A.Warren 5-69), Derbyshire 190 (W.Ringrose 6-78) & 96-1. *Lost by nine wickets*

**Sheffield**, June 19, 20, 21: Yorkshire 61 (T.G.Wass 7-28) & 227 (J.R.Gunn 7-78), Nottinghamshire 122 (S.Haigh 6-34) & 39 (S.Haigh 6-21). *Won by 127 runs*

**Dewsbury**, June 22, 23: Yorkshire 153 (S.Hargreave 5-64) & 108 (S.Santall 5-26), Warwickshire 138 (W.Rhodes 5-48) & 57 (S.Haigh 5-26, W.Rhodes 5-26). *Won by 66 runs*

**Headingley**, June 26, 27, 28: Yorkshire 295 & 243-7dec (G.H.Hirst 103*), Sussex 294 (C.B.Fry 111) & 77-3. *Match drawn*

**Hull**, June 29, 30: Yorkshire 77 (C.Blythe 6-40) & 162 (C.Blythe 5-49), Kent 124 (H.Myers 7-15) & 116-4. *Lost by six wickets*

**Harrogate**, July 6, 7: Yorkshire 474 (W.Rhodes 108), Somerset 125 (G.Deyes 5-75) & 200. *Won by an innings and 149 runs*

**Tunbridge Wells**, July 13, 14: Kent 142 (W.Ringrose 6-66) & 174 (G.H.Hirst 5-43), Yorkshire 239 & 81-2. *Won by eight wickets*
**Bournemouth**, July 17, 18: Yorkshire 491 (D.Denton 165, J.W.Rothery 118), Hampshire 172 & 152 (H.Myers 5-48). *Won by an innings and 167 runs*
**The Oval**, July 20, 21, 22: Yorkshire 442 (G.H.Hirst 232*, N.A.Knox 5-162), Surrey 116 (G.H.Hirst 5-43) & 218 (T.W.Hayward 115). *Won by an innings and 108 runs*
**Sheffield**, July 24, 25, 26: Yorkshire 261 (T.Jayes 6-78) & 295-8dec, Leicestershire 137 (W.Ringrose 7-51) & 174 (S.Haigh 5-43). *Won by 245 runs*
**Trent Bridge**, July 27, 28: Nottinghamshire 114 (W.Rhodes 5-34) & 174, Yorkshire 343. *Won by an innings and 55 runs*
**Bradford**, July 31, August 1, 2: Gloucestershire 245 & 141, Yorkshire 504-7dec (D.Denton 172). *Won by an innings and 118 runs*
**Hull**, August 3, 4, 5: Yorkshire 303-4dec (D.Denton 133*), Hampshire 88-3. *Match drawn*
**Sheffield**, August 7, 8, 9: Yorkshire 76 (W.Brearley 7-35) & 285 (W.Brearley 6-122), Lancashire 177 (W.Rhodes 5-66) & 140. *Won by 44 runs*
**Headingley**, August 10, 11: Surrey 171 (W.Rhodes 6-73) & 91, Yorkshire 231 (J.N.Crawford 7-90) & 33-5. *Won by five wickets*
**Huddersfield**, August 17, 18, 19: Yorkshire 423-6dec (D.Denton 134), Essex 172 (W.Ringrose 6-79) & 58 (W.Rhodes 6-9). *Won by an innings and 193 runs*
**Bradford**, August 21, 22, 23: Middlesex 285 & 87 (W.Rhodes 7-45), Yorkshire 281 & 59-0. *Match drawn*
**Leyton**, August 24, 25, 26: Essex 521 (F.L.Fane 106, C.McGahey 105), Yorkshire 98 (J.W.H.T.Douglas 5-31) & 227-7. *Match drawn*
**Hove**, August 28, 29, 30: Yorkshire 203 (G.R.Cox 5-71) & 154-5dec, Essex 137 (G.H.Hirst 6-41) & 119-1. *Match drawn*

## NOTES and HIGHLIGHTS

For the third time in six seasons the two Rose counties occupied the top two places in the Championship. Although both sides lost only three games, Yorkshire's 18 wins contrasted convincingly with Lancashire's 12. Yorkshire began well, winning all of their first four games but they then lost three games out of six. Victories in ten of the next eleven meant that it did not matter that the last three games were all drawn. Ten of the 18 victories were by an innings and the bowlers were the most convincing part of the team.

In a remarkable innings at Leicester, Hirst came to the wicket with the score at 22-3. He proceeded to score 341 in seven hours and this remains Yorkshire's highest-ever individual innings. The county were facing a Leicestershire score of 419 but Hirst hit one six and 53 fours and made his runs out of 495 while he was at the wicket – 68%. Although little time was left after Yorkshire had been all out for 515, the home side collapsed to 121-7 and hung on for a draw.

Lancashire had won the first Roses match comfortably and the return game was a vital encounter, with the Red Rose county just ahead in the table, over the (early) August Bank Holiday week-end. Unfortunately Yorkshire immediately collapsed and were all out for a disappointing 76, mainly to the pace of Walter Brearley. Although Lancashire began well they, too, collapsed and with Jackson taking four of the last five wickets, the visitors' lead was only 101. The home side gave a much-improved performance in the second innings with Denton (96) and Rhodes (74) leading the way and setting Lancashire a target of 184. Despite the top four managing almost a hundred runs between them another collapse ensued and the White Rose county ran out winners by 44 runs. Brearley (match figures of 13-157) did not deserve to be on the losing side but the all-round efforts of Jackson (75 runs and five wickets) and Rhodes (match figures of 9-115) made the telling difference between the two sides.

Yorkshire were lucky to escape with a draw in their penultimate match. Essex began with 521 at Leyton and promptly dismissed Yorkshire for 98 with Johnny Douglas taking a hat-trick. They were saved when following on, mainly by Tunnicliffe (59) and Hirst (90) who battled for 3½ hours in tandem to wear down the bowling. Ernest Smith made an invaluable 0 not out in the last hour which concluded with Yorkshire still 196 behind and only three wickets left.

Denton and Hubert Myers played throughout the campaign. Jackson's 530 runs at 29.44 gave him fourth place in the averages but Hirst came fourth in the national averages and sixth in the bowling. The latter were led by

Haigh with Rhodes just two places behind. Haigh took five wickets in an innings on seven occasions in five consecutive matches taking 45 wickets at 8.64. Hunter came second in the wicket-keepers' list but the county also gave a debut to Arthur Dolphin who was to be the regular stumper from 1910 until well into the 1920s. Noted for his speed behind the wickets, almost one-third of his 829 Yorkshire dismissals were stumpings.

## PLAYER of the SEASON

The batting averages were topped, with some comfort, by George Hirst who vied with Rhodes for the accolade of being the best all-rounder in England. By a remarkable coincidence he also was born in Kirkheaton, batted right-handed and bowled with the left. Unlike Rhodes, however, Hirst's bowling was of the medium-fast variety and he had a settled middle-order position in the batting order.

Hirst was born in 1871 and made his county debut at the age of 19. His bowling made most impact at first but he secured his first 'double' in 1896 and played in the first of his 24 Test matches 18 months later. His bowling contained much variety, especially of pace, and his batting was aggressive, particularly on the leg-side. He was to achieve the 'double' on 14 occasions and his best performances were the innings of 341 referred to above and an analysis of 9-23 in the 1910 Headingley Roses fixture. His greatest success, however, came in 1906 when he became the only player in history to achieve a 'double double' with 2385 runs and 208 wickets in all first-class matches.

Hirst retired after the end of the 1921 season to become coach at Eton, although his final first-class match was in 1929. He died in Lindley, Huddersfield in 1954. The opposite of Rhodes, in many respects, Hirst was genial, warm and friendly and played the game with obvious enthusiasm.

### 1906 and 1907

Kent and Nottinghamshire, respectively, both won their first official titles in these two seasons. Yorkshire gained the runners-up position in both campaigns, a spot they shared with Worcestershire in 1907. Hirst had a remarkable season in 1906 scoring 1771 runs and taking 182 wickets in Championship matches alone – an unprecedented feat.

# 1908

## TOP FIVE COUNTIES

|  | Pld | W | L | D | Pts | % |
|---|---|---|---|---|---|---|
| Yorkshire | 28 | 16 | 0 | 12 | 16 | 100.00 |
| Kent | 25 | 17 | 3 | 5 | 14 | 70.00 |
| Surrey | 29 | 13 | 4 | 12 | 9 | 52.94 |
| Middlesex | 19 | 6 | 3 | 10 | 3 | 33.33 |
| Sussex | 28 | 6 | 4 | 18 | 2 | 20.00 |

## LEADING YORKSHIRE AVERAGES

### BATTING

|  | M | I | NO | Runs | HS | Avge | 100 | 50 |
|---|---|---|---|---|---|---|---|---|
| G.H.Hirst | 28 | 41 | 8 | 1332 | 128* | 40.36 | 1 | 10 |
| D.Denton | 28 | 44 | 4 | 1488 | 110 | 37.20 | 1 | 13 |
| W.Rhodes | 27 | 43 | 1 | 1412 | 146 | 33.61 | 3 | 5 |
| W.H.Wilkinson | 28 | 42 | 3 | 1111 | 99 | 28.48 | - | 7 |

### BOWLING

|  | O | M | R | W | Avge | 5WI | 10WM | BB |
|---|---|---|---|---|---|---|---|---|
| S.Haigh | 412.1 | 113 | 860 | 71 | 12.11 | 6 | - | 6-13 |
| G.H.Hirst | 896.5 | 238 | 1941 | 156 | 12.44 | 15 | 3 | 7-51 |
| J.T.Newstead | 804.4 | 221 | 1700 | 115 | 14.78 | 9 | 3 | 7-18 |
| W.Rhodes | 592.1 | 183 | 1295 | 78 | 16.60 | 3 | - | 6-17 |

### FIELDING and WICKET-KEEPING

47 (43 ct, 4 st) D.Hunter
23 W.H.Wilkinson
21 G.H.Hirst, J.T.Newstead

# RESULTS

**Northampton**, May 7, 8: Yorkshire 356-8dec (D.Denton 110, R.W.R.Hawtin 5-78), Northamptonshire 27 (G.H.Hirst 6-12) & 15 (G.H.Hirst 6-7). *Won by an innings and 314 runs*
**Bradford**, May 18, 19: Kent 77 & 46 (S.Haigh 5-24), Yorkshire 101 & 25-1. *Won by nine wickets*
**Leyton**, May 21, 22, 23: Essex 226 (G.H.Hirst 5-69) & 226-9dec, Yorkshire 188 (J.W.H.T.Douglas 5-62) & 210-4. *Match drawn*
**Headingley**, May 25, 26: Surrey 90 (S.Haigh 6-13) & 69 (G.H.Hirst 6-23), Yorkshire 113 (W.C.Smith 5-46) & 48-3. *Won by seven wickets*
**Chesterfield**, May 28, 29, 30: Yorkshire 190 & 352-5dec (G.H.Hirst 128*), Derbyshire 102 (S.Haigh 5-23) & 244. *Won by 193 runs*
**Edgbaston**, June 1, 2, 3: Yorkshire 339, Warwickshire 121 & 166-4. *Match drawn*
**Worcester**, June 4, 5, 6: Yorkshire 130 (J.A.Cuffe 5-63) & 228, Worcestershire 197 (S.Haigh 5-48) & 92 (G.H.Hirst 6-34). *Won by 69 runs*
**Sheffield**, June 8, 9, 10: Yorkshire 209 (W.Brearley 7-116) & 210 (W.Brearley 5-89), Lancashire 129 (G.H.Hirst 6-41) & 97 (G.H.Hirst 5-47). *Won by 193 runs*
**Leicester**, June 11, 12: Yorkshire 437, Leicestershire 58 (W.Rhodes 6-17) & 58 (J.T.Newstead 7-18). *Won by an innings and 321 runs*
**Huddersfield**, June 15, 16, 17: Northamptonshire 196 (G.H.Hirst 6-68), Yorkshire 347. *Match drawn*
**Lord's**, June 18, 19: Middlesex 130 & 153 (G.H.Hirst 6-54), Yorkshire 157 (F.A.Tarrant 6-59) & 127-7 (A.E.Trott 5-34). *Won by three wickets*
**Bradford**, June 22, 23, 24: Warwickshire 294 & 159, Yorkshire 239 (F.E.Field 6-64) & 216-7 (F.E.Field 5-75). *Won by three wickets*
**Trent Bridge**, June 25, 26, 27: Yorkshire 179 & 374-6dec (J.T.Newstead 100*), Nottinghamshire 207 (J.T.Newstead 7-68) & 66-4. *Match drawn*
**Dewsbury**, June 29, 30: Somerset 160 (G.H.Hirst 6-53) & 132 (J.T.Newstead 5-42), Yorkshire 240 & 53-2. *Won by eight wickets*
**Dover,** July 6, 7, 8: Yorkshire 401 (J.W.Rothery 161) & 90-3, Kent 242 (J.T.Newstead 6-106). *Match drawn*
**Huddersfield**, July 9, 10, 11: Sussex 290, Yorkshire 164 (J.H.Vincent 5-12). *Match drawn*
**Headingley**, July 13, 14, 15: Yorkshire 189 (T.W.Wass 7-93) & 132 (A.W.Hallam 5-59, T.G.Wass 5-72), Nottinghamshire 113 (G.H.Hirst 7-51) & 68 (W.Rhodes 6-33). *Won by 140 runs*

**Hull**, July 16, 17, 18: Essex 42-3 v Yorkshire *Match drawn*
**Sheffield**, July 20, 21: Gloucestershire 153 (G.H.Hirst 5-40) & 92 (S.Haigh 5-19), Yorkshire 340. *Won by an innings and 95 runs*
**Harrogate**, July 23, 24, 25: Yorkshire 325 (W.Rhodes 122, E.W.Astill 5-102, T.Jayes 5-105) & 69-0, Leicestershire 309 (G.H.Hirst 5-102). *Match drawn*
**Headingley**, July 27, 28, 29: Derbyshire 127 (J.T.Newstead 6-43) & 136, Yorkshire 394-8dec (B.B.Wilson 109). *Won by an innings and 131 runs*
**Old Trafford**, August 1, 3, 4: Yorkshire 206 (W.Brearley 7-81) & 243 (W.Brearley 6-115), Lancashire 144 & 115 (J.T.Newstead 5-44). *Won by 190 runs*
**Bradford**, August 10, 11, 12: Yorkshire 279 (J.T.Hearne 9-78) & 153-1dec, Middlesex 164 (W.Rhodes 5-49) & 232-8 (J.Douglas 109). *Match drawn*
**The Oval**, August 13, 14, 15: Surrey 117 (J.T.Newstead 5-44, G.H.Hirst 5-58) & 177 (J.T.Newstead 5-48), Yorkshire 162 & 135-3. *Won by seven wickets*
**Sheffield**, August 17, 18, 19: Yorkshire 378 (W.Rhodes 146), Worcestershire 24-1. *Match drawn*
**Cheltenham**, August 20, 21, 22: Yorkshire 219 & 222 (E.G.Dennett 6-85), Gloucestershire 83 & 176 (J.T.Newstead 7-66). *Won by 182 runs*
**Taunton**, August 24, 25, 26: Yorkshire 210 (W.T.Greswell 7-67) & 240-6dec (E.Robson 5-44), Somerset 101 (G.H.Hirst 5-21) & 64-3. *Match drawn*
**Hove**, August 27, 28, 29: Sussex 105 (S.Haigh 6-60) & Yorkshire 111-3. *Match drawn*

## NOTES and HIGHLIGHTS

Yorkshire equalled their feat of 1900 in going through the whole season without losing a single match. This was a great surprise to many observers as it was felt that they would be weak in batting. However it was a wet summer, Haigh, Hirst and Rhodes performed well yet again and the sudden development of John Newstead (733 runs and 155 wickets) gave the side an extra dimension. Being in the process of re-building meant that many players were young and this helped the fielding – another important factor in the success.

Yorkshire were never dismissed for fewer than 100 but their opponents were dealt with in like manner on 13 occasions. Three of their first four games finished in two days, their opponents' best innings total being 90. In these four matches Hirst took 34 wickets at 7.88 and Haigh 26 at 8.07.

The first game of the season was Northamptonshire's first against Yorkshire since joining the Championship. They were completely out-played to the extent that the combined total of their two innings – 42 runs – is still a record low for an inter-county game. Hirst (12-19) and Haigh (6-19) bowled unchanged throughout and the whole demolition process took just 2¼ hours.

No batsman came in the top ten of the national averages but the bowling was led by Haigh and Hirst with Newstead (fourth) and Rhodes (seventh) also in the top ten. Denton, Hirst, Newstead and William Wilkinson did not miss a single game.

1908 was the last of the record eight titles that were won under the leadership of Lord Hawke. He led the county for 28 seasons, finishing in 1910 and then became the Club's president, a post that he held until his death in 1938. His importance to Yorkshire CCC is immeasurable – his off-the-field innovations did much to encourage the players to develop their characters and they were able to approach their cricket more confidently as a result.

Major Booth was one of the young players to make his debut in 1908. A fine all-rounder, he would score over 4000 runs and take over 500 wickets for the county as well as play in two Tests. Tragically he lost his life at the age of only 29 during the First World War.

## PLAYER of the SEASON

The leading run aggregate in 1908 was achieved by David Denton, who, with an eventual tally of 33,282 runs, would become Yorkshire's second-most prolific batsman after Herbert Sutcliffe. Making the pivotal number three spot his own, he batted right-handed in a stylish manner with a great variety of strokes. He enjoyed his fair share of luck but scored his runs at a fast rate and the highest of his 69 centuries came in 1912. Another string to his bow was his fine fielding in the deep. He was quick on his feet and possessed a fast and accurate throw as well as a very safe pair of hands.

Denton was born and died in Thornes, near Wakefield, living from 1874 to 1950. His career with Yorkshire lasted from 1894 to 1920. He played in eleven Tests in the late 1900s and, successively, became Yorkshire's scorer and an umpire on retirement.

## 1909-1911

The champions, in chronological order, were Kent, Kent and Warwickshire and Yorkshire finished third, eighth and seventh respectively. A new name was therefore added to the list of title-holders. For 1911 a new points system was devised. This gave five points for a win and three (for first innings lead) or one in a drawn match. The counties were ranked according to percentage of points gained divided by the number of possible points. Drawn games in which no decision was made on the first innings were designated as 'No Result' matches and not included when totaling up the number of possible points.

## 1912

### TOP FIVE COUNTIES

|  | Pld | W | L | D | Pts | % |
|---|---|---|---|---|---|---|
| Yorkshire | 28 | 13 | 1 | 14 | 90 | 72.00 |
| Northamptonshire | 18 | 10 | 1 | 7 | 60 | 70.58 |
| Kent | 26 | 14 | 5 | 7 | 82 | 65.60 |
| Lancashire | 22 | 8 | 2 | 12 | 55 | 64.70 |
| Middlesex | 20 | 7 | 4 | 9 | 52 | 57.77 |

### LEADING YORKSHIRE AVERAGES

#### BATTING

|  | M | I | NO | Runs | HS | Avge | 100 | 50 |
|---|---|---|---|---|---|---|---|---|
| D.Denton | 26 | 38 | 4 | 1831 | 221 | 53.85 | 6 | 4 |
| W.Rhodes | 20 | 32 | 4 | 965 | 176 | 34.46 | 2 | 3 |
| B.B.Wilson | 26 | 41 | 3 | 1086 | 150 | 28.57 | 1 | 3 |
| G.H.Hirst | 24 | 32 | 0 | 880 | 109 | 27.50 | 1 | 5 |

#### BOWLING

|  | O | M | R | W | Avge | 5WI | 10WM | BB |
|---|---|---|---|---|---|---|---|---|
| S.Haigh | 615.5 | 196 | 1101 | 96 | 11.46 | 8 | 2 | 9-25 |
| A.Drake | 494.5 | 141 | 1110 | 67 | 16.56 | 6 | - | 6-24 |
| M.W.Booth | 560.2 | 122 | 1525 | 85 | 17.94 | 6 | 2 | 8-47 |
| G.H.Hirst | 662.3 | 194 | 1492 | 78 | 19.12 | 3 | 2 | 6-30 |

## FIELDING and WICKET-KEEPING

37 (27 ct, 10 st) A.Dolphin
18 A.Drake, G.H.Hirst
17 W.Rhodes

# RESULTS

**Leicester**, May 9, 10, 11: Yorkshire 344 & 117-1, Leicestershire 143 (A.Drake 5-26) & 317. *Won by nine wickets*
**Sheffield**, May 13, 14, 15: Hampshire 80 (M.W.Booth 6-31) & 260-4 (C.P.Mead 111*), Yorkshire 471 (D.Denton 107, J.A.Newman 6-160). *Match drawn*
**Headingley**, May 20, 21, 22: Yorkshire 96 (F.E.Woolley 6-42), Kent 103-2. *Match drawn*
**Bradford**, May 27, 28: Lancashire 76 (A.Drake 6-33) & 165 (S.Haigh 5-25), Yorkshire 226 (W.Rhodes 107, W.Huddleston 6-77) & 17-0. *Won by ten wickets*
**Dewsbury**, May 30, 31, June 1: Yorkshire 146 (E.Robson 5-53, W.T.Greswell 5-56) & 111-8dec (E.Robson 5-50), Somerset 73 (S.Haigh 5-14) & 45-3. *Match drawn*
**Sheffield**, June 3, 4, 5: Yorkshire v Surrey *Match abandoned*
**Huddersfield**, June 6, 7, 8: Yorkshire 242 (W.Mead 6-92), Essex 103 (A.Drake 6-35). *Match drawn*
**Lord's**, June 13, 14, 15: Yorkshire 157 & 166 (F.A.Tarrant 6-73), Middlesex 185 & 139-6. *Lost by four wickets*
**Headingley**, June 17, 18, 19: Yorkshire 82 & 170 (E.G.Dennett 5-58), Gloucestershire 68 (S.Haigh 9-25) & 110 (S.Haigh 5-40). *Won by 74 runs*
**Trent Bridge**, June 20, 21, 22: Nottinghamshire 261 & 132, Yorkshire 145 & 249-5. *Won by five wickets*
**Bradford**, June 24, 25, 26: Yorkshire 241-9dec, Northamptonshire 74 & 24-7. *Match drawn*
**Edgbaston**, June 27, 28, 29: Yorkshire 451-4dec (D.Denton 200*, B.B.Wilson 150), Warwickshire 183 & 63-3. *Match drawn*
**Dewsbury,** July 4, 5, 6: Yorkshire 129 (E.G.Arnold 6-24) & 345-9dec (G.H.Hirst 109), Worcestershire 85 (S.Haigh 5-37) & 175 (S.Haigh 5-57). *Won by 214 runs*

**Bristol**, July 8, 9, 10: Yorkshire 134 (E.G.Dennett 8-74) & 411-9dec (D.Denton 182), Gloucestershire 132 (S.Haigh 6-46) & 166. *Won by 247 runs*
**Tunbridge Wells**, July 11, 12, 13: Yorkshire 543 (D.Denton 221), Kent 310 (S.Haigh 5-62) & 188. *Won by an innings and 45 runs*
**Sheffield**, July 15, 16, 17: Yorkshire 350 & 115-2, Leicestershire 140 (M.W.Booth 8-52) & 324 (A.E.Knight 147). *Won by eight wickets*
**Northampton**, July 18, 19, 20: Yorkshire 330 (D.Denton 111, W.Wells 5-113) & 27-0, Northamptonshire 233 (M.W.Booth 5-91). *Match drawn*
**The Oval**, July 22, 23, 24: Yorkshire 233 (J.W.Hitch 6-78) & 229-6dec, Surrey 267 & 93-1. *Match drawn*
**Southampton**, July 25, 26, 27: Hampshire 441 (C.B.Fry 186, E.I.M.Barrett 120*) & 95 (G.H.Hirst 6-47), Yorkshire 492 (D.Denton 191, A.S.Kennedy 6-181) & 45-1. *Won by nine wickets*
**Bradford**, July 29, 30, 31: Yorkshire 178 (A.E.Relf 5-82), Sussex 28-2. *Match drawn*
**Hull**, August 1, 2, 3: Warwickshire 59 (A.Drake 6-25) & 64-3, Yorkshire 88 (F.R.Foster 7-42). *Match drawn*
**Old Trafford**, August 5, 6, 7: Lancashire 347 (R.H.Spooner 109), Yorkshire 103 (H.Dean 7-54) & 105-7 (W.Huddleston 5-33). *Match drawn*
**Leyton**, August 8, 9, 10: Essex 129 (M.W.Booth 7-50) & 187 (M.W.Booth 5-69), Yorkshire 278 (C.P.Buckenham 6-33) & 40-0. *Won by ten wickets*
**Headingley**, August 12, 13, 14: Yorkshire 92 (F.A.Tarrant 7-40) & 215, Middlesex 110 (A.Drake 5-23) & 90 (M.W.Booth 8-47). *Won by 107 runs*
**Harrogate**, August 15, 16, 17: Yorkshire 389 (W.Rhodes 176), Nottinghamshire 161 (W.Rhodes 5-68) & 126 (A.Drake 6-24). *Won by an innings and 102 runs*
**Worcester**, August 22, 23, 24: Worcestershire 134 v Yorkshire. *Match drawn*
**Taunton**, August 26, 27, 28: Yorkshire 330 (W.T.Greswell 5-105), Somerset 69 (G.H.Hirst 6-30) & 125 (G.H.Hirst 6-37). *Won by an innings and 136 runs*
**Hove**, August 29, 30, 31: Yorkshire 141, Sussex 154-8. *Match drawn*

# NOTES and HIGHLIGHTS

The summer of 1912 was the second worst of the entire 20$^{th}$ century, weather-wise, this being the main explanation for half of Yorkshire's matches ending in draws. Northamptonshire, who have never won the title, were surprising runners-up and ran Yorkshire close. The White Rose county's overall success was not as convincing as in previous Championships, with only three of the 13 victories being by an innings. The main contributors to the success, other than Denton, were the all-rounders. Of the five bowlers who took over 35 wickets (as per the above plus Rhodes) only Haigh did not score over 600 runs.

The most interesting game of the season was at Southampton where Hampshire, despite a first innings score of 441, lost by nine wickets. After each side had batted once the pitch became rain-affected, the home side collapsed and Yorkshire were presented with an easy target.

Despite the prevailing conditions Denton had an outstanding season. He came second in the national averages and for Yorkshire his aggregate and average were 745 and 19.39 runs ahead of his nearest rivals. In mid-season he scored four centuries, including two doubles, in six consecutive games making 925 runs at the outstanding average of 132.14. His 221 against Kent at Tunbridge Wells was the highest score of his career.

Haigh's innings bowling figures of nine for 25 against Gloucestershire at Headingley was the best performance for the entire season and the best of his own illustrious career. He finished in third place in the national averages. Booth also had career best figures – against Middlesex at Headingley.

No player appeared in more than 26 matches and the side was led by Sir Archibald White, who was in charge for the first of three seasons.

# PLAYER of the SEASON

The bowling averages for 1912 were led by Schofield Haigh who formed, with Hirst and Rhodes, a Huddersfield area-born trio of bowlers the like of whom any county has rarely had on its books simultaneously. Haigh bowled right-handed, unlike the other two, and his fast-medium pace, combined with the ability to bowl off-spin, enabled him to eventually snare 1876 victims (average 15.61) in his career for Yorkshire. His best performance is referred to above but his best season had come six years earlier when he took 174 wickets in 1906.

Haigh was born in 1871 and made his county debut at the age of 24. He was a bright cricketer in both senses of the term and represented his country in eleven Tests spread over a period of 13 years – scant reward for a player of his ability. He retired in 1913 and became coach at Winchester but his second career was cut short when he died suddenly in his hometown in 1921.

## 1913 and 1914

For these two seasons Kent and Surrey were the champion counties with Yorkshire finishing second and fourth, respectively. In 1914 Alonzo Drake, a left-arm slow medium bowler, took all ten Somerset wickets in an innings for 35 runs at Weston-super-Mare. He was the first Yorkshire bowler to achieve the feat and he and Booth bowled unchanged throughout the entire match.

*Four of the best bowlers to have played for the county. Clockwise from back left: Alonzo Drake, Schofield Haigh, George Hirst and Wilfred Rhodes. Drake was the first Yorkshire bowler to take ten wickets in an innngs.*

# Bowlers Dominant

*Yorkshire's Championship-winning team of 1919. From left: back row – A.Dolphin, R.Kilner, A.Waddington, A.C.Williams, H.Sutcliffe; middle row – G.H.Hirst, W.Rhodes, D.C.F.Burton, E.R.Wilson, D.Denton; front row – P.Holmes, E.Robinson. It was the only season that consisted entirely of two-day matches.*

# 1919-1929

# Bowlers Dominant

Following the break for the Great War (later named the First World War) the Championship resumed with two-day matches, for the only season in its history. Worcestershire did not take part and the ranking was decided on percentages of wins to matches played.

## 1919

### TOP SIX COUNTIES

|  | Pld | W | L | D | % |
|---|---|---|---|---|---|
| Yorkshire | 26 | 12 | 3 | 11 | 46.15 |
| Kent | 14 | 6 | 1 | 7 | 42.85 |
| Nottinghamshire | 14 | 5 | 1 | 8 | 35.71 |
| Surrey | 20 | 7 | 3 | 10 | 35.00 |
| Lancashire | 24 | 8 | 4 | 12 | 33.33 |
| Somerset | 12 | 4 | 3 | 5 | 33.33 |

*NOTE: Somerset's total of drawn games includes one tied match.*

## LEADING YORKSHIRE AVERAGES

### BATTING

|  | M | I | NO | Runs | HS | Avge | 100 | 50 |
|---|---|---|---|---|---|---|---|---|
| H.Sutcliffe | 26 | 36 | 3 | 1601 | 174 | 48.51 | 5 | 6 |
| P.Holmes | 26 | 37 | 3 | 1471 | 140 | 43.26 | 5 | 4 |
| D.Denton | 24 | 32 | 2 | 1070 | 122 | 35.66 | 4 | 5 |
| R.Kilner | 26 | 34 | 4 | 955 | 115 | 31.89 | 2 | 6 |
| G.H.Hirst | 25 | 29 | 2 | 829 | 120 | 30.70 | 2 | 4 |

## BOWLING

|  | O | M | R | W | Avge | 5WI | 10WM | BB |
|---|---|---|---|---|---|---|---|---|
| W.Rhodes | 797.3 | 236 | 1764 | 142 | 12.42 | 11 | 4 | 8-44 |
| R.Kilner | 273.5 | 97 | 573 | 38 | 15.07 | - | - | 4-12 |
| A.Waddington | 662.3 | 176 | 1676 | 95 | 17.64 | 8 | 1 | 6-66 |

## FIELDING and WICKET-KEEPING

65 (42 ct, 23 st) A.Dolphin
30 P.Holmes
24 W.Rhodes
22 R.Kilner

# RESULTS

**Gloucester**, May 26, 27: Yorkshire 277 (R.Kilner 112), Gloucestershire 125 (W.Rhodes 7-47) & 89 (W.E.Blackburne 5-39). *Won by an innings and 63 runs*
**Leyton**, June 4, 5: Essex 354 (C.A.G.Russell 118) & 55-1, Yorkshire 348 (G.H.Hirst 120). *Match drawn*
**Old Trafford,** June 9, 10: Lancashire 319 (J.W.H.Makepeace 105, W.Rhodes 5-74) & 206-9dec, Yorkshire 232 (C.H.Parkin 6-88) & 153 (C.H.Parkin 8-35). *Lost by 140 runs*
**Edgbaston**, June 13, 14: Yorkshire 371-8dec (G.H.Hirst 120), Warwickshire 115 (W.Rhodes 5-16) & 193. *Won by an innings and 63 runs*
**Bradford**, June 20, 21: Derbyshire 74 (W.E.Blackburne 5-17) & 172, Yorkshire 221 (J.Horsley 6-78) & 26-0. *Won by ten wickets*
**Sheffield**, June 27, 28: Yorkshire 112 & 238 (T.L.Richmond 6-89), Nottinghamshire 236 (W.Rhodes 7-74) & 117-4. *Lost by six wickets*
**Headingley**, June 30, July 1: Kent 169 (W.Rhodes 5-35), Yorkshire 64 (W.J.Fairservice 6-35) & 8-0. *Match drawn*
**Chesterfield**, July 2, 3: Derbyshire 87, Yorkshire 251-6. *Match drawn*
**Trent Bridge**, July 4, 5: Nottinghamshire 197 & 74-4, Yorkshire 232 (P.Holmes 100). *Match drawn*
**Hull**, July 7, 8: Yorkshire 241 (J.W.H.T.Douglas 6-98), Essex 106 & 77 (A.Waddington 5-30). *Won by an innings and 58 runs*

**Dewsbury**, July 11, 12: Yorkshire 401-8dec (D.C.F.Burton 142*, W.Rhodes 135), Hampshire 82 (A.C.Williams 9-29) & 176 (W.Rhodes 6-66). *Won by an innings and 143 runs*
**Sheffield**, July 14, 15: Yorkshire 85 (W.Wells 8-35) & 273, Northamptonshire 149 & 135. *Won by 74 runs*
**Huddersfield**, July 18, 19: Yorkshire 215 (A.Skelding 7-98) & 314-6dec (D.Denton 110), Leicestershire 223 (A.Waddington 6-66) & 127-4. *Match drawn*
**Bradford**, July 21, 22: Yorkshire 264 & 25-0, Surrey 143 & 145 (A.Waddington 5-61). *Won by ten wickets*
**Northampton**, July 23, 24: Yorkshire 380-3dec (H.Sutcliffe 145, P.Holmes 133), Northamptonshire 72 & 112 (W.Rhodes 6-33). *Won by an innings and 196 runs*
**Headingley**, July 25, 26: Yorkshire 448-4dec (D.Denton 122, H.Sutcliffe 118, R.Kilner 115*), Gloucestershire 121 (A.Waddington 6-58) & 202 (A.Waddington 6-68). *Won by an innings and 125 runs*
**Harrogate**, August 1, 2: Yorkshire 187 (A.E.Relf 6-65) & 228, Sussex 271 (W.Rhodes 5-46) & 145-5. *Lost by five wickets*
**Sheffield**, August 4, 5: Lancashire 124 & 271-6 (C.Hallows 102*, A.C.Williams 5-67), Yorkshire 317-5dec (H.Sutcliffe 132, P.Holmes 123). *Match drawn*
**Leicester**, August 8, 9: Leicestershire 161 (E.Robinson 5-64) & 136 (A.Waddington 5-42), Yorkshire 423 (P.Holmes 140, W.E.Benskin 5-142). *Won by an innings and 126 runs*
**The Oval**, August 11, 12: Surrey 324 (D.J.Knight 114) & 189-4dec (D.J.Knight 101), Yorkshire 243 & 110-4. *Match drawn*
**Headingley**, August 15, 16: Yorkshire 190 & 358-8dec (D.Denton 120), Middlesex 208 (A.Waddington 5-75, W.Rhodes 5-80) & 153 (W.Rhodes 5-42). *Won by 187 runs*
**Bradford**, August 18, 19: Warwickshire 183 (E.Robinson 5-42) & 107 (W.Rhodes 8-44), Yorkshire 381. *Won by an innings and 91 runs*
**Lord's**, August 21, 22: Yorkshire 187 (H.Sutcliffe 103, N.E.Haig 5-34) & 279-3dec (P.Holmes 133), Middlesex 128 (E.R.Wilson 6-28) & 234-8. *Match drawn*
**Dover**, August 25, 26: Yorkshire 375-8dec (H.Sutcliffe 174, D.Denton 114), Kent 168 (A.Waddington 5-57) & 78-2. *Match drawn*
**Southampton**, August 27, 28: Hampshire 201 (C.P.Mead 100*), Yorkshire 242-3. *Match drawn*
**Hove**, August 29, 30: Sussex 100 & 38-2, Yorkshire 187-6dec. *Match drawn*

# NOTES and HIGHLIGHTS

The re-building process following the First World War, despite the loss of Booth and Drake, was less of a burden to Yorkshire than some other counties. Rhodes' career as a bowler was revived and three newcomers – Emmott Robinson, Herbert Sutcliffe and Abram Waddington – all made a huge impact.

The two-day match experiment resulted in a proliferation of drawn games (45% in total), despite the reasonable summer. This saw that it was not to be repeated.

Percy Holmes and Sutcliffe started their famous partnership on June 30 against Kent. Before the season was through they had compiled five of their eventual total of 69 opening stands for the county. The first was an impressive 279 against Northamptonshire at Northampton and they also shared a double-century stand against Lancashire at Sheffield.

Rhodes and skipper David Burton established the current Yorkshire record partnership for the seventh wicket with a stand of 254 against Hampshire at Dewsbury. Yorkshire scored so quickly that they were able to declare on 401-8 shortly after tea. The visitors were then bowled out before the end of the day for a humiliating 82. The innings saw the best bowling performance of the entire Championship campaign - from Ambrose Williams who took nine for 29, in only 77 balls, with eight of his victims being bowled. He had last played for the county in 1911, when he had made just two appearances. He played in a few more games in 1919 but had no more real success and disappeared from the first-class scene.

Four bowlers appeared in the top ten of the national averages; the way was led by Rhodes with Roy Kilner (third), Rockley Wilson (sixth) and Waddington (tenth) also appearing. Wilson's 26 victims were taken at an average of 16.03. Dolphin was the country's leading wicket-keeper, his total of victims being 16 more than second-placed Herbert Strudwick of Surrey.

No less than four players - Holmes, Kilner, Rhodes and Sutcliffe - played right through the season without missing a single game. Burton led the team to the Championship in his first season as captain.

Both Sutcliffe and Waddington were playing in their first seasons. Robinson - another debutant - was to be remembered more for his character, memorably described by Neville Cardus, than his deeds. Despite scoring 1000 runs and taking 100 wickets in a season only twice and once, respectively, he always seemed to be making valuable contributions, especially in the field.

## PLAYER of the SEASON

Despite 1919 being only his first season, Abe Waddington took 100 wickets in all first-class matches and the impact that he made has been described as the main reason for Yorkshire winning the Championship. Unfortunately he was to play for the county for only eight more seasons. He made his debut at the age of 26, because of the First World War, and had to retire after the 1927 season due to a shoulder injury. Nevertheless he made a very significant impact with his left-arm fast-medium bowling taking a total of 835 wickets for the county at an average of fewer than twenty.

*Abe Waddington bowling on the second day of the match against Surrey at The Oval in 1919.*

Born in Bradford in 1893 he soon succeeded in league cricket, as he did later in the first-class game, with the ability to make the batsman hurry his strokes. He bowled fluently and with rhythm but played in only two Tests without any success. He died near Scarborough in 1959 with the satisfaction of knowing that he had played a leading role in no fewer than five Championship-winning sides.

## 1920 and 1921

Middlesex were champions for both of these two seasons with Yorkshire finishing third and fourth, respectively. Glamorgan joined the elite for the 1921 season bringing the total of participants to 17 – a number that was to last for 65 seasons, this representing the most stable period in the Championship's history. One of the highlights of 1920 was an innings of 302 not out made by Holmes against Hampshire at Portsmouth.

## 1922

### TOP FIVE COUNTIES

|                  | Pld | W  | L | D  | Pts | %     |
|------------------|-----|----|---|----|-----|-------|
| Yorkshire        | 30  | 19 | 2 | 9  | 107 | 73.79 |
| Nottinghamshire  | 28  | 17 | 5 | 6  | 93  | 71.53 |
| Surrey           | 24  | 13 | 1 | 10 | 77  | 66.95 |
| Kent             | 28  | 16 | 3 | 9  | 86  | 63.70 |
| Lancashire       | 30  | 15 | 7 | 8  | 79  | 56.42 |

### LEADING YORKSHIRE AVERAGES

### BATTING

|             | M  | I  | NO | Runs | HS   | Avge  | 100 | 50 |
|-------------|----|----|----|------|------|-------|-----|----|
| E.Oldroyd   | 30 | 39 | 5  | 1534 | 151* | 45.11 | 5   | 7  |
| H.Sutcliffe | 30 | 41 | 3  | 1674 | 232  | 44.05 | 2   | 11 |
| W.Rhodes    | 30 | 36 | 6  | 1181 | 110  | 39.36 | 4   | 4  |
| P.Holmes    | 30 | 41 | 3  | 1489 | 220* | 39.18 | 5   | 3  |
| R.Kilner    | 30 | 38 | 2  | 1085 | 124  | 30.13 | 2   | 6  |

## BOWLING

|               | O     | M   | R    | W   | Avge  | 5WI | 10WM | BB   |
|---------------|-------|-----|------|-----|-------|-----|------|------|
| W.Rhodes      | 605.4 | 231 | 1068 | 84  | 12.71 | 5   | -    | 6-13 |
| G.G.Macaulay  | 721.4 | 182 | 1598 | 120 | 13.31 | 8   | 2    | 7-47 |
| R.Kilner      | 916.1 | 354 | 1454 | 101 | 14.39 | 5   | 2    | 6-13 |
| A.Waddington  | 838.4 | 191 | 1956 | 127 | 15.40 | 9   | 2    | 8-34 |
| E.Robinson    | 513.5 | 180 | 941  | 51  | 18.45 | 2   | -    | 5-20 |

## FIELDING and WICKET-KEEPING

49 (36 ct, 13 st) A.Dolphin
38 A.Waddington
30 E.Robinson
27 G.G.Macaulay
25 W.Rhodes

# RESULTS

**Northampton**, May 6, 8: Northamptonshire 81 (G.G.Macaulay 6-8) & 42 (G.G.Macaulay 5-23), Yorkshire 112 (J.V.Murdin 6-38) & 12-0. *Won by ten wickets*
**Cardiff**, May 10, 11: Glamorgan 78 (G.G.Macaulay 6-12) & 68, Yorkshire 404-2dec (E.Oldroyd 151*, P.Holmes 138). *Won by an innings and 258 runs*
**Dudley**, May 13, 15: Worcestershire 111 (W.Rhodes 5-24) & 90, Yorkshire 421 (E.Oldroyd 121, R.Kilner 117). *Won by an innings and 220 runs*
**Derby**, May 17, 18, 19: Yorkshire 147 (A.Morton 5-55) & 314-4dec, Derbyshire 130 & 80 (A.Waddington 7-31). *Won by 251 runs*
**Headingley**, May 20, 22, 23: Yorkshire 342 (R.Kilner 124), Northamptonshire 69 (A.Waddington 8-34) & 88. *Won by an innings and 185 runs*
**Leicester**, May 27, 29, 30: Leicestershire 298 & 180-6dec, Yorkshire 283. *Match drawn*
**Sheffield**, June 3, 5, 6: Lancashire 307 (G.E.Tyldesley 178) & 144, Yorkshire 306 (R.K.Tyldesley 6-70) & 148-4. *Won by six wickets*
**Edgbaston**, June 7, 8, 9: Yorkshire 453-2dec (P.Holmes 209, E.Oldroyd 138*), Warwickshire 123 (W.Rhodes 5-12) & 178. *Won by an innings and 152 runs*

**Bradford**, June 10, 12, 13: Surrey 317 (G.G.Macaulay 5-67) & 133-2, Yorkshire 283 (H.Sutcliffe 114). *Match drawn*
**Lord's**, June 14, 15, 16: Middlesex 138 (G.G.Macaulay 5-31) & 180, Yorkshire 339-7dec (P.Holmes 129). *Won by an innings and 21 runs*
**Sheffield**, June 17, 19: Yorkshire 140 (T.L.Richmond 6-50) & 138, Nottinghamshire 353 (A.Waddington 5-97). *Lost by an innings and 75 runs*
**Huddersfield**, June 21, 22: Yorkshire 495-5dec (P.Holmes 220*), Warwickshire 99 & 125. *Won by an innings and 271 runs*
**Headingley**, June 24, 26, 27: Kent 163 (A.Waddington 8-39) & 131, Yorkshire 273-9dec (G.C.Collins 5-69) & 24-0. *Won by ten wickets*
**Headingley**, July 1, 3, 4: Glamorgan 161 & 165, Yorkshire 429-7dec (E.Oldroyd 143, W.Rhodes 110). *Won by an innings and 103 runs*
**Sheffield**, July 5, 6, 7: Derbyshire 99 & 69-3, Yorkshire 202-6dec. *Match drawn*
**Hull**, July 8, 10, 11: Sussex 95 (W.Rhodes 6-43) & 20 (A.Waddington 7-6), Yorkshire 125 (A.E.R.Gilligan 6-20). *Won by an innings and 10 runs*
**Bradford**, July 12, 13, 14: Worcestershire 116 (A.Waddington 5-39) & 149-7, Yorkshire 214-4dec. *Match drawn*
**Harrogate**, July 15, 17, 18: Yorkshire 314-7dec (W.Rhodes 108*, G.G.Macaulay 101*), Essex 105 (R.Kilner 5-29) & 149-9 (R.Kilner 6-22). *Match drawn*
**Maidstone**, July 19, 20, 21: Yorkshire 344 (P.Holmes 107, A.P.Freeman 8-127) & 228, Kent 259 (A.Waddington 5-106) & 147 (A.Waddington 5-52). *Won by 166 runs*
**Trent Bridge**, July 22, 24, 25: Nottinghamshire 257 & 74 (R.Kilner 5-14, E.Robinson 5-20), Yorkshire 222 (T.L.Richmond 5-79) & 110-5. *Won by five wickets*
**Dewsbury**, July 26, 27: Gloucestershire 134 (G.G.Macaulay 7-47) & 87 (G.G.Macaulay 5-29, A.Waddington 5-35), Yorkshire 228. *Won by an innings and 7 runs*
**Sheffield**, July 29, 31, August 1: Leicestershire 97 (E.Robinson 5-36) & 114 (G.G.Macaulay 5-30), Yorkshire 410 (E.Oldroyd 128, A.Skelding 5-96). *Won by an innings and 199 runs*
**Old Trafford**, August 5, 7, 8: Lancashire 118 & 135, Yorkshire 122 & 129-8. *Match drawn*

**Bristol**, August 9, 10, 11: Gloucestershire 172 & 58 (W.Rhodes 5-24), Yorkshire 66 (C.W.L.Parker 9-36) & 167-4. *Won by six wickets*
**Bradford**, August 12, 14, 15: Yorkshire 56 (A.S.Kennedy 7-28) & 116 (G.S.Boyes 6-53), Hampshire 113 (A.Waddington 8-35) & 60-5. *Lost by five wickets*
**Headingley**, Yorkshire 266 (W.Rhodes 105) & 144-5dec, Middlesex 170 (R.Kilner 5-38) & 85-2. *Match drawn*
**The Oval**, August 19, 21, 22: Surrey 339 (E.R.Wilson 5-91) & 165-3, Yorkshire 539-5dec (H.Sutcliffe 232). *Match drawn*
**Bournemouth**, August 23, 24, 25: Hampshire 272 & 44 (R.Kilner 6-13), Yorkshire 293 (W.Rhodes 106) & 25-0. *Won by ten wickets*
**Hove**, August 26, 28: Yorkshire 42 (H.E.Roberts 5-20, M.W.Tate 5-20) & 228, Sussex 95 & 83 (W.Rhodes 6-13). *Won by 92 runs*
**Leyton**, August 30, 31, September 1: Essex 5-1 v Yorkshire. *Match drawn*

## NOTES and HIGHLIGHTS

This was the first of four consecutive Championships for Yorkshire and came with a new captain at the helm – Geoffrey Wilson. Although the gap between the top two teams was narrow, the fact that Yorkshire won two more games and lost three fewer than their nearest rival, Nottinghamshire, meant that the county's victory was well-deserved. Many of Yorkshire's victories were so emphatic that in 13 of the 19 winning games the team did not lose any second innings wickets.

There were many low scores, Yorkshire dismissing their opponents for fewer than 100 on 19 occasions, although the situation was reversed only three times. Sussex's all-out total of 20 at Hull (Waddington 7-4-6-7) was the third-lowest against Yorkshire and still remains as such. The wicket was rain-affected and the weather interrupted the game regularly. What play there was meant that the game lasted only five hours and despite only scoring 125, Yorkshire managed to win by an innings!

Similarly the county made only 112 against Northamptonshire at Northampton but needed to score only 12 runs in the second innings to win by ten wickets. The Roses match at Old Trafford was also a low-scoring, rain-affected game but with a nail-biting finish. When stumps were drawn

Yorkshire needed just three to win with, in theory, two wickets left. However had Lancashire taken just one more wicket they would have won as the Yorkshire skipper, Geoffrey Wilson, was in hospital recovering from an operation.

The return match with Sussex, at Hove, was another remarkable game in that Yorkshire, despite being all out for 42 after 90 minutes' play, went on to win by 92 runs. The home side could only manage 95 and although Sutcliffe's 48, when the visitors batted again, was the highest score of the match, Sussex were set 176 to win. They looked comfortable at 34-0 but all ten wickets fell for 49 runs, thanks mainly to Rhodes who took his six wickets in just six overs.

Yorkshire passed 400 seven times during the season (a feat not managed by their opponents at all) and on two of these occasions lost only two wickets in the process. Holmes took a particular liking to the Warwickshire bowlers scoring two double-centuries against them (209 and 220 not out) and sharing in three century partnerships including one of 333 with Oldroyd for the second wicket at Edgbaston.

Four bowlers appeared in the top ten of the national averages, including Rhodes (first) and George Macaulay (third) as well as Kilner and Waddington. Yorkshire took 500 wickets during the season and 483 of these were taken by the five bowlers in the above averages. Particularly economical innings analyses were achieved by Macaulay (11.3-8-8-6 against Northamptonshire at Northampton), and Kilner (42-31-22-6 against Essex at Harrogate, 18-8-14-5 against Nottinghamshire at Trent Bridge and 15.1-8-13-6 against Hampshire at Bournemouth). Waddington's figures in the home game against Northamptonshire were the best of his career. There was some success for opposing bowlers, in particular Charlie Parker's 9-36 for Gloucestershire at Bristol was, at the time, the fourth-best innings analysis ever recorded against Yorkshire.

For the first 13 games of the season – taking in the whole of May and June – Yorkshire fielded exactly the same eleven players. These were the nine mentioned in the above averages plus Wilson and Norman Kilner. A total of seven players - Holmes, R.Kilner, Oldroyd, Rhodes, Robinson, Sutcliffe and Waddington – did not miss a single game throughout the whole Championship campaign.

The 1922 season saw the start of a 49-year association with Arthur Mitchell. A first-class career record of almost 20,000 runs in over 400 matches, including six Tests, would be followed by 26 seasons as Yorkshire's first full-time coach, this lasting until 1970.

## PLAYER of the SEASON

*Edgar Oldroyd, one of Yorkshire's most consistent number three batsmen.*

In topping the county batting averages Edgar Oldroyd would eventually look back on 1922 as being the best season of his career. Despite making his debut in 1910, it was not until the 1921 season that he had established himself in the side having taken up the crucial number three spot, vacated by Denton, with dedication and consistency. Hailing from Batley, being born there in 1888, he began a club career as an off-spinner. His skilled batsmanship, especially on difficult pitches, soon became invaluable, however, and he often scored important runs in low-scoring matches. His highest score came in 1923 but his courage against hostile bowling would be tested three years later when a ball from the Lancastrian Ted MacDonald knocked him unconscious. Fortunately there were no long-term effects but he remained out of the side for the rest of the season and the incident seemed to cloud the rest of his career.

Oldroyd continued to score consistently - he passed 1000 runs in each of ten consecutive seasons - but he lacked some of his previous confidence. He was not retained after the 1931 season and it is worth noting that of the 19 Yorkshire batsmen who have scored over 15,000 runs, only six have a better average than Oldroyd's 35.23. He did not play in any representative type of fixture and thus remains, along with Tunnicliffe, one of the best 'Yorkies' not to receive a Test cap. He died in Truro, Cornwall in 1964.

## 1923

## TOP FIVE COUNTIES

|  | Pld | W | L | D | Pts | % |
|---|---|---|---|---|---|---|
| Yorkshire | 32 | 25 | 1 | 6 | 133 | 85.80 |
| Nottinghamshire | 26 | 15 | 3 | 8 | 85 | 68.00 |
| Lancashire | 30 | 15 | 2 | 13 | 87 | 60.00 |
| Surrey | 26 | 11 | 2 | 13 | 67 | 58.26 |
| Kent | 28 | 15 | 9 | 4 | 75 | 55.55 |

# LEADING YORKSHIRE AVERAGES

## BATTING

|  | M | I | NO | Runs | HS | Avge. | 100 | 50 |
|---|---|---|---|---|---|---|---|---|
| H.Sutcliffe | 29 | 42 | 2 | 1453 | 139 | 36.32 | 1 | 9 |
| P.Holmes | 31 | 44 | 1 | 1546 | 199 | 35.95 | 2 | 8 |
| R.Kilner | 29 | 38 | 6 | 1126 | 79 | 35.18 | - | 6 |
| W.Rhodes | 31 | 38 | 5 | 1023 | 126 | 31.00 | 2 | 3 |
| E.Oldroyd | 32 | 45 | 4 | 1237 | 194 | 30.17 | 1 | 7 |
| M.Leyland | 32 | 46 | 11 | 1006 | 89 | 28.74 | - | 7 |

## BOWLING

|  | O | M | R | W | Avge | 5WI | 10WM | BB |
|---|---|---|---|---|---|---|---|---|
| W.Rhodes | 833.4 | 315 | 1353 | 120 | 11.27 | 8 | 1 | 7-15 |
| R.Kilner | 1071.3 | 455 | 1586 | 139 | 11.41 | 7 | 1 | 8-26 |
| G.G.Macaulay | 939.3 | 227 | 1989 | 149 | 13.34 | 11 | 3 | 7-13 |
| E.Robinson | 693.3 | 214 | 1343 | 95 | 14.13 | 2 | 1 | 7-26 |
| A.Waddington | 453.3 | 107 | 1110 | 57 | 19.47 | 2 | 1 | 6-21 |

## FIELDING and WICKET-KEEPING

68 (45 ct, 23 st)  A.Dolphin
33 E.Robinson
30 A.Waddington
26 G.G.Macaulay, W.Rhodes
20 P.Holmes, R.Kilner

# RESULTS

**Cardiff**, May 5, 7, 8: Glamorgan 63 (G.G.Macaulay 7-13) & 112 (R.Kilner 8-26), Yorkshire 93 & 83-1. *Won by nine wickets*
**Worcester**, May 9, 10: Worcestershire 76 & 169 (W.Rhodes 5-35), Yorkshire 358 (E.Oldroyd 194, C.F.Root 6-93). *Won by an innings and 113 runs*
**Bradford**, May 12, 14, 15: Yorkshire 411-9dec (W.Rhodes 126, J.W.Hearne 7-99), Middlesex 122 (W.Rhodes 5-29) & 60 (R.Kilner 6-14). *Won by an innings and 229 runs*

**Old Trafford**, May 19, 21, 22: Lancashire 108 (R.Kilner 5-33), Yorkshire 126-5. *Match drawn*

**Edgbaston**, May 23, 24, 25: Yorkshire 113 (H.Howell 10-51) & 162-6dec, Warwickshire 110 (G.G.Macaulay 5-42) & 81. *Won by 85 runs*

**Sheffield**, May 26, 28, 29: Kent 136 (W.Rhodes 6-37) & 48-5, Yorkshire 180-6dec. *Match drawn*

**Derby**, May 30, 31: Derbyshire 104 & 72 (R.Kilner 5-32), Yorkshire 302-9dec. *Won by an innings and 126 runs*

**Headingley**, June 2, 4, 5: Nottinghamshire 200 & 95 (W.Rhodes 6-23), Yorkshire 134 (S.J.Staples 5-45, F.C.Matthews 5-46) & 158 (S.J.Staples 5-37). *Lost by 3 runs*

**Lord's**, June 9, 11, 12: Middlesex 289 (J.W.Hearne 175*) & 102, Yorkshire 168 (F.J.Durston 5-25) & 225-4. *Won by six wickets*

**Northampton**, June 13, 14: Northamptonshire 50 (A.Waddington 6-21) & 198 (G.G.Macaulay 5-59), Yorkshire 308 (W.Wells 6-51). *Won by an innings and 60 runs*

**Sheffield**, June 16, 18, 19: Yorkshire 278 & 129, Surrey 224 & 158 (R.Kilner 6-22). *Won by 25 runs*

**Tonbridge**, June 20, 21, 22: Yorkshire 255 & 239, Kent 130 (G.G.Macaulay 5-21) & 244 (F.E.Woolley 138, E.Robinson 7-26). *Won by 120 runs*

**Leyton**, June 23, 25, 26: Essex 251 (A.Waddington 5-78) & 64 (W.Rhodes 5-8) Yorkshire 152 (G.M.Louden 5-59) & 164-3. *Won by seven wickets*

**Bradford**, June 27, 28: Yorkshire 312, Northamptonshire 78 & 79 (G.G.Macaulay 6-18). *Won by an innings and 155 runs*

**Headingley**, June 30, July 2, 3: Yorkshire 412 (A.E.R.Gilligan 6-127), Sussex 182 & 197. *Won by an innings and 33 runs*

**Hull**, July 4, 5, 6: Yorkshire 170 (H.Howell 6-80) & 311-9dec, Warwickshire 249 & 136 (G.G.Macaulay 6-54). *Won by 96 runs*

**Hull**, July 7, 9, 10: Yorkshire 446-6dec (P.Holmes 199, H.Sutcliffe 139), Somerset 226 & 90. *Won by an innings and 130 runs*

**Dewsbury**, July 14, 16, 17: Yorkshire 195 (J.W.H.T.Douglas 5-86) & 332-6dec (W.Rhodes 102), Essex 96 & 151. *Won by 280 runs*

**Huddersfield**, July 18, 19, 20: Yorkshire 376, Leicestershire 71 & 132 (E.Robinson 5-46). *Won by an innings and 173 runs*

**Sheffield**, July 21, 23, 24: Gloucestershire 183 & 133, Yorkshire 280-3dec (P.Holmes 122*) & 38-0. *Won by ten wickets*

**Bristol**, July 25, 26, 27: Gloucestershire 95 (W.Rhodes 7-15) & 239, Yorkshire 352-9dec (N.Kilner 102*). *Won by an innings and 18 runs*
**Trent Bridge**, July 28, 30, 31: Nottinghamshire 131 (R.Kilner 6-42) & 50-5, Yorkshire 216 (S.J.Staples 5-57). *Match drawn*
**Harrogate**, August 1, 2, 3: Worcestershire 42 (G.G.Macaulay 5-11) & 163 (G.G.Macaulay 5-58), Yorkshire 242-2dec. *Won by an innings and 37 runs*
**Bradford**, August 4, 6, 7: Lancashire 188 & 73, Yorkshire 213 (R.K.Tyldesley 7-71) & 51-2. *Won by eight wickets*
**Leicester**, August 8, 9, 10: Leicestershire 129 & 108, Yorkshire 311. *Won by an innings and 74 runs*
**Bradford**, August 11, 13, 14: Derbyshire 197 (W.Rhodes 7-60) & 121, Yorkshire 196 (J.Horsley 5-69) & 124-2. *Won by eight wickets*
**Headingley**, Yorkshire 246 & 206-5dec, Hampshire 327 (C.P.Mead 123). *Match drawn*
**Sheffield**, August 18, 20, 21: Glamorgan 110 & 89 (W.Rhodes 5-26), Yorkshire 233 (T.Arnott 6-98). *Won by an innings and 34 runs*
**The Oval**, August 22, 23: Surrey 360 (R.Kilner 5-93), Yorkshire 88-2. *Match drawn*
**Portsmouth**, Hampshire 66 (G.G.Macaulay 5-25) & 52 (G.G.Macaulay 6-27), Yorkshire 206 (J.A.Newman 5-50). *Won by an innings and 88 runs*
**Hove**, August 29, 30, 31: Yorkshire 135 & 170-5dec, Sussex 129 & 48-5. *Match drawn*
**Taunton**, September 1, 3, 4: Somerset 134 & 124 (G.G.Macaulay 5-65), Yorkshire 180 (J.J.Bridges 5-59) & 81-3. *Won by seven wickets*

## NOTES and HIGHLIGHTS

This was the most conclusive victory in the Championship's entire history. Yorkshire's feat of winning 25 matches is unsurpassed, the nearest being Surrey's 23 wins in 1955, and this included a run of 13 consecutive victories lasting for virtually the whole of June and July. Thirteen of the victories were by an innings and Yorkshire's only defeat was by a mere three runs against Nottinghamshire at Headingly. This was caused mainly by a second innings collapse; the visitors had gained a first innings lead of 66 but Rhodes, in particular, ensured that Yorkshire's final target was no more than 162. At 133-4 the odds were firmly on a home victory but four wickets fell for eight runs and the visitors won a pulsating match.

The batting was consistent rather than heavy-scoring, none of Yorkshire's players appearing in the top ten of the national averages. Of the 56 half-centuries made, only seven were converted into hundreds. Oldroyd's near-double century against Worcestershire at Worcester was the highest score of his career. The bowling was outstanding, however, with five players averaging fewer than 15.

Remarkably, E.H.Bryant's 41 for the home county at Worcester was the highest innings made against Yorkshire in whole of the month of May. Although J.W.Hearne scored 60% of Middlesex's total in the match at Lord's, each of Yorkshire's five bowlers took four wickets and a century opening stand by Holmes and Sutcliffe ensured a comfortable victory. At Sheffield in June, Surrey needed only 184 to win and looked comfortable at 143-4 but Roy Kilner took all of the last five wickets to give himself impressive innings figures of 25.2-15-22-6.

Norman Kilner, in his last season before moving to Warwickshire, made a century against Gloucestershire at Bristol from the number nine batting position, he and Macaulay sharing a ninth wicket stand of 114.

Despite Waddington being injured for much of the season the main five bowlers sent down over 95% of the overs bowled by Yorkshire. Rhodes (first), Kilner (second), Macaulay and Robinson were all in the top five of the national averages. Particularly economical analyses were achieved by Macaulay (13.2-8-13-7 against Glamorgan at Cardiff and 11.5-6-11-5 against Worcestershire at Harrogate) as well as Kilner (15.4-7-14-6 against Middlesex at Bradford and 40-20-33-5 against Lancashire at Old Trafford).

Morris Leyland, Oldroyd and Robinson played in every match of the campaign and Kilner and Rhodes became the first pair of Yorkshire players to complete the season double since Hirst and Rhodes in 1904. Dolphin came second in the leading wicket-keepers' list.

## PLAYER of the SEASON

In the 1923 season Roy Kilner achieved two career bests: his innings bowling figures against Glamorgan at Cardiff and his season's total of wickets. He was an authentic left-handed all-rounder and one of the most popular players ever to represent the county. Testimony to this fact was later proved in 1928 when an estimated 100,000 lined the streets of his native Wombwell for his funeral. He had contracted a fever on a coaching trip to India and died at the age of 37. He was born in 1890 and first played for Yorkshire at the age of twenty.

Kilner first made an impact in the county team as an aggressive batsman and his best season came as early as 1913, when he scored 1586 runs. After the 1914-18 hostilities his bowling was needed more and his slow, nagging spinners with subtle variations of pace and flight made him a vital part of a successful side. He completed the 'double' on four occasions and ended his county career with over 13,018 runs and 857 wickets. His highest score was an innings of 206 not out against Derbyshire at Bramall Lane in 1920.

Aside from his undoubted cricketing talents, Kilner will be remembered by those who knew him for his sense of humour and easy disposition.

For the 1924 season five points would be awarded for a win and three or one for a drawn match, depending on first innings lead. Ranking would be decided by percentage of points to possible points.

## 1924

## TOP FIVE COUNTIES

|  | Pld | W | L | D | Pts | % |
|---|---|---|---|---|---|---|
| Yorkshire | 30 | 16 | 3 | 11 | 88 | 76.52 |
| Middlesex | 22 | 11 | 3 | 8 | 69 | 69.00 |
| Surrey | 24 | 9 | 1 | 14 | 67 | 67.00 |
| Lancashire | 30 | 11 | 2 | 17 | 79 | 63.20 |
| Kent | 28 | 12 | 4 | 12 | 81 | 62.30 |

*NOTE: Kent's total of drawn games includes one tied match.*

# LEADING YORKSHIRE AVERAGES

## BATTING

|            | M  | I  | NO | Runs | HS   | Avge  | 100 | 50 |
|------------|----|----|----|------|------|-------|-----|----|
| H.Sutcliffe | 23 | 33 | 4  | 1342 | 255* | 46.27 | 3   | 7  |
| E.Oldroyd  | 30 | 42 | 5  | 1373 | 138  | 37.10 | 3   | 5  |
| P.Holmes   | 28 | 41 | 5  | 1308 | 118* | 36.33 | 4   | 7  |
| M.Leyland  | 30 | 41 | 7  | 1138 | 133* | 33.47 | 2   | 5  |
| W.Rhodes   | 30 | 37 | 5  | 826  | 100  | 25.81 | 1   | 4  |

## BOWLING

|              | O     | M   | R    | W   | Avge  | 5WI | 10WM | BB   |
|--------------|-------|-----|------|-----|-------|-----|------|------|
| G.G.Macaulay | 950   | 282 | 1866 | 159 | 11.73 | 11  | 4    | 7-21 |
| R.Kilner     | 868   | 351 | 1370 | 113 | 12.12 | 10  | 3    | 7-37 |
| W.Rhodes     | 551.3 | 187 | 1085 | 81  | 13.39 | 4   | -    | 6-25 |
| E.Robinson   | 501.4 | 165 | 1084 | 55  | 19.70 | 3   | -    | 6-87 |
| A.Waddington | 450.2 | 110 | 1067 | 52  | 20.51 | 2   | -    | 7-43 |

## FIELDING and WICKET-KEEPING

49 (24 ct, 25 st) A.Dolphin
30 E.Robinson
25 G.G.Macaulay, A.Waddington

# RESULTS

**Cardiff**, May 7, 8: Yorkshire 275, Glamorgan 48 (G.G.Macaulay 5-15) & 50 (R.Kilner 5-25). *Won by an innings and 177 runs*

**Gloucester**, May 10, 12, 13: Gloucestershire 68 (G.G.Macaulay 5-19) & 42 (G.G.Macaulay 7-21), Yorkshire 98 & 14-2. *Won by 8 wickets*

**Headingley**, May 17, 19, 20: Yorkshire 262 (E.Oldroyd 103, H.A.Peach 5-32), Surrey 169-7. *Match drawn*

**Northampton**, May 21, 22, 23: Northamptonshire 84 (G.G.Macaulay 6-26) & 123 (R.Kilner 5-34), Yorkshire 159 & 49-5. *Won by five wickets*

**Bradford**, May 24, 26, 27: Nottinghamshire 147 & 92 (W.Rhodes 5-30), Yorkshire 161 (F.Barrett 5-58) & 79-7 (S.J.Staples 5-22). *Won by three wickets*

**Lord's**, May 28, 29, 30: Yorkshire 192 & 121, Middlesex 465-8dec (G.T.S.Stevens 114, H.L.Dales 113). *Lost by an innings and 152 runs*
**Hull**, May 31, June 2, 3: Yorkshire 257 (A.P.Freeman 5-59), Kent 128-9. *Match drawn*
**Headingley**, June 7, 9, 10: Lancashire 113 (G.G.Macaulay 6-40) & 74, Yorkshire 130 (C.H.Parkin 5-46) & 33 (R.K.Tyldesley 6-18). *Lost by 24 runs*
**Edgbaston**, June 11, 12, 13: Warwickshire 139 (R.Kilner 6-48), Yorkshire 120-3. *Match drawn*
**Chesterfield**, June 14, 16, 17: Yorkshire 169 (J.Horsley 6-42) & 205, Derbyshire 74 & 163. *Won by 137 runs*
**Dewsbury**, June 18, 19: Somerset 132 & 100, Yorkshire 434-8dec (H.Sutcliffe 213). *Won by an innings and 202 runs*
**Sheffield**, June 21, 23, 24: Yorkshire 200 & 343-3dec (H.Sutcliffe 160), Sussex 192 (M.W.Tate 102*, E.Robinson 6-87) & 125 (G.G.Macaulay 5-60). *Won by 226 runs*
**Hull**, June 28, 30, July 1: Yorkshire 299 (J.W.H.T.Douglas 6-97) & 111 (J.W.H.T.Douglas 5-49), Essex 248 (G.G.Macaulay 5-73) & 68-6. *Match drawn*
**Sheffield**, July 5, 7, 8: Middlesex 358 (E.Robinson 5-59) & 268, Yorkshire 334 (N.E.Haig 6-79) & 43-0. *Match drawn*
**Southend-on-Sea**, July 9, 10, 11: Essex 132 & 208, Yorkshire 471-5dec (H.Sutcliffe 255*, E.Oldroyd 138). *Won by an innings and 131 runs*
**Maidstone**, July 12, 14, 15: Kent 230 (R.Kilner 5-48) & 273 (H.T.W.Hardinge 140, E.Robinson 5-84), Yorkshire 205 (A.P.Freeman 5-39) & 196-3 (P.Holmes 105*). *Match drawn*
**Weston-super-Mare**, July 16, 17, 18: Yorkshire 342 (W.Rhodes 100), Somerset 174 & 127 (W.Rhodes 5-28). *Won by an innings and 41 runs*
**Trent Bridge**, July 19, 21, 22: Nottinghamshire 216 (G.G.Macaulay 6-72), Yorkshire 206-9 (P.Holmes 112). *Match drawn*
**Bradford**, July 23, 24, 25: Glamorgan 116 & 106, Yorkshire 248-3dec (P.Holmes 118*). *Won by an innings and 26 runs*
**Headingley**, July 26, 28, 29: Yorkshire 137-2 v Gloucestershire. *Match drawn*
**Huddersfield**, July 30, 31, August 1: Yorkshire 300-7dec (P.Holmes 107), Derbyshire 111 (W.Rhodes 6-25) & 78-8. *Match drawn*
**Old Trafford**, August 2, 4, 5: Yorkshire 359 (M.Leyland 133*), Lancashire 78-2. *Match drawn*
**Leicester**, August 6, 7, 8: Leicestershire 114 (A.Waddington 7-43) & 166, Yorkshire 228 (G.Geary 5-35) & 53-2. *Won by eight wickets*

**Sheffield**, August 9, 11: Warwickshire 170 & 107 (G.G.Macaulay 7-66), Yorkshire 275 (H.Howell 5-94) & 4-0. *Won by ten wickets*
**Dewsbury**, August 13, 14, 15: Northamptonshire 163 & 187 (W.Rhodes 6-40), Yorkshire 328 & 23-0. *Won by ten wickets*
**Bradford**, August 16, 18, 19: Yorkshire 119 (E.W.Astill 6-45) & 203, Leicestershire 71 (G.G.Macaulay 7-31) & 159 (A.Waddington 5-57). *Won by 92 runs*
**Harrogate**, August 20, 21, 22: Yorkshire 291-2dec (E.Oldroyd 122*, M.Leyland 100*), Hampshire 137-7. *Match drawn*
**The Oval**, August 23, 25, 26: Surrey 209 (R.Kilner 5-58) & 202 (R.Kilner 5-95), Yorkshire 100 (W.C.H.Sadler 5-29) & 202 (W.C.H.Sadler 5-42, P.G.H.Fender 5-45). *Lost by 109 runs*
**Portsmouth**, August 27, 28: Hampshire 74 (G.G.Macaulay 5-31, R.Kilner 5-33) & 97 (R.Kilner 6-15), Yorkshire 136 (A.S.Kennedy 7-41) & 38-0. *Won by ten wickets*
**Hove**, August 30, September 1: Sussex 60 (R.Kilner 5-18) & 83 (R.Kilner 7-37), Yorkshire 253-9dec. *Won by an innings and 110 runs*

## NOTES and HIGHLIGHTS

Despite the humiliation of being dismissed by Lancashire for a mere 33 (when requiring only 57 to win) at Headingley and losing three games in total, Yorkshire won the title with some comfort. The county's best performances of the season came in their first two, and last two, matches. At the beginning of the campaign their opponents (Glamorgan and Gloucestershire) lost 40 wickets for 208 runs and at the end Hampshire and Sussex were dismissed for a combined total of 314 runs.

Although the bowlers dominated the season, two of the batsmen recorded significant feats. On two occasions Sutcliffe (who finished sixth in the national averages) made a double century - against Somerset at Dewsbury and Essex at Southend, the latter innings being the highest score for the entire season and one in which he shared a stand of 314 with Oldroyd for the second wicket. Both times he scored more than 50% of the side's runs. Holmes had a purple patch of form in July when he scored three centuries in four innings and four in six. His run of scores was 59 & 105*, 6, 112, 118*, 5, 107.

Macaulay and Kilner both had excellent seasons the pair coming first and second, respectively, in the national bowling averages with Rhodes not far behind in sixth place. Kilner took at least ten wickets in each of the last two games, his overall figures being 23 for 103, while Macaulay dominated the first two matches with 19 for 67. Kilner's full second innings figures against Hampshire at Portsmouth were 20-12-15-6.

Five members of the team – Dolphin, Leyland, Oldroyd, Rhodes and Robinson – played in all of the season's 30 matches.

The end of the season signalled the end of Geoffrey Wilson's career. He had led the county for three seasons and they had won the Championship in all three. He resigned from the leadership following a disciplinary problem in a game against Middlesex, who threatened not to play against Yorkshire in the following season.

## PLAYER of the SEASON

George Macaulay, who topped Yorkshire's wicket aggregate and bowling averages for 1924, was one of the most aggressive spin bowlers in the history of the game. He began as a fast-medium bowler but advice from Hirst made him slow down and this enabled him to give the ball a sharp turn. He continued to trade in both forms and thus played a versatile role in the team, never losing his place for fifteen seasons.

Macaulay was born in Thirsk in 1897 and made his debut for the county in 1920. Not only was he a vital part of the four 1922-25 Championship-winning sides he actually took more wickets in these four seasons than any other bowler, his tally being 604 at the very cheap rate of 13.46. He played in eight Test matches over a period of eleven years and his best season was in 1925 when he took 211 wickets at 15.48 in all matches. His final total for Yorkshire was 1774 victims (average 17.22) and this remains the county's fourth best. His best innings performance was an analysis of 8-21 against the Indians at Harrogate in 1932.

Macaulay died in a flying accident in the Shetland Islands in 1940, leaving many spectators and batsmen with a memory of highly effective, varied and successful hostile bowling.

# 1925

## TOP FIVE COUNTIES

|  | Pld | W | L | D | Pts | % |
|---|---|---|---|---|---|---|
| Yorkshire | 32 | 21 | 0 | 11 | 117 | 86.66 |
| Surrey | 26 | 14 | 2 | 10 | 84 | 76.36 |
| Lancashire | 32 | 19 | 4 | 9 | 117 | 75.48 |
| Nottinghamshire | 26 | 15 | 3 | 8 | 84 | 67.20 |
| Kent | 28 | 15 | 7 | 6 | 79 | 65.83 |

## LEADING YORKSHIRE AVERAGES

### BATTING

|  | M | I | NO | Runs | HS | Avge | 100 | 50 |
|---|---|---|---|---|---|---|---|---|
| P.Holmes | 31 | 41 | 7 | 2123 | 315* | 62.44 | 5 | 9 |
| H.Sutcliffe | 30 | 40 | 5 | 1787 | 235 | 51.05 | 5 | 8 |
| M.Leyland | 31 | 35 | 4 | 1391 | 138 | 44.87 | 3 | 9 |
| W.Rhodes | 32 | 35 | 7 | 1234 | 157 | 44.07 | 2 | 9 |
| E.Oldroyd | 32 | 39 | 8 | 1228 | 109* | 39.61 | 1 | 9 |

### BOWLING

|  | O | M | R | W | Avge | 5WI | 10WM | BB |
|---|---|---|---|---|---|---|---|---|
| G.G.Macaulay | 1107.4 | 264 | 2678 | 176 | 15.21 | 4 | 15 | 7-13 |
| R.Kilner | 1036.2 | 402 | 1891 | 116 | 16.30 | - | 5 | 6-92 |
| W.Rhodes | 447.4 | 220 | 928 | 52 | 17.84 | - | - | 4-40 |
| A.Waddington | 723.4 | 165 | 1786 | 91 | 19.62 | - | 3 | 7-96 |
| E.Robinson | 659.3 | 150 | 1528 | 69 | 22.14 | - | 3 | 5-44 |

### FIELDING and WICKET-KEEPING

48 (30 ct, 18 st) A.Dolphin
28 P.Holmes
26 E.Robinson, H.Sutcliffe
23 E.Oldroyd
21 G.G.Macaulay

# RESULTS

**Cardiff**, May 6, 7, 8: Yorkshire 134-1 v Glamorgan. *Match drawn*
**Bristol**, May 9, 11, 12: Yorkshire 166 (C.W.L.Parker 5-49) & 77-4dec, Gloucestershire 82 & 42 (G.G.Macaulay 6-30). *Won by 119 runs*
**Worcester**, May 13, 14: Worcestershire 213 (R.Kilner 5-74) & 65 (G.G.Macaulay 7-20), Yorkshire 295 (H.O.Rogers 8-85). *Won by an innings and 17 runs*
**Sheffield**, May 16, 18, 19: Yorkshire 412 (E.Robinson 112*), Northamptonshire 148 & 127 (E.Robinson 5-44). *Won by an innings and 137 runs*
**Chesterfield**, May 20, 21, 22: Yorkshire 330-7dec (P.Holmes 125), Derbyshire 61 (G.G.Macaulay 7-13) & 109. *Won by an innings and 160 runs*
**Headingley**, May 23, 25, 26: Yorkshire 39-0 v Kent. *Match drawn*
**Old Trafford**, May 30, June 1, 2: Yorkshire 232 & 186-6, Lancashire 265 (C.Hallows 111*). *Match drawn*
**Edgbaston**, June 3, 4, 5: Yorkshire 265 & 275-3dec (H.Sutcliffe 130), Warwickshire 195 & 203 (R.Kilner 6-92). *Won by 142 runs*
**Lord's**, June 6, 8, 9: Middlesex 118 (E.Robinson 5-52) & 271, Yorkshire 538-6dec (P.Holmes 315*). *Won by an innings and 149 runs*
**Bradford**, June 10, 11, 12: Gloucestershire 137 & 229, Yorkshire 365 (M.Leyland 131*) & 4-0. *Won by ten wickets*
**Sheffield**, June 13, 15, 16: Nottinghamshire 139 & 165 (G.G.Macaulay 7-76), Yorkshire 157 (F.Barratt 7-71) & 148-5. *Won by five wickets*
**Huddersfield**, June 17, 18, 19: Glamorgan 246 (A.Waddington 7-96) & 197 (G.G.Macaulay 7-81), Yorkshire 579-6dec (P.Holmes 130, H.Sutcliffe 121, E.Robinson 108*). *Won by an innings and 136 runs*
**Hull**, June 20, 22, 23: Yorkshire 451-3dec (P.Holmes 194, H.Sutcliffe 129), Leicestershire 85 (G.G.Macaulay 6-34) & 206 (R.Kilner 5-56). *Won by an innings and 160 runs*
**Hull**, June 24, 25, 26: Hampshire 139 & 153 (G.G.Macaulay 6-73), Yorkshire 408. *Won by an innings and 116 runs*
**Bradford**, June 27, 29: Surrey 105 (G.G.Macaulay 5-36) & 175 (G.G.Macaulay 6-68), Yorkshire 233 & 49-0. *Won by ten wickets*
**Headingley**, July 1, 2: Yorkshire 423-8dec (W.Rhodes 157), Derbyshire 128 & 136. *Won by an innings and 159 runs*
**Harrogate**, July 4, 6: Yorkshire 414-9dec (W.Rhodes 114*), Somerset 148 (E.Robinson 5-65) & 116. *Won by an innings and 150 runs*

**Harrogate**, July 8, 9, 10: Worcestershire 215 (G.G.Macaulay 5-71) & 235 (G.G.Macaulay 5-96), Yorkshire 438 (M.Leyland 138) & 14-0. *Won by ten wickets*

**Maidstone**, July 11, 13, 14: Yorkshire 196 (A.C.Wright 6-52) & 333 (F.E.Woolley 5-90), Kent 259 (Waddington 6-90) & 160. *Won by 110 runs*

**Sheffield**, July 15, 16, 17: Essex 250 & 182, Yorkshire 303 & 68-2. *Match drawn*

**Trent Bridge**, July 18, 20, 21: Yorkshire 386 & 142-4dec, Nottinghamshire 312 & 103 (A.Waddington 6-59). *Match drawn*

**Kettering**, July 22, 23: Northamptonshire 107 & 42 (G.G.Macaulay 6-19) Yorkshire 259-4dec (E.Oldroyd 109*). *Won by an innings and 110 runs*

**Headingley,** July 25, 27, 28: Yorkshire 528-6dec (H.Sutcliffe 235, M.Leyland 110), Middlesex 184 & 149-4. *Match drawn*

**Sheffield**, August 1, 3, 4: Lancashire 320 & 74-6 (R.Kilner 5-14), Yorkshire 277. *Match drawn*

**Leicester**, August 5, 6, 7: Leicestershire 222 & 195-5, Yorkshire 197. *Match drawn*

**Dewsbury**, August 8, 10, 11: Yorkshire 507-8dec (H.Sutcliffe 206, R.Kilner 124), Warwickshire 323 (S.Santall 119*) & 128. *Won by an innings and 56 runs*

**Leyton**, August 12, 13, 14: Essex 218-3dec, Yorkshire 80-1. *Match drawn*

**Bradford**, August 15, 17: Yorkshire 119 & 230 (F.B.R.Browne 7-62), Sussex 87 (R.Kilner 5-14) & 239 (E.H.Bowley 105, G.G.Macaulay 7-67). *Won by 23 runs*

**Southampton**, August 19, 20, 21: Yorkshire 264 (P.Holmes 159), Hampshire 114-4. *Match drawn*

**The Oval**, August 22, 24, 25: Surrey 246-8dec, Yorkshire 82-0. *Match drawn*

**Hove**, August 29, 31, September 1: Sussex 156 & 237 (G.G.Macaulay 5-65), Yorkshire 305 (A.F.Wensley 6-76) & 89-1. *Won by nine wickets*

**Taunton**, September 2, 3, 4: Somerset 235 & 147 (G.G.Macaulay 6-45), Yorkshire 362 (J.C.White 5-82) & 22-0. *Won by ten wickets*

## NOTES and HIGHLIGHTS

Yorkshire won the Championship for the fourth consecutive season and this was the first time that this had been achieved by any county since the official competition had begun in 1890. Yorkshire's average number of runs scored for each wicket (38.57) was more than twice that of their opponents (18.03). The campaign included a sequence of twelve consecutive victories and it was the first time since 1908 (also Yorkshire) that any county had gone through a season without losing a single game. Yorkshire passed 400 runs on ten occasions but their opponents did not manage to do so at all. In the game against Somerset at Harrogate the away team's top four batsmen scored a total of 20 runs in their two innings. Yorkshire faced defeat against Sussex at Bradford when the visitors needed only 40 runs to win with seven wickets in hand. However, Macaulay took five wickets in six overs for only eight runs and Yorkshire's unbeaten record remained.

Holmes made the highest score of his career, and the second-highest for the county to date, in the match at Lord's against Middlesex in an innings that took a mere six hours and fifty minutes. More significantly, it was the highest innings ever scored at the ground and passed a record that had stood for 105 years. Unfortunately, Holmes's record stood for only one year but with Sutcliffe (who was eighth in the national averages) he was involved in two consecutive double-century opening partnerships – 221 against Glamorgan at Huddersfield and 272 against Leicestershire at Hull.

Macaulay was in fifth place in the national bowling averages with Kilner seventh. In the game against Derbyshire at Chesterfield, Macaulay's full match analysis was an amazing 30-18-19-8. Only five wickets were taken, throughout the whole campaign, by bowlers other than those listed in the above averages. In fact, in all four Championship-winning seasons, 1922-25, only 24 wickets were the responsibility of bowlers outside this illustrious quintet, who themselves snared 2007 victims.

The team was led for the first time by Major A.W.Lupton, who had previously played in only one match for Yorkshire – 17 years previously in 1908! Although he instilled a sense of discipline, his influence over tactics was minimal, to say the least. He was one of four players who played throughout the season, the others being Oldroyd, Rhodes and Waddington.

# PLAYER of the SEASON

Percy Holmes's record 315 not out at Lord's was the highest score for the entire season and he was also top of the national batting averages. His run aggregate of 2453 was the best of his career. He will always be best-known for being half of the most prolific opening partnership in the history of the game. He would eventually take part in no fewer than 74 century opening partnerships with Herbert Sutcliffe, 69 of these being for Yorkshire, including 64 in the Championship. In 1919, their first season together, they broke the record stand for Roses matches and in the following year Holmes became the first Yorkshire player to score two centuries in a match against Lancashire.

Holmes was born in Oakes, near Huddersfield, in 1886 and made his debut for the county in 1913. He soon became noticed as a batsman with flair, someone always looking to attack with his brilliant footwork. Sadly for Holmes he was a contemporary of Jack Hobbs and Andrew Sandham and thus received little opportunity at international level. His seven Tests were spread over a period of twelve years and his best season's average was 58.42 in 1928. Four years later he and Sutcliffe broke the world record partnership for any wicket with a stand of 555 against Essex at Leyton.

Following his non-retention at the end of 1933, Holmes spent most of the rest of his cricketeing life as coach at Scarborough College. He died in Marsh, Huddersfield, in 1971 with a record that includes five of Yorkshire's ten highest innings.

## 1926-1929

Lancashire became the third county, following Surrey and Yorkshire, to win a hat-trick of titles, over the first three years of this period. Nottinghamshire won in 1929. Yorkshire's positions were second, third, fourth and third, respectively. 1928 was a season dominated by batting, from Yorkshire's point of view, so much so that the team passed 400 on 13 occasions. However 18 of their 26 games were draws, the others all being victories – a campaign, therefore, in which they remained unbeaten.

In 1929 every county played 28 matches – the first time that the Championship had had a sense of equality about it. However it was not possible for every county to play every other county home and away and the system became random again after only four years.

# Almost Complete Domination

*Yorkshire's Championship-winning team of 1931 pictured at Scarborough. From left: A.Wood, W.Barber, M.Leyland, G.G.Macaulay, H.Verity, W.E.Bowes, F.E.Greenwood (capt.), H.Sutcliffe, E.Robinson, E.Oldroyd, P.Holmes. This began a period of eight titles in ten seasons.*

# 1930-1939

# Almost Complete Domination

### 1930

Lancashire were again champions, for the fourth time in five seasons, with Yorkshire finishing as runners-up.

For the 1931 season 15 points were to be awarded for a win with five or three points for a draw, depending on first innings lead.

### 1931

### TOP FIVE COUNTIES

|  | Pld | W | L | D | Pts |
|---|---|---|---|---|---|
| Yorkshire | 28 | 16 | 1 | 11 | 287 |
| Gloucestershire | 28 | 11 | 4 | 13 | 219 |
| Kent | 28 | 12 | 7 | 9 | 216 |
| Sussex | 28 | 10 | 6 | 12 | 205 |
| Nottinghamshire | 28 | 9 | 3 | 16 | 202 |

## LEADING YORKSHIRE AVERAGES

### BATTING

|  | M | I | NO | Runs | HS | Avge | 100 | 50 |
|---|---|---|---|---|---|---|---|---|
| H.Sutcliffe | 23 | 27 | 6 | 2049 | 230 | 97.57 | 8 | 9 |
| P.Holmes | 27 | 34 | 3 | 1211 | 250 | 39.06 | 3 | 5 |
| A.Mitchell | 22 | 23 | 4 | 681 | 134 | 35.84 | 1 | 3 |
| M.Leyland | 27 | 28 | 4 | 823 | 124 | 34.29 | 1 | 5 |
| E.Oldroyd | 21 | 23 | 2 | 707 | 93 | 33.66 | - | 5 |

## BOWLING

|             | O     | M   | R    | W   | Avge  | 5WI | 10WM | BB    |
|-------------|-------|-----|------|-----|-------|-----|------|-------|
| H.Verity    | 789.2 | 251 | 1703 | 138 | 12.34 | 12  | 3    | 10-36 |
| W.E.Bowes   | 731.3 | 177 | 1667 | 109 | 15.29 | 12  | 4    | 7-80  |
| G.G.Macaulay| 725.5 | 281 | 1170 | 76  | 15.39 | 4   | -    | 7-24  |

## FIELDING and WICKET-KEEPING

57 (39 ct, 18 st) A.Wood
31 A.Mitchell
20 F.E.Greenwood
16 E.Robinson

## RESULTS

**Leyton**, May 9, 11, 12: Essex 106 & 215 (H.Verity 7-77), Yorkshire 329. *Won by an innings and 8 runs*
**Headingley**, May 16, 18: Warwickshire 201 & 72 (H.Verity 10-36), Yorkshire 298 (J.H.Mayer 6-76). *Won by an innings and 25 runs*
**Old Trafford**, May 23, 25, 26: Yorkshire 231 & 76-2, Lancashire 128 (H.Verity 5-54). *Match drawn*
**Edgbaston**, May 27, 28, 29: Yorkshire 468-8dec (P.Holmes 250, H.Sutcliffe 129), Warwickshire 64-6. *Match drawn*
**Bradford**, May 30, June 1, 2: Kent 296-4 (F.E.Woolley 188). *Match drawn*
**Sheffield**, June 3, 4, 5: Gloucestershire 4-0dec & 171 (H.Verity 7-64), Yorkshire 4-0dec & 124 (T.W.J.Goddard 5-21). *Lost by 47 runs*
**Hull**, June 6, 8, 9: Yorkshire v Sussex. *Match abandoned*
**Sheffield**, June 13, 15, 16: Yorkshire 263 & 167-2dec, Leicestershire 157 (W.E.Bowes 5-57) & 29-1. *Match drawn*
**Hull**, June 17, 18, 19: Yorkshire 135 (A.S.Kennedy 7-45) v Hampshire. *Match drawn*
**Lord's**, June 20, 22: Yorkshire 302 (H.Sutcliffe 120*), Middlesex 111 (W.E.Bowes 5-39) & 126 (W.E.Bowes 6-63). *Won by an innings and 65 runs*
**Portsmouth**, June 24, 25, 26: Yorkshire 387-8dec (A.Mitchell 119*, H.Sutcliffe 107), Hampshire 136 (W.E.Bowes 5-64) & 180 (W.E.Bowes 5-68). *Won by an innings and 71 runs*

**Folkestone**, June 27, 29, 30: Yorkshire 467-9dec (H.Sutcliffe 230, A.P.Freeman 5-189), Kent 167 (W.E.Bowes 5-40) & 188 (H.Verity 5-53). *Won by an innings and 112 runs*
**Dewsbury**, July 1, 2, 3: Somerset 309 (G.G.Macaulay 6-69) & 107 (H.Verity 6-32), Yorkshire 451-9dec (H.Sutcliffe 183, A.W.Wellard 5-114). *Won by an innings and 35 runs*
**Bradford**, July 4, 6, 7: Surrey 165 (W.E.Bowes 6-93) & 61 (H.Verity 6-11), Yorkshire 281-3dec (M.Leyland 124). *Won by an innings and 55 runs*
**Sheffield**, July 11, 13, 14: Nottinghamshire 288 (A.Staples 131, W.E.Bowes 5-118) & 1-0, Yorkshire 313. *Match drawn*
**Headingley**, July 15, 16, 17: Essex 108 (G.G.Macaulay 7-24) & 119 (T.A.Jacques 5-33), Yorkshire 109 (M.S.Nichols 6-26) & 119-0. *Won by ten wickets*
**Trent Bridge**, July 18, 20, 21: Nottinghamshire 201 (W.E.Bowes 7-80) & 95 (E.Robinson 7-27), Yorkshire 204-6dec (P.Holmes 133) & 93-1. *Won by nine wickets*
**Swansea**, July 22, 23, 24: Glamorgan 62 (H.Verity 6-21) & 91 (H.Verity 8-33), Yorkshire 178-8dec (F.P.Ryan 5-86). *Won by an innings and 25 runs*
**Bristol**, July 25, 27, 28: Gloucestershire 182-9dec & 70 (G.G.Macaulay 6-27), Yorkshire 118-9dec (C.W.L.Parker 5-38) & 137-1. *Won by nine wickets*
**Taunton**, July 29, 30, 31: Somerset 176 & 177 (E.F.Longrigg 100, W.E.Bowes 5-79), Yorkshire 314 (A.Mitchell 134) & 43-0. *Won by ten wickets*
**Sheffield**, August 1, 3, 4: Yorkshire 484-7dec (H.Sutcliffe 195, P.Holmes 125), Lancashire 221 & 165-2. *Match drawn*
**Leicester**, August 5, 6, 7: Yorkshire 447-4dec (H.Sutcliffe 187), Leicestershire 241 (W.E.Bowes 5-95) & 181 (G.G.Macaulay 6-52). *Won by an innings and 25 runs*
**Bradford**, August 8, 10, 11: Northamptonshire 4-0dec & 86 (H.Verity 7-62), Yorkshire 4-0dec & 88-5. *Won by five wickets*
**Scarborough**, August 12, 13, 14: Yorkshire 378 (F.P.Ryan 5-108), Glamorgan 105 (H.Verity 5-62) & 153 (W.E.Bowes 7-71). *Won by an innings and 120 runs*
**Headingley**, August 15, 17, 18: Middlesex 190-5dec, Yorkshire 141-3. *Match drawn*
**Northampton** August 19, 20, 21: Northamptonshire 163, Yorkshire 38-0. *Match drawn*

**The Oval**, August 22, 24, 25: Yorkshire 233 & 178-4 (H.Sutcliffe 101*), Surrey 300 (J.B.Hobbs 133*). *Match drawn*
**Hove**, August 26, 27: Sussex 106 (H.Verity 6-52) & 165 (H.Verity 7-93), Yorkshire 148 (J.Langridge 6-59) & 124-1. *Won by nine wickets*

## NOTES and HIGHLIGHTS

The only game that Yorkshire lost was to runners-up Gloucestershire in what was effectively a one-innings match at Bramall Lane. The first two days were lost to rain, following the loss of the last two days of the previous game, against Kent at Bradford. The Championship title was richly deserved as the county won more matches and lost fewer games than any of their rivals. During the middle part of the season the team achieved five consecutive victories by an innings. In a sequence of 15 games Yorkshire lost only two second innings wickets except in two drawn matches, the rest all being won by convincing margins. Over the whole season Yorkshire's average number of runs per wicket (35.95) was more than twice that of their opponents (16.53).

Sutcliffe scored four centuries in consecutive innings, against four different opponents – Middlesex, Hampshire, Kent and Somerset – Yorkshire winning by an innings in each case. He had two triple-century partnerships with Holmes – 323 against Lancashire and 309 against Warwickshire – this being the only such example for Yorkshire in one season. Holmes's 250 against Warwickshire at Edgbaston was the highest score for the whole season.

The three main bowlers were all in the top ten of the averages, Verity finishing second in his first full season. The feat of taking ten wickets in an innings against Warwickshire came in only his fourteenth championship match. He was only the second Yorkshire bowler to achieve the feat and took four wickets in one over. At Bradford, on the occasion of Macaulay's benefit, Verity's full innings analysis was 14-7-11-6. When Bowes took eleven wickets against Middlesex at Lord's nine of his victims were all bowled or lbw.

Weather-wise, the season was a wet one, overall being the worst one since 1912 and the fourth-worst in the entire century.

The campaign saw the last games for Oldroyd and Robinson. The all-round skills of Robinson resulted in him being only the seventh player to score over 8000 runs and take over 800 wickets for Yorkshire.

## PLAYER of the SEASON

Herbert Sutcliffe easily topped the national averages for 1931, being nearly forty runs ahead of anyone else and creating a new record. He was already one of the greatest batsmen of all time and this was his best season, his aggregate for all first-class matches being 3336. His Test career average – which would end up as 60.73 – is the highest by any English player and he was most fortunate in being able to sustain outstanding opening partnerships with Jack Hobbs for England and Percy Holmes for Yorkshire. Many, many records fell Sutcliffe's way: the first English player to score two centuries in a Test match; the only English player to complete 1000 runs in his first ten Tests; the only player to score 1000 runs in each season from 1919 to 1939; the only player to score 2000 runs in as many as 14 consecutive seasons.

Although born in Summerbridge in Nidderdale, in 1894, Sutcliffe is always regarded as a son of Pudsey, his family moving there while he was still a baby. He made his debut for the county in 1919 and made an immediate impact. He soon showed the ability to bat according to the conditions and his outstanding judgement of length, pace and direction meant that he could score very rapidly off either foot. He had an impeccable technique and an imperturbable temperament. His highest score would come in the 1932 555-run record stand with Holmes and this was part of his peak period (1928-1932) when he scored 3000 runs in three seasons and topped the national averages three times consecutively.

With Hobbs, the pair became the first duo to bat throughout the entirety of a day's play in a Test and their Test career average partnership of 87.81 has never been beaten. His 38,558 runs for Yorkshire are a county record as is his total of 112 centuries. Even in his final full season (1939) at the age of 44 he broke the record for being the oldest cricketer to carry his bat through an innings. Although he spent some time as a Test selector, Sutcliffe was largely lost to the game after retirement and he died near Keighley in 1978. The 'Sutcliffe Gates' at Headingley are inscribed 'In Honour of a great Yorkshire and England cricketer' and never have these words had a truer ring.

## 1932

## TOP FIVE COUNTIES

|  | Pld | W | L | D | Pts |
|---|---|---|---|---|---|
| Yorkshire | 28 | 19 | 2 | 7 | 315 |
| Sussex | 28 | 14 | 1 | 13 | 262 |
| Kent | 28 | 14 | 3 | 11 | 248 |
| Nottinghamshire | 28 | 13 | 4 | 11 | 241 |
| Surrey | 28 | 9 | 2 | 17 | 210 |

## LEADING YORKSHIRE AVERAGES

### BATTING

|  | M | I | NO | Runs | HS | Avge | 100 | 50 |
|---|---|---|---|---|---|---|---|---|
| H.Sutcliffe | 24 | 35 | 5 | 2624 | 313 | 87.46 | 12 | 7 |
| M.Leyland | 22 | 29 | 2 | 1624 | 189 | 60.11 | 5 | 7 |
| P.Holmes | 16 | 23 | 3 | 946 | 224* | 47.30 | 2 | 6 |
| W.Barber | 26 | 34 | 2 | 932 | 162 | 29.12 | 3 | 2 |
| A.Mitchell | 26 | 35 | 3 | 929 | 177* | 29.03 | 2 | 3 |

### BOWLING

|  | O | M | R | W | Avge | 5WI | 10WM | BB |
|---|---|---|---|---|---|---|---|---|
| H.Verity | 948.1 | 339 | 1856 | 135 | 13.74 | 11 | 4 | 10-10 |
| W.E.Bowes | 992.1 | 218 | 2364 | 160 | 14.77 | 13 | 4 | 9-121 |
| G.G.Macaulay | 750.3 | 252 | 1323 | 66 | 20.45 | 4 | - | 7-66 |

## FIELDING and WICKET-KEEPING

64 (55 ct, 9 st) A.Wood
34 A.Mitchell
25 G.G.Macaulay
20 H.Sutcliffe

## RESULTS

**Bradford**, May 14, 16, 17: Lancashire 263 (E.Paynter 152, H.Verity 8-107), Yorkshire 46 (F.M.Sibbles 7-10) & 167 (F.M.Sibbles 5-58). *Lost by an innings and 50 runs*
**Edgbaston**, May 18, 19, 20: Yorkshire 403-5dec (H.Sutcliffe 109), Warwickshire 17-0. *Match drawn*
**Chesterfield**, May 21, 23, 24: v Derbyshire. *Match abandoned*
**Bath**, May 25, 26: Somerset 78 (H.Verity 6-28) & 94, Yorkshire 115 (H.L.Hazell 5-30) & 58-1. *Won by nine wickets*
**Sheffield**, May 28, 30, 31: v Kent. No play. *Match abandoned*
**Headingley**, June 1, 2, 3: Hampshire 199 & 203, Yorkshire 183 (A.S.Kennedy 5-62) & 170 (H.Sutcliffe 104*, A.S.Kennedy 5-77). *Lost by 49 runs*
**Hull**, June 4, 6, 7: Yorkshire 229 & 326-6dec (H.Sutcliffe 153*), Warwickshire 285 (N.Kilner 119, W.E.Bowes 6-118) & 54-1. *Match drawn*
**Bristol**, June 8, 9, 10: Yorkshire 418 (A.Mitchell 140), Gloucestershire 173 (W.E.Bowes 5-49) & 150 (W.E.Bowes 5-56). *Won by an innings and 95 runs*
**Tonbridge**, June 11, 13: Kent 196 & 75 (W.Rhodes 6-48), Yorkshire 207 (A.P.Freeman 8-105) & 67-6. *Won by four wickets*
**Leyton**, June 15, 16, 17: Yorkshire 555-1dec (H.Sutcliffe 313, P.Holmes 224*), Essex 78 (H.Verity 5-8) & 164 (H.Verity 5-45, W.E.Bowes 5-47). *Won by an innings and 313 runs*
**Lord's**, June 18, 20: Middlesex 152 & 134 (W.E.Bowes 7-46), Yorkshire 254 (W.Barber 102, F.J.Durston 6-73) & 34-0. *Won by ten wickets*
**Headingley**, June 22, 23, 24: Yorkshire 500-8dec (H.Sutcliffe 270, J.H.Parks 7-99), Sussex 259 (W.Rhodes 5-70) & 258-4. *Match drawn*
**Sheffield**, June 25, 27, 28: Middlesex 340 (E.H.Hendren 123, C.H.Hall 6-71) & 196-5 (J.H.A.Hulme 114*), Yorkshire 481-7dec (M.Leyland 189, W.Barber 162). *Match drawn*

**Northampton**, June 29, 30, July 1: Northamptonshire 89 (H.Verity 8-39) & 113 (G.G.Macaulay 7-66), Yorkshire 251-6dec. *Won by an innings and 49 runs*
**Sheffield**, July, 2, 4, 5: Yorkshire 241 & 160 (F.R.Brown 5-41), Surrey 126 & 97 (H.Verity 5-39, W.E.Bowes 5-43). *Won by 178 runs*
**Bradford**, July 6, 7, 8: Yorkshire 472-7dec (A.Mitchell 177*) & 240-6dec (H.Sutcliffe 132), Gloucestershire 404 (W.R.Hammond 147, R.A.Sinfield 110) & 175 (G.G.Macaulay 5-67). *Won by 133 runs*
**Headingley**, July 9, 11, 12: Nottinghamshire 234 & 67 (H.Verity 10-10), Yorkshire 163-9dec (H.Larwood 5-73) & 139-0. *Won by ten wickets*
**Huddersfield**, July 20, 21, 22: Yorkshire 384-9dec, Northamptonshire 161 (W.E.Bowes 5-68) & 207 (G.G.Macaulay 6-35). *Won by an innings and 16 runs*
**Trent Bridge**, July 23, 25, 26: Nottinghamshire 168 (G.G.Macaulay 5-49), Yorkshire 169-6. *Match drawn*
**Old Trafford**, July 30, August 1, 2: Lancashire 170 & 187 (H.Verity 5-35), Yorkshire 362-9dec (H.Sutcliffe 135). *Won by an innings and 5 runs*
**Leicester**, August 3, 4: Yorkshire 365 (M.Leyland 153, H.A.Smith 5-80), Leicestershire 155 & 141 (W.E.Bowes 5-32). *Won by an innings and 69 runs*
**Headingley**, August 6, 8: Derbyshire 78 (H.Verity 6-32) & 249 (T.S.Worthington 102, H.Verity 5-37), Yorkshire 416-7dec (H.Sutcliffe 182, M.Leyland 113, G.H.Pope 6-116). *Won by an innings and 89 runs*
**Scarborough**, August 10, 11, 12: Essex 325 (R.M.Taylor 106, M.S.Nichols 105, W.E.Bowes 9-121) & 143, Yorkshire 476-9dec (H.Sutcliffe 194). *Won by an innings and 8 runs*
**Bradford**, August 13, 15: Yorkshire 467-7dec (M.Leyland 166, W.Barber 110), Leicestershire 111 (H.Fisher 6-11) & 72 (C.H.Hall 5-27, W.E.Bowes 5-39). *Won by an innings and 284 runs*
**Sheffield**, August 17, 18: Somerset 93 (H.Fisher 5-12) & 171, Yorkshire 357-8dec (H.Sutcliffe 136). *Won by an innings and 93 runs*
**The Oval**, August 20, 22, 23: Surrey 231 & 118 (W.E.Bowes 6-49), Yorkshire 215 (M.J.C.Allom 6-75) & 135-7. *Won by three wickets*
**Bournemouth**, August 24, 25, 26: Yorkshire 307 (H.Sutcliffe 112, J.Bailey 7-83) & 199-5dec (M.Leyland 153*), Hampshire 174 & 160 (W.E.Bowes 5-40). *Won by 172 runs*
**Hove**, August 27, 29, 30: Yorkshire 258 (M.W.Tate 6-79) & 225-3dec (H.Sutcliffe 122*), Sussex 166 (W.E.Bowes 8-62) & 150 (H.Verity 6-48). *Won by 167 runs*

# NOTES and HIGHLIGHTS

Despite a very slow start to the season – the county winning only one game in the whole of May - the title was won with some comfort. For the second consecutive season the county's average number of runs per wicket (36.09) was more than twice that of their opponents (17.67). Yorkshire won all of their last nine matches, including six consecutive victories by an innings, four of these being completed within two days. The defeat by Lancashire in the opening game of the campaign, Yorkshire starting with an all-out total of 46, did not bode well, and poor weather in the first month meant that the team was not able to build up a consistent pattern of success.

Sutcliffe's season was again outstanding. His run aggregate created a new record for Yorkshire and this still stands, being over 400 runs more than his nearest rival and the third best in the entire history of the Championship. He again topped the national averages, being over 20 runs ahead of his nearest rival. Leyland (fourth) and Holmes were also in the top ten. Sutcliffe's triple-century at Leyton (the highest score of his career) is Yorkshire's third highest innings of all time and his stand of 555 with Holmes set a new world record for any wicket. Although it has been since beaten, it still stands as the highest partnership in England, and in the Championship. The whole stand was scored at the rate of 75 runs per hour and almost ended in farce as the scoreboard was turned back one run to the old record before a no-ball was conveniently found. Sutcliffe's innings, together with his 270 against Sussex at Headingley, were the best two scores for the entire season. He scored four centuries in six consecutive innings and his 194 against Essex at Scarborough took only 165 minutes – the last 94 runs coming in only 40 minutes! Barber and Leyland set the present county record of 346 for the second wicket when they batted together against Middlesex at Sheffield.

An even more remarkable feat than that of Sutcliffe and Holmes came the way of Verity. His astonishing feat of taking all ten wickets for a mere ten runs, including the hat-trick, at Headingley against Nottinghamshire, may never be beaten. Sixteen of his 19.4 overs were maidens as the bemused batsmen had no answer to his flight and guile. Against Essex at Leyton his full innings figures were a remarkable 7-3-8-5. The bowling tended to rely on him, Bowes (the pair coming second and third in the national averages) and Macaulay, although Horace Fisher did in fact have the best average with 19 wickets at 12.52, taking a hat-trick against Somerset at Sheffield, all of his victims being given out lbw. In the previous match against Leicestershire at Bradford he had recorded the economical innings figures of 17-8-11-6. Bowes' analysis against Essex at Scarborough was the best of his career.

Frank Greenwood retired at the end of the season, having led the county to the title in both of his seasons as Yorkshire's captain. 1932 was the debut season for Brian Sellers and Frank Smailes, both of whom were to play significant roles for the county in the remainder of the decade and beyond.

## PLAYER of the SEASON

Despite Verity's record-breaking feat, the highest wicket aggregate for the season was that achieved by Bill Bowes and, in the game against Essex at Scarborough, he produced an analysis that would remain the best of his career. His efforts would eventually show that was one of the most effective swing bowlers Yorkshire has ever produced. His contribution to the highly successful team of the 1930s may be measured by the fact that he was only once outside the top ten in the national averages during that decade, and only three times outside the top three. Born in Elland in 1908, Bowes made his first-class debut for MCC in 1928 and his county debut in the following season. He learnt to use his height (6 ft 5 in) to gain considerable bounce as well as the ability to bowl with variety of movement and pace.

Bowes's 15 Tests were spread over a period of 15 years (including the years of the Second World War) and his most famous moment came when he bowled Bradman for a duck at Melbourne on the infamous 'Bodyline' tour of 1932-33. Although he played in only one of the five Tests on this trip, he was fully supportive of skipper Jardine's policy regarding the mode of attack as being a natural evolution of the game. His limited batting (he scored fewer first-class runs than he took wickets) and laboured fielding probably militated against him playing in more Tests but his 68 wickets (average 22.33), including five wickets in an innings on six occasions, justified his appearances.

Bowes's career-best performance was typical of his attitude when he persevered on a hot day on a batsman's pitch to bowl forty overs in three-and-a-half hours. His best season would come in 1935 when his 193 victims were snared at an average of 15.44. During the War he spent two years in prison camps and lost four stones in weight but he still came back to rebuild his career with indomitable spirit. He retired, however, after the 1947 season having taken a total of 1351 wickets for his county. He was a most intelligent bowler and was soon able to build a second career in the game – as a journalist. He became cricket correspondant for two Yorkshire papers, successively, and continued in this role until 1973, just 14 years before his death in Otley. The game had lost a perceptive cricketer and a real gentleman.

For 1933 the determination of rankings would again be decided by percentage of points obtained to points possible.

## 1933

## TOP FIVE COUNTIES

|  | Pld | W | L | D | Pts | % |
|---|---|---|---|---|---|---|
| Yorkshire | 30 | 19 | 3 | 8 | 315 | 70.00 |
| Sussex | 32 | 18 | 5 | 9 | 311 | 64.79 |
| Kent | 30 | 15 | 8 | 7 | 253 | 56.22 |
| Essex | 28 | 13 | 8 | 7 | 224 | 53.33 |
| Lancashire | 28 | 9 | 1 | 18 | 210 | 50.00 |

## LEADING YORKSHIRE AVERAGES

### BATTING

|  | M | I | NO | Runs | HS | Avge | 100 | 50 |
|---|---|---|---|---|---|---|---|---|
| M.Leyland | 28 | 39 | 4 | 1969 | 210* | 56.25 | 6 | 9 |
| A.Mitchell | 28 | 40 | 8 | 1547 | 150* | 48.34 | 5 | 5 |
| H.Sutcliffe | 27 | 40 | 3 | 1635 | 205 | 44.19 | 4 | 5 |
| W.Barber | 30 | 42 | 4 | 1477 | 124 | 38.86 | 4 | 8 |

## BOWLING

|  | O | M | R | W | Avge | 5WI | 10WM | BB |
|---|---|---|---|---|---|---|---|---|
| H.Verity | 924.4 | 363 | 1826 | 153 | 11.93 | 14 | 6 | 9-44 |
| G.G.Macaulay | 914.2 | 327 | 1761 | 115 | 15.31 | 8 | 3 | 7-9 |
| W.E.Bowes | 778 | 179 | 2139 | 123 | 17.39 | 11 | 4 | 8-69 |

### FIELDING and WICKET-KEEPING

62 (43 ct, 19 st) A.Wood
29 A.B.Sellers
28 A.Mitchell, H.Sutcliffe
24 A.C.Rhodes
20 G.G.Macaulay

## RESULTS

**Hull**, May 13, 15: Derbyshire 51 (H.Verity 6-12) & 78 (H.Verity 6-41), Yorkshire 96 (L.F.Townsend 6-38) & 35-4. *Won by six wickets*
**Dewsbury**, May 17, 18, 19: Essex 64 (H.Verity 5-34) & 68 (H.Verity 6-40), Yorkshire 128-4dec & 5-0. *Won by ten wickets*
**Bradford**, May 20, 22: Leicestershire 65 (G.G.Macaulay 6-25) & 39 (G.G.Macaulay 6-22), Yorkshire 250-7dec. *Won by an innings and 146 runs*
**Cardiff**, May 24, 25, 26: Yorkshire 299 (W.Barber 120*, J.C.Clay 6-72) & 236-3dec (A.Mitchell 108*), Glamorgan 208 & 161 (W.E.Bowes 6-82). *Won by 166 runs*
**Headingley**, May 27, 29: Yorkshire 286 (A.P.Freeman 5-113), Kent 90 (W.E.Bowes 6-44) & 172 (W.E.Bowes 6-73). *Won by an innings and 24 runs*
**Sheffield**, May 31, June 1, 2: Gloucestershire 245 (W.E.Bowes 5-112) & 148 (W.Rhodes 5-46), Yorkshire 369 & 25-0. *Won by ten wickets*
**Old Trafford**, June 3, 5: Yorkshire 341 (A.Mitchell 123), Lancashire 93 (G.G.Macaulay 7-28) & 92 (G.G.Macaulay 5-21). *Won by an innings and 156 runs*
**Edgbaston**, June 7, 8, 9: Yorkshire 591-6dec (H.Sutcliffe 205, W.Barber 124), Warwickshire 319 (N.Kilner 197) & 127-4. *Match drawn*
**Sheffield**, June 10, 11, 12: Yorkshire 500-9dec (A.Mitchell 142, M.Leyland 133), Worcestershire 231 & 104. *Won by an innings and 165 runs*

**Kettering**, June 14, 15: Northamptonshire 27 (G.G.Macaulay 7-9) & 68, Yorkshire 301 (H.Sutcliffe 113, (V.W.C.Jupp 6-99). *Won by an innings and 206 runs*

**Gloucester**, June 17, 19, 20: Yorkshire 227 & 153 (T.W.J.Goddard 8-77), Gloucestershire 144 (H.Verity 6-55) & 135 (W.E.Bowes 8-69). *Won by 101 runs*

**Headingley**, June 21, 22: Yorkshire 229, Warwickshire 63 & 101 (H.Verity 5-25, G.G.Macaulay 5-33). *Won by an innings and 65 runs*

**Trent Bridge**, June 24, 25, 27: Nottinghamshire 241 (W.E.Bowes 7-89) & 199-8dec (W.E.Bowes 6-87), Yorkshire 155 (H.J.Butler 5-36) & 176-4 (W.Barber 109*). *Match drawn*

**Hull**, June 28, 29, 30: Sussex 378 (J.Langridge 159*, M.Leyland 5-67) & 17-0, Yorkshire 131 & 263. *Lost by ten wickets*

**Sheffield**, July 1, 3, 4: Yorkshire 253 & 195, Surrey 134 (W.E.Bowes 7-68) & 252 (D.R.Jardine 105, W.E.Bowes 5-72). *Won by 62 runs*

**Headingley**, July 8, 10, 11: Yorkshire 349-7dec (M.Leyland 192), Northamptonshire 63 (H.Verity 7-35) & 135 (H.Verity 6-67). *Won by an innings and 151 runs*

**Leyton**, July 12, 13, 14: Yorkshire 340 (W.Barber 101, T.P.B.Smith 5-122), Essex 104 (H.Verity 8-47) & 64 (H.Verity 9-44). *Won by an innings and 172 runs*

**Bradford**, July 15, 17, 18: Middlesex 305 (H.Verity 6-103) & 114 (G.G.Macaulay 7-52), Yorkshire 367 (H.Sutcliffe 177, J.M.Sims 5-69) & 53-0. *Won by ten wickets*

**Bournemouth**, July 22, 24, 25: Hampshire 177 & 330-8dec, Yorkshire 255 & 58-3. *Match drawn*

**Headingley**, July 26, 27: Middlesex 136 (H.Verity 5-43) & 192 (H.Verity 6-49), Yorkshire 302 (J.M.Sims 6-106) & 28-0. *Won by ten wickets*

**Sheffield**, July 29, 31, August 1: Hampshire 268 (W.E.Bowes 5-74) & 68-2, Yorkshire 338 (M.Leyland 133, R.H.Palmer 5-93, G.S.Boyes 5-96). *Match drawn*

**Scarborough**, August 2, 3: Yorkshire 308 & 4-0, Glamorgan 157 (W.E.Bowes 7-39) & 154. *Won by ten wickets*

**Headingley**, August 5, 7, 8: Yorkshire 296 & 153-3, Lancashire 431 (J.L.Hopwood 120, C.Hawkwood 113). *Match drawn*

**Leicester**, August 9, 10, 11: Yorkshire 550 (H.Sutcliffe 174), Leicestershire 154 & 145 (M.Leyland 6-46). *Won by an innings and 251 runs*

**Chesterfield**, August 12, 14, 15: Derbyshire 245 & 330-8dec (L.F.Townsend 100), Yorkshire 218 (T.B.Mitchell 6-66) & 137-2. *Match drawn*
**Bradford**, August 16, 17, 18: Nottinghamshire 324 (W.W.Keeton 110) & 202, Yorkshire 515 (A.Mitchell 138, M.Leyland 134) & 12-0. *Won by ten wickets*
**Dover**, August 19, 21, 22: Kent 332 & 133 (H.Verity 9-59), Yorkshire 333-6dec (M.Leyland 210*) & 88 (A.P.Freeman 6-51). *Lost by 44 runs*
**The Oval**, August 23, 24, 25: Surrey 560-6dec (H.S.Squires 178, H.T.Barling 112), Yorkshire 233 & 219-5. *Match drawn*
**Hove**, August 26, 28: Yorkshire 115 & 114 (G.S.Pearce 5-34), Sussex 249. *Lost by an innings and 20 runs*
**Worcester**, August 30, 31, September 1: Yorkshire 223 & 421-3 (A.Mitchell 150*, M.Leyland 117*), Worcestershire 420 (M.Nichol 154, S.H.Martin 144). *Match drawn*

## NOTES and HIGHLIGHTS

Although the final Championship table suggested otherwise, this was a very emphatic victory for Yorkshire in the first season under their new captain, Brian Sellers. On no fewer than 14 occasions they dismissed their opponents for under 100, including six matches when they achieved the feat twice. Essex and Northamptonshire were each dismissed three times for less than 100, the latter being dismissed at Kettering for a mere 27, Macaulay's full figures being a remarkable 14-7-9-7. The county got off to an excellent start by winning all of their first seven games, eleven from the first twelve, and the only real downside to the season was to lose twice to the eventual runners-up, Sussex.

The success was dominated by the bowlers, three in particular. After the first three games Verity had taken 29 wickets at an average of 5.85 and Macaulay 24 at 5.83. The latter's full match figures in the game against Essex at Dewsbury were the highly economical ones of 38-19-31-5. Verity's feat of taking 17 wickets at Leyton against Essex remains unsurpassed in the history of Yorkshire cricket and his analysis was the best for the whole season. His full figures in his first innings of the season, in the game against Derbyshire, were 13.3-7-12-6. His feat of taking nine wickets in an innings on two occasions in the same season was also unprecedented for the county, although he was to repeat the feat in 1936 and Johnny Wardle was to do so in 1954. Verity was top of the national averages, with Macaulay third and Bowes seventh. Even Leyland took ten wickets in a match – for 94 runs against Leicestershire at Leicester – for the only time in his career.

Although Sutcliffe was not as dominant as in the previous two seasons Leyland, Mitchell and Wilf Barber all increased their aggregates, both Leyland (fourth) and Mitchell being in the top ten of the national averages.

Sellers' reputation for leading his side by example in the field was soon put into practice at Leyton where he took seven catches, including five in the first innings. Neither he, Barber nor Arthur Wood missed a single game. Holmes was not re-engaged after the end of the season and thus was concluded a distinguished career.

The weather for much of the season was warm and sunny, it being, overall, the best summer since 1921.

## PLAYER of the SEASON

With the leading run aggregate and average for Yorkshire's season, Morris Leyland (usually known as Maurice) was already gaining a reputation as one of the county's best-ever left-handed batsmen. Dependable, courageous, solid and yet enthusiastic, Leyland was born in Harrogate in 1900 and first played for the county in 1920. He gained his cap in 1922 and scored at least 1000 runs in each of the following 17 seasons, making his Test debut in 1928. He would be an England regular for ten years, averaging an excellent 56.83 in twenty Tests against Australia (1705 runs) and scoring, in all, 2764 runs (average 46.06) in 41 Tests. He set records for three of Yorkshire's wicket partnerships, all of which still stand, as well as the England second wicket record of 382 with Len Hutton at The Oval in 1938 against Australia.

Leyland always stood very still at the crease and gave himself time to play the ball, especially with his nimble footwork. He would have had more opportunity to ply his left-arm spinners, had not Rhodes, Kilner and Verity been contemporaries. Even so, 466 first-class wickets with a best of 8-63 against Hampshire at Huddersfield in 1938 show that he was not entirely kept in the shade. He was also a brilliant outfielder.

Leyland retired from playing in 1946 and became Yorkshire coach, having a cheerful approach with his young players. He battled against Parkinson's disease in later life and died near Knaresborough in 1967, having displayed the same courage as he had when facing the best fast bowlers.

## 1934

Lancashire continued the northern domination of the inter-war period with Yorkshire slipping to sixth place – their lowest position since 1911.

## 1935

## TOP FIVE COUNTIES

|  | Pld | W | L | D | Pts | % |
|---|---|---|---|---|---|---|
| Yorkshire | 30 | 19 | 1 | 10 | 321 | 71.33 |
| Derbyshire | 28 | 16 | 6 | 6 | 266 | 63.33 |
| Middlesex | 24 | 11 | 5 | 8 | 202 | 56.11 |
| Lancashire | 28 | 12 | 6 | 10 | 227 | 54.04 |
| Nottinghamshire | 28 | 10 | 3 | 15 | 213 | 50.71 |

## LEADING YORKSHIRE AVERAGES

### BATTING

|  | M | I | NO | Runs | HS | Avge | 100 | 50 |
|---|---|---|---|---|---|---|---|---|
| H.Sutcliffe | 26 | 36 | 3 | 1966 | 212 | 59.57 | 8 | 6 |
| W.Barber | 26 | 36 | 3 | 1678 | 255 | 50.88 | 4 | 8 |
| A.Mitchell | 26 | 36 | 3 | 1239 | 98 | 37.54 | - | 10 |
| A.Wood | 29 | 41 | 11 | 1087 | 123* | 36.23 | 1 | 7 |
| M.Leyland | 23 | 31 | 2 | 915 | 95 | 31.55 | - | 7 |

## BOWLING

|  | O | M | R | W | Avge | 5WI | 10WM | BB |
|---|---|---|---|---|---|---|---|---|
| H.Verity | 906.3 | 306 | 2196 | 161 | 13.63 | 18 | 5 | 8-28 |
| W.E.Bowes | 811 | 223 | 1819 | 138 | 15.18 | 12 | 5 | 8-17 |
| T.F.Smailes | 558.2 | 132 | 1453 | 70 | 20.75 | 2 | 1 | 7-47 |

## FIELDING and WICKET-KEEPING

60 (43 ct, 17 st) A.Wood
26 A.B.Sellers
24 C.Turner
22 H.Verity
20 A.Mitchell

## RESULTS

**Neath**, May 8, 9, 10: Glamorgan 270 (W.E.Bowes 7-89) & 211-4dec, Yorkshire 262 (H.Sutcliffe 135*) & 72-3. *Match drawn*

**Chesterfield**, May 11, 13, 14: Derbyshire 382 (D.Smith 189, H.Verity 5-118) & 211-6dec (A.E.Alderman 100, H.Verity 5-74), Yorkshire 328 & 102-4. *Match drawn*

**Gloucester**, May 18, 20, 21: Gloucestershire 128 (C.Turner 7-54) & 116 (H.Verity 6-45), Yorkshire 166 & 79-2. *Won by eight wickets*

**Headingley**, May 25, 27: Yorkshire 421 (W.Barber 191), Sussex 86 & 212. *Won by an innings and 123 runs*

**Sheffield**, May 29, 30: Worcestershire 92 (W.E.Bowes 8-40) & 189 (W.E.Bowes 5-48), Yorkshire 445-5dec (H.Sutcliffe 200*, A.Wood 123*). *Won by an innings and 164 runs*

**Bradford**, June 1, 3: Kent 182 & 140 (G.G.Macaulay 5-40, Verity 5-52), Yorkshire 131 (A.P.Freeman 6-47) & 192-8 (H.Sutcliffe 110, A.P.Freeman 7-108). *Won by two wickets*

**Hull**, June 5, 6: Hampshire 63 (H.Verity 7-31) & 117 (H.Verity 7-47), Yorkshire 315-5dec (H.Sutcliffe 100). *Won by an innings and 135 runs*

**Old Trafford**, June 8, 10, 11:Lancashire 153 & 80-0, Yorkshire 140 (R.Pollard 6-56). *Match drawn*

**Edgbaston**, June 12, 13, 14: Warwickshire 254 & 221 (T.F.Smailes 6-65), Yorkshire 161 (R.E.S.Wyatt 6-47) & 225-3. *Match drawn*

**Lord's**, June 15, 17, 18: Middlesex 108 (T.F.Smailes 5-23), Yorkshire 307-6 (W.Barber 107). *Match drawn*

**Headingley**, June 19, 20, 21: Leicestershire 153 (H.Verity 5-69) & 55 (H.Verity 8-28), Yorkshire 93 (H.A.Smith 6-31) & 75-2. *Match drawn*

**Bradford**, June 26, 27, 28: Yorkshire 423-7dec (H.Sutcliffe 121, W.Barber 120), Glamorgan 178 & 145. *Won by an innings and 100 runs*

**Kettering**, June 29, July 1: Northamptonshire 62 (W.E.Bowes 8-18) & 52 (W.E.Bowes 8-17), Yorkshire 280. *Won by an innings and 166 runs*

**Colchester**, July 3, 4, 5: Yorkshire 253 & 228-5dec, Essex 150 (W.E.Bowes 7-58) & 105 (H.Verity 5-17). *Won by 226 runs*

**Sheffield**, July 6, 8, 9: Yorkshire 582-7dec (W.Barber 255), Surrey 206 (M.Leyland 5-46) & 256 (H.S.Squires 120*, W.E.Bowes 5-54). *Won by an innings and 120 runs*

**Tonbridge**, July 10, 11, 12: Yorkshire 326 (A.P.Freeman 6-114) & 245, Kent 171 (W.E.Bowes 6-42) & 247 (H.Verity 7-53). *Won by 153 runs*

**Harrogate**, July 17, 18, 19: Yorkshire 459-8dec, Northamptonshire 289 & 94 (H.Verity 5-20). *Won by an innings and 76 runs*

**Trent Bridge**, July 20, 22, 23: Yorkshire 268 & 20-1, Nottinghamshire 402 (A.Staples 125*). *Match drawn*

**Hull**, July 24, 25, 26: Yorkshire 260 & 294-9dec (T.W.J.Goddard 5-99), Gloucestershire 203 & 154 (H.Verity 6-53). *Won by 197 runs*

**Sheffield**, July 27, 29, 30: Nottinghamshire 232 (W.W.Keeton 120) & 286-8, Yorkshire 421 (P.A.Gibb 157*, H.Sutcliffe 135). *Match drawn*

**Huddersfield**, July 31, August 1: Yorkshire 31 (H.D.Read 6-11) & 99 (M.S.Nichols 7-37), Essex 334 (M.S.Nichols 146). *Lost by an innings and 204 runs*

**Bradford**, August 3, 5, 6: Yorkshire 225 (F.M.Sibbles 5-56) & 181-3, Lancashire 53 (W.E.Bowes 6-16) & 352 (F.B.Watson 141, W.E.Bowes 6-83). *Won by seven wickets*

**Leicester**, August 7, 8, 9: Leicestershire 274 & 130, Yorkshire 393 (H.Sutcliffe 212, W.H.Marlow 5-116) & 15-0. *Won by ten wickets*

**Bradford**, August 10, 12: Yorkshire 354 & 4-0, Warwickshire 105 (W.E.Bowes 6-32) & 250 (W.E.Bowes 5-49). *Won by ten wickets*

**Scarborough**, August 14, 15: Yorkshire 304 & 5-0, Derbyshire 133 & 174. *Won by ten wickets*

**Headingley**, August 17, 19, 20: Yorkshire 367 (L.Hutton 131), Middlesex 183 (H.Verity 6-53) & 102 (H.Verity 5-20). *Won by an innings and 82 runs*

**Worcester**, August 21, 22: Worcestershire 154 & 144 (H.Verity 5-48), Yorkshire 358 (H.Sutcliffe 138, R.Howorth 5-80). *Won by an innings and 60 runs*
**The Oval**, August 24, 26, 27: Yorkshire 299-8dec, Surrey 44 (H.Verity 6-24) & 26-3. *Match drawn*
**Hove**, August 28, 29, 30: Sussex 274 (T.F.Smailes 7-47) & 121, Yorkshire 220 & 28-1. *Match drawn*
**Portsmouth**, August 31, September 2: Yorkshire 309-8dec, Hampshire 99 (H.Verity 6-52) & 94 (H.Verity 7-55). *Won by an innings and 116 runs*

# NOTES and HIGHLIGHTS

A solitary blip at Huddersfield against Essex did not prevent Yorkshire from winning the Championship with some comfort despite the vagaries of the points scoring system. Essex dismissed Yorkshire inside an hour on the first morning of the match (for their lowest score for 26 years) and the game was over before one o'clock on the second day, Morris Nichols finishing with match figures of eleven for 52, to add to his century. He was only the fifth all-rounder to score a century and take ten wickets in the same match against Yorkshire, and the first since 1911. The season's best game was against Kent at Bradford where, largely due to Sutcliffe being the only one to play 'Tich' Freeman with any confidence, the hosts won by two wickets after being 120-6 chasing 192. Yorkshire had previously conceded a first innings lead of 51 in a low-scoring game. On twelve occasions Yorkshire's opponents were dismissed for fewer than a hundred.

The game against Nottinghamshire at Sheffield saw Paul Gibb scoring a century on his first appearance for the county, only the second player to do so. It remained his highest score for Yorkshire and he added 178 runs to the total in a sixth-wicket partnership with Sutcliffe. Gibb had previously played for Scotland and Cambridge University. Wood scored over 1000 runs in a season for the only time in his career and Barber's double-century against Surrey at Sheffield was his highest score. Sutcliffe topped the national averages for the fourth and final time, with Barber in third place.

Bowes and Verity were second and third, respectively, in the national bowling averages. Bowes' remarkable match analysis of sixteen for 35 against Northamptonshire at Kettering remains the second best for Yorkshire in all matches. The wickets were taken in 29.3 overs, of which 18 were maidens.

1935 was the final season of George Macaulay's outstanding career. His haul of 1774 wickets (av. 17.22) in all first-class matches remains the fourth best for Yorkshire.

## PLAYER of the SEASON

In 1935 Arthur Wood scored the only century of his career but, more importantly, became the first Yorkshire wicket-keeper to score 1000 runs in a season. His all-round contribution was vital to the side's success throughout the very successful period during which he played. An effervescent character, Wood soon had to learn how to keep wicket against highly skilled bowlers, whose turn and swing could be most pronounced, especially on unpredictable pitches.

Born in Bradford, Wood first played for the county in 1927 and was to create a Yorkshire record by playing in 225 consecutive matches. He would lift the team, even on its most difficult days, with his humour and ebullient 'keeping. Stocky and squat, he was agile and fast, especially down the leg-side, and always took the ball cleanly. He eventually totalled 855 victims (612 catches and 243 stumpings) for the county. The main aspect of his batting was that he could always perform according to the needs of the side, either doggedly or in a swashbuckling manner. He ended his county career with over 8500 runs. He would gain four Test caps in the latter part of the 1930s, the first of these being won just five days before his fortieth birthday.

Wood played his final season in 1946 and died in Ilkley in 1973. An extremely popular player, both with spectators and team-mates, he had been at the heart of a side doing his job with skill and humour.

# 1936

Derbyshire claimed the only title in their history, Yorkshire finishing in third place.

*Herbert Sutcliffe (left) and Arthur Mitchell going out to open Yorkshire's innings on the second day of the Roses match at Headingley in 1936. Their stand was worth 114 in a rain-affected drawn game.*

# 1937

## TOP FIVE COUNTIES

|  | Pld | W | L | D | Pts | % |
|---|---|---|---|---|---|---|
| Yorkshire | 28 | 18 | 2 | 8 | 302 | 71.90 |
| Middlesex | 24 | 15 | 4 | 5 | 246 | 68.33 |
| Derbyshire | 28 | 14 | 6 | 8 | 240 | 57.14 |
| Gloucestershire | 30 | 15 | 10 | 5 | 244 | 54.22 |
| Sussex | 32 | 13 | 7 | 12 | 247 | 51.45 |

## LEADING YORKSHIRE AVERAGES

### BATTING

|  | M | I | NO | Runs | HS | Avge | 100 | 50 |
|---|---|---|---|---|---|---|---|---|
| L.Hutton | 22 | 36 | 5 | 1728 | 271* | 55.74 | 5 | 7 |
| H.Sutcliffe | 27 | 45 | 5 | 1822 | 189 | 45.55 | 4 | 9 |
| W.Barber | 25 | 37 | 5 | 1270 | 115 | 39.68 | 3 | 5 |
| A.Mitchell | 26 | 42 | 6 | 1286 | 105 | 35.72 | 2 | 7 |
| M.Leyland | 19 | 25 | 1 | 856 | 167 | 35.66 | 3 | 2 |
| C.Turner | 23 | 32 | 4 | 861 | 84 | 30.75 | - | 6 |

### BOWLING

|  | O | M | R | W | Avge | 5WI | 10WM | BB |
|---|---|---|---|---|---|---|---|---|
| H.Verity | 1078.3 | 395 | 2270 | 157 | 14.45 | 16 | 6 | 9-43 |
| W.E.Bowes | 593.1 | 158 | 1330 | 66 | 20.15 | 4 | 1 | 7-56 |
| E.P.Robinson | 548.4 | 143 | 1528 | 66 | 23.15 | 3 | 1 | 7-45 |
| T.F.Smailes | 891.1 | 216 | 2219 | 93 | 23.86 | 4 | - | 6-29 |

### FIELDING and WICKET-KEEPING

51 (36 ct, 15 st) A.Wood
38 A.Mitchell
27 C.Turner
24 A.B.Sellers

# RESULTS

**Old Trafford**, May 15, 17, 18: Lancashire 106 (H.Verity 6-32) & 197, Yorkshire 270 & 35-0. *Won by ten wickets*

**Edgbaston**, May 19, 20, 21: Yorkshire 492-9dec (T.F.Smailes 109), Warwickshire 496-8 (R.E.S.Wyatt 152, A.J.W.Croom 118, H.E.Dollery 110, H.Verity 5-110). *Match drawn*

**Sheffield**, May 22, 24, 25: Yorkshire 465 (W.Barber 104) & 166-5, Sussex 566 (J.G.Langridge 175, H.W.Parks 104, T.F.Smailes 5-130). *Match drawn*

**Headingley**, May 26, 27, 28: Yorkshire 157 (T.W.J.Goddard 6-57) & 147 (T.W.J.Goddard 7-85), Gloucestershire 77 (E.P.Robinson 7-45) & 87. *Won by 140 runs*

**Chesterfield**, May 29, 31, June 1: Derbyshire 248 & 106, Yorkshire 261 (T.B.Mitchell 6-101) & 94-4. *Won by six wickets*

**Stourbridge**, June 2, 3, 4: Yorkshire 460 (M.Leyland 167, L.Hutton 101), Worcestershire 190 (H.Verity 5-53) & 189 (H.Verity 5-60). *Won by an innings and 81 runs*

**Bradford**, June 5, 7, 8: Yorkshire 297 (A.B.Sellers 109, A.E.Watt 6-99) & 328-7dec (F.E.Woolley 6-125), Kent 254 & 84 (T.F.Smailes 5-16). *Won by 287 runs*

**Lord's**, June 9, 10, 11: Yorkshire 218 (C.I.J.Smith 6-75) & 131 (J.M.Sims 5-36), Middlesex 371 (E.P.Robinson 6-157). *Lost by an innings and 22 runs*

**Tonbridge**, June 12, 14: Yorkshire 462-8dec (L.Hutton 136), Kent 141 (H.Verity 6-46) & 270 (H.Verity 5-82). *Won by an innings and 51 runs*

**Sheffield**, June 19, 21, 22: Derbyshire 145 (C.Turner 5-45) & 281, Yorkshire 525-4dec (L.Hutton 271*). *Won by an innings and 99 runs*

**Hull**, June 23, 24, 25: Yorkshire 523-3dec (H.Sutcliffe 189, L.Hutton 153, M.Leyland 118*) & 77-4, Leicestershire 458 (C.S.Dempster 146, G.S.Watson 122). *Match drawn*

**Headingley**, June 26, 28, 29: Nottinghamshire 191 & 346 (W.E.Bowes 6-69), Yorkshire 379 (W.Barber 115) & 7-0. *Match drawn*

**Ilford**, June 30, July 1: Yorkshire 440 (L.Hutton 124), Essex 152 & 80 (H.Verity 6-10). *Won by an innings and 208 runs*

**Bradford**, July 3, 5, 6: Yorkshire 398 (H.Sutcliffe 138) & 199-7, Surrey 187 (E.P.Robinson 6-33) & 409 (L.B.Fishlock 146, H.Verity 5-113). *Won by three wickets*

**Sheffield**, July 7, 8, 9: Yorkshire 238 (H.G.Owen-Smith 5-74) & 128-4, Middlesex 267. *Match drawn*

**Hull**, July 14, 15, 16: Hampshire 180 & 182 (T.F.Smailes 6-50), Yorkshire 244 & 119-6 (G.Hill 5-42). *Won by four wickets*

**Trent Bridge**, July 17, 19, 20: Nottinghamshire 326 & 145-7dec, Yorkshire 209 (A.B.Sellers 103*) & 101-3. *Match drawn*

**Cardiff**, July 21, 22, 23: Yorkshire 255 (D.E.Davies 5-57) & 103-5dec, Glamorgan 150 (H.Verity 5-38) & 104-5. *Match drawn*

**Bristol**, July 24, 26, 27: Yorkshire 346 (B.H.Lyon 5-72) & 273-4dec (W.Barber 107*), Gloucestershire 286 (B.O.Allen 102) & 214 (W.E.Bowes 5-36). *Won by 119 runs*

**Huddersfield**, July 28, 29, 30: Essex 184 & 163 (W.E.Bowes 7-56), Yorkshire 279 & 69-0. *Won by ten wickets*

**Sheffield**, July 31, August 2, 3: Yorkshire 246 (H.Sutcliffe 122, R.Pollard 5-59) & 168 (J.Iddon 9-42), Lancashire 324 & 91-5. *Lost by five wickets*

**Leicester**, August 4, 5, 6: Yorkshire 333-9dec (H.Sutcliffe 109, A.Mitchell 100, H.A.Smith 5-94) & 183-9dec, Leicestershire 202 & 185 (L.Hutton 6-76). *Won by 129 runs*

**Headingley**, August 7, 9, 10: Warwickshire 205 (H.Verity 9-43) & 180 (H.Verity 5-49), Yorkshire 282 (W.E.Hollies 5-89) & 106-1. *Won by nine wickets*

**Bradford**, August 14, 16, 17: Yorkshire 258-8dec, Worcestershire 120 (H.Verity 7-38) & 129 (T.F.Smailes 6-29). *Won by an innings and 9 runs*

**Scarborough**, August 18, 19, 20: Yorkshire 356 (A.Mitchell 105) & 171-7dec, Glamorgan 243 (H.Verity 5-76) & 199 (H.Verity 5-71). *Won by 85 runs*

**The Oval**, August 21, 23, 24: Yorkshire 463 (N.W.D.Yardley 101, A.R.Gover 6-130), Surrey 273 (L.B.Fishlock 113) & 295-6 (R.J.Gregory 109, L.B.Fishlock 105). *Match drawn*

**Eastbourne**, August 25, 26, 27: Yorkshire 457 (M.Leyland 101), Sussex 198 (H.Verity 8-80) & 143 (H.Verity 6-52). *Won by an innings and 116 runs*

**Bournemouth**, August 28, 30, 31: Hampshire 93 (W.E.Bowes 6-36) & 185, Yorkshire 191 (G.E.M.Heath 5-66) & 88-0. *Won by ten wickets*

## NOTES and HIGHLIGHTS

Other than Verity, the bowlers were not up to the standard expected of the county and it was the batsmen who were more collectively responsible for winning the title. All of those who played in at least five games averaged at least 15 with the bat – even Bowes! - but only Verity averaged fewer then 20 with the ball. Yorkshire won six of their last seven matches as they sneaked home in a close race for the title with Middlesex. Although the victory at Tonbridge was secured on the second day, it came in the last five minutes of the extra half-hour. The best match of the season was Mitchell's Benefit game against Surrey at Bradford; at the end of an encounter which see-sawed throughout, Yorkshire scored the 199 runs needed for victory in 101 minutes – seven minutes to spare. After the end of the season Yorkshire beat Middlesex in an unofficial challenge match played at The Oval by the very satisfactory margin of an innings and 115 runs.

Len Hutton scored four centuries in consecutive innings against four different opponents – Kent, Derbyshire, Leicestershire and Essex. Between the matches against the last two counties he scored 0 and 1 on his Test debut against New Zealand at Lord's. Against Leicestershire at Hull Sutcliffe and Hutton made a stand of 315 for the first wicket and the latter, who came fourth in the national averages, shared in 20 of Yorkshire's 36 century partnerships throughout the season. Norman Yardley came third in the averages with 616 runs at 44.00. Surrey's Laurie Fishlock scored three centuries in the two games against Yorkshire. He was the eighth player to score two centuries in one match against the county and the first for 18 years.

In the match against Warwickshire at Headingley, Verity took nine wickets in an innings for the eighth and last time in his Championship career. In the first match against Lancashire his full match figures were a remarkably economical 79.1-28-75-10 and his second innings figures against Essex at Ilford were 10.5-7-10-6. He finished in second place in the national averages.

# PLAYER of the SEASON

In taking 64 wickets more than his nearest rival, Hedley Verity continued to confirm his prowess as the country's leading left-arm spinner. He had succeeded Rhodes as the latest in the line of Yorkshire's great practitioners of this art. Possibly the greatest of this sequence, he dominated the 1930s like no other domestic bowler and his astonishing feat of taking ten wickets for ten runs in 1932 may never be beaten.

Verity was born in Headingley in 1905 and did not play his first game for Yorkshire until he was aged 25, after time in the Lancashire League and a trial with Warwickshire. An average of 12.42 in his first season showed signs of something special and he played in the first of his forty Test matches in the following season. His control of spin and flight, when combined with subtle variations of pace and length, as well as his ability to extract additional bounce, due to his height, made even the best batsmen suffer. Testimony to this is that no bowler would take Don Bradman's wicket on more occasions than Verity's record of ten (including eight times in Tests – also a record).

Other records that eventually came his way defy belief. He took over 200 wickets in a season on three occasions, at least nine in an innings nine times, five wickets in an innings 164 times and ten in a match on 54 occasions. Almost 2000 wickets at an average of fewer than 15 in a ten-year career pay testimony to a very high degree of skill. Quiet and unassuming, Verity went about his work with efficiency and little fuss.

Tragically, his life ended during the Second World War. He was mortally wounded leading his company into battle and died in an Italian hospital in 1943. His bravery typified the conscientious approach that he had employed in his cricketing life and he was admired by all, in death, as in life.

For 1938 the number of points for a win would be reduced to 12 with four being given for first innings lead in a drawn match. The final rankings were to be decided by the average number of points gained per match, rather than by percentage.

## 1938

## TOP FIVE COUNTIES

|  | Pld | W | L | D | Pts | Avge |
|---|---|---|---|---|---|---|
| Yorkshire | 30 | 20 | 2 | 8 | 256 | 9.14 |
| Middlesex | 22 | 15 | 5 | 2 | 184 | 8.36 |
| Surrey | 25 | 12 | 6 | 7 | 172 | 6.88 |
| Lancashire | 28 | 14 | 6 | 8 | 192 | 6.85 |
| Derbyshire | 25 | 11 | 8 | 6 | 160 | 6.40 |

## LEADING YORKSHIRE AVERAGES

### BATTING

|  | M | I | NO | Runs | HS | Avge | 100 | 50 |
|---|---|---|---|---|---|---|---|---|
| M.Leyland | 27 | 38 | 4 | 1441 | 135 | 42.38 | 3 | 8 |
| H.Sutcliffe | 25 | 37 | 2 | 1451 | 142 | 41.45 | 5 | 6 |
| A.Mitchell | 23 | 33 | 1 | 1108 | 133 | 34.62 | 3 | 7 |
| W.Barber | 27 | 40 | 3 | 1244 | 157 | 33.62 | 3 | 5 |
| A.B.Sellers | 30 | 39 | 6 | 999 | 93* | 30.27 | - | 5 |

### BOWLING

|  | O | M | R | W | Avge | 5WI | 10WM | BB |
|---|---|---|---|---|---|---|---|---|
| H.Verity | 746 | 260 | 1526 | 111 | 13.74 | 11 | 2 | 7-18 |
| W.E.Bowes | 752.5 | 249 | 1424 | 100 | 14.24 | 6 | - | 6-32 |
| E.P.Robinson | 628.1 | 151 | 1788 | 90 | 19.86 | 5 | - | 7-122 |
| T.F.Smailes | 653.3 | 177 | 1689 | 80 | 21.11 | 5 | 1 | 8-68 |

## FIELDING and WICKET-KEEPING

46 (28 ct, 18 st) A.Wood
38 E.P.Robinson
35 A.Mitchell
22 A.B.Sellers
21 C.Turner

## RESULTS

**Ilford**, May 11, 12, 13: Essex 327 (J.O'Connor 129) & 218 (H.Verity 5-75), Yorkshire 289 (M.Leyland 114, T.P.B.Smith 5-99) & 257-6. *Won by four wickets*

**Gloucester**, May 14, 16, 17: Yorkshire 266 (H.Sutcliffe 110, R.A.Sinfield 5-93) & 58-0, Gloucestershire 428-9dec (W.R.Hammond 124). *Match drawn*

**Sheffield**, May 18, 19, 20: Yorkshire 171 (M.S.Nichols 7-62) & 177, Essex 131 (T.F.Smailes 6-59) & 90 (H.Verity 7-40). *Won by 127 runs*

**Headingley**, May 21, 23, 24: Sussex 260 (W.E.Bowes 6-39) & 115-3, Yorkshire 401 (L.Hutton 107, H.E.Hammond 5-86). *Match drawn*

**Hull**, May 28, 30, 31: Kent 78-1 v Yorkshire. *Match drawn*

**Huddersfield**, June 1, 2, 3: Yorkshire 202 (G.S.Boyes 6-73) & 24-3, Hampshire 188 (M.Leyland 8-63). *Match drawn*

**Bradford**, June 4, 6, 7: Lancashire 232 & 138 (H.Verity 6-49), Yorkshire 273 & 98-2. *Won by eight wickets*

**Edgbaston**, June 8, 9, 10: Yorkshire 415 (H.Sutcliffe 142, J.H.Mayer 7-75), Warwickshire 41 (W.E.Bowes 5-14) & 232 (E.P.Robinson 5-65). *Won by an innings and 142 runs*

**Headingley**, June 11, 13: Middlesex 105 & 148, Yorkshire 173 & 84-3. *Won by seven wickets*

**Cardiff**, June 15, 16, 17: Yorkshire 343 (M.Leyland 127, T.F.Smailes 117, W.Wooller 5-90) & 221-4dec, Glamorgan 250 (E.P.Robinson 5-93) & 184 (H.Verity 7-63). *Won by 130 runs*

**Sheffield**, June 18, 20: Yorkshire 416 (W.Barber 157, T.F.Smailes 116), Surrey 52 (W.E.Bowes 6-32) & 162 (L.Hutton 5-45). *Won by an innings and 202 runs*

**Hull**, June 22, 23, 24: Yorkshire 273 (D.E.Davies 5-83) & 68-5dec, Glamorgan 179 (T.F.Smailes 6-35) & 150 (T.F.Smailes 8-68). *Won by 12 runs*

**Bradford**, June 25, 27, 28: Nottinghamshire 87 & 95-5, Yorkshire 133. *Match drawn*

**Worcester**, June 29, 30, July 1: Yorkshire 359-9dec, Worcestershire 118 (W.E.Bowes 5-35) & 223. *Won by an innings and 18 runs*

**Bradford**, July 6, 7, 8: Worcestershire 227 (E.P.Robinson 5-99), Yorkshire 93-4. *Match drawn*

**Chesterfield**, July 9, 11, 12: Yorkshire 198 (G.H.Pope 6-37) & 210-7dec, Derbyshire 158 & 87. *Won by 163 runs*

**Peterborough**, July 13, 14, 15: Northamptonshire 196 & 177, Yorkshire 435-5dec (A.Mitchell 133, H.Sutcliffe 104). *Won by an innings and 62 runs*

**Lord's**, July 16, 18: Yorkshire 144 & 103, Middlesex 205 (W.E.Bowes 5-67) & 43-2. *Lost by eight wickets*

**Bournemouth**, July 20, 21, 22: Hampshire 199 (F.Wilkinson 7-68) & 211 (E.P.Robinson 6-73), Yorkshire 254 (W.Barber 111) & 159-3. *Won by seven wickets*

**The Oval**, July 23, 24, 25: Surrey 264 & 383-3dec (E.W.Whitfield 174*), Yorkshire 100 & 285 (F.Berry 5-61). *Lost by 262 runs*

**Scarborough**, July 27, 28, 29: Northamptonshire 283 (H.Verity 5-114) & 155 (H.Verity 5-52), Yorkshire 311 & 128-4. *Won by six wickets*

**Old Trafford**, July 30, August 1, 2: Lancashire 133 (E.P.Robinson 5-57) & 120 (H.Verity 5-21), Yorkshire 453 (M.Leyland 135, A.E.Nutter 5-68). *Won by an innings and 200 runs*

**Leicester**, August 3, 4, 5: Leicestershire 297 (M.Leyland 5-77) & 69 (W.E.Bowes 5-28, H.Verity 5-36), Yorkshire 440-6dec (W.Barber 130). *Won by an innings and 74 runs*

**Sheffield**, August 6, 8: Yorkshire 192 & 232-9dec (T.S.Worthington 5-44), Derbyshire 113 (T.F.Smailes 5-39) & 101. *Won by 210 runs*

**Headingley**, August 10, 11, 12: Warwickshire 263 (H.E.Dollery 126*) & 14-1, Yorkshire 324 (A.Mitchell 124, J.H.Mayer 5-72). *Match drawn*

**Bradford**, August 13, 15: Leicestershire 62 (H.Verity 7-18) & 125, Yorkshire 328 (H.Sutcliffe 105, H.A.Smith 6-132). *Won by an innings and 141 runs*

**Scarborough**, August 17, 18: Yorkshire 346 (C.J.Scott 5-51), Gloucestershire 119 (T.F.Smailes 5-32) & 147 (H.Verity 6-43). *Won by an innings and 80 runs*

**Trent Bridge**, August 20, 22, 23: Yorkshire 320 (H.Sutcliffe 100, G.F.H.Hearne 6-74) & 267-5, Nottinghamshire 403 (C.B.Harris 103, E.P.Robinson 7-122). *Match drawn*

**Dover**, August 27, 29: Yorkshire 326-8dec (L.J.Todd 5-64), Kent 168 (H.Verity 5-42) & 109. *Won by an innings and 49 runs*
**Hove**, August 31, September 1, 2: Sussex 77 & 322 (G.Cox 142), Yorkshire 330-9dec (A.Mitchell 100) & 70-6. *Won by four wickets*

## NOTES and HIGHLIGHTS

In the second half of July Yorkshire lost two out of three consecutive games but lost none of the final ten to hold off the threat of Middlesex. Such was Yorkshire's dominance in the final run-in that four of the last five victories (in seven matches) were concluded in two days. Their opponents were dismissed for double figures on eight occasions, including twice by Leicestershire.

*Bill Bowes (6-32) and Frank Smailes (4-16) return to the pavilion at Bramall Lane, Sheffield on June 20th, 1938 after dismissing Surrey for 52 in 75 minutes.*

The squad was strong all-round and it needed to be. Injuries and the demands of the Test selectors meant that a total of 22 players were used. Five of the team – Bowes, Hutton, Leyland, Verity and Wood – were all chosen for England for the fifth Test at The Oval.

Although none were in the top ten of the national averages, a total of eight batsmen averaged more than 30. In addition to the above list, Hutton (631 runs, av. 45.07), Gibb (332, 36.88) and Cyril Turner (581, 34.17) all played their part. In the game against Glamorgan at Hull Smailes took all of his 14 wickets on the final day. Against Warwickshire at Edgbaston Bowes had the economical figures of 14.2-8-14-5. Three bowlers were in the top ten of the national averages, including Verity (first) and Bowes (third). In addition to those in the above list, two other bowlers took their wickets at an average of fewer than 20. These were Leyland (48 wkts, av. 17.52) and Frank Wilkinson (24, 19.62).

Sellers was the only player who did not miss a game. The campaign saw the debut of Harry Halliday who became a regular after the War and whose 8361 runs (av 32.03) and 12 centuries would have been considerably more but for that interruption to the cricket.

## PLAYER of the SEASON

Arthur Mitchell was one of the more thorough and methodical batsmen to have represented Yorkshire and these attributes he would carry with him into his second career as the county coach. Born in Bradford in 1902, he made his first-class debut at the tender age of 19 but did not fully establish himself in the side until 1928. He usually batted in the vital number three position as successor to Edgar Oldroyd and, although he often played in a dogged and determined manner, he could score quickly when the situation required.

Mitchell's highest innings came as early as 1926, when he scored 189 at Northampton, and his best season was that of 1933 when he made 2300 runs at the commendable average of 58.97. His Test career was limited to just six caps, in the mid-1930s. He was also a brilliant close fielder, specialising in front of the wicket, and would take more catches (171) from the bowling of Verity than any other player (Sellers took 101). He took over as Yorkshire's coach on retirement following the Second World War and attempted to instill into his pupils the same standards of meticulous approach that he had utilised himself. He was employed in this capacity for 25 years and died in 1976. The county had lost one of its most dedicated and hard-working practitioners.

## 1939

## TOP FIVE COUNTIES

|  | Pld | W | L | D | Pts | Avge |
|---|---|---|---|---|---|---|
| Yorkshire | 28 | 20 | 4 | 4 | 260 | 9.28 |
| Middlesex | 22 | 14 | 6 | 2 | 180 | 8.18 |
| Gloucestershire | 26 | 15 | 7 | 4 | 196 | 7.53 |
| Essex | 24 | 12 | 10 | 2 | 170 | 7.08 |
| Kent | 26 | 14 | 9 | 3 | 180 | 6.92 |

## LEADING YORKSHIRE AVERAGES

### BATTING

|  | M | I | NO | Runs | HS | Avge | 100 | 50 |
|---|---|---|---|---|---|---|---|---|
| L.Hutton | 26 | 40 | 4 | 2167 | 280* | 60.19 | 9 | 6 |
| H.Sutcliffe | 19 | 26 | 2 | 1230 | 234* | 51.25 | 6 | 2 |
| M.Leyland | 24 | 33 | 5 | 1191 | 180* | 42.53 | 3 | 3 |
| W.Barber | 27 | 41 | 5 | 1388 | 141 | 38.55 | 3 | 6 |
| A.Mitchell | 27 | 42 | 4 | 1086 | 136 | 28.57 | 2 | 4 |
| N.W.D.Yardley | 26 | 35 | 2 | 875 | 108 | 26.51 | 2 | 5 |

### BOWLING

|  | O | M | R | W | Avge | 5WI | 10WM | BB |
|---|---|---|---|---|---|---|---|---|
| H.Verity | 797.6 | 236 | 2097 | 165 | 12.70 | 11 | 2 | 8-38 |
| W.E.Bowes | 549.7 | 112 | 1389 | 96 | 14.46 | 8 | 1 | 7-50 |
| E.P.Robinson | 599.7 | 121 | 2039 | 102 | 19.99 | 6 | 2 | 8-35 |

## FIELDING and WICKET-KEEPING

65 (38 ct, 27 st) A.Wood
43 A.Mitchell
37 E.P.Robinson
31 L.Hutton
24 H.Verity

# RESULTS

**Headingley**, May 13, 15, 16: Yorkshire 169 & 171-9dec (L.J.Todd 5-56), Kent 100 & 139 (E.P.Robinson 6-42). *Won by 101 runs*

**Bradford**, May 17, 18, 19: Yorkshire 252 (M.Leyland 112, T.W.J.Goddard 5-76, C.J.Scott 5-91) & 162-7dec (C.J.Scott 6-87), Gloucestershire 227 & 190-4. *Lost by six wickets*

**Ilford**, May 20, 22, 23: Essex 209 (M.Leyland 5-74) & 165 (H.Verity 5-27), Yorkshire 141 (T.P.B.Smith 5-31) & 237-3. *Won by seven wickets*

**Old Trafford**, May 27, 29, 30: Lancashire 300 & 185 (W.E.Bowes 6-43), Yorkshire 528-8dec (H.Sutcliffe 165, A.Mitchell 136). *Won by an innings and 43 runs*

**Edgbaston**, May 31, June 1, 2: Warwickshire 219 (W.E.Bowes 7-50) & 144 (H.Verity 5-38, W.E.Bowes 5-46), Yorkshire 417 (L.Hutton 158, W.E.Hollies 5-131). *Won by an innings and 54 runs*

**Sheffield**, June 3, 5, 6: Hampshire 174 & 190, Yorkshire 493-1dec (L.Hutton 280*, H.Sutcliffe 116). *Won by an innings and 129 runs*

**Hull**, June 7, 8, 9: Leicestershire 366 (C.S.Dempster 165*) & 104 (H.Verity 8-38), Yorkshire 500-7dec (H.Sutcliffe 234*). *Won by an innings and 30 runs*

**Lord's**, June 10, 12: Yorkshire 430-5dec (M.Leyland 180*, H.Sutcliffe 175), Middlesex 62 (W.E.Bowes 5-20) & 122. *Won by an innings and 246 runs*

**Headingley**, June 14, 15, 16: Northamptonshire 180 (W.E.Bowes 6-57), Yorkshire 207-8 (A.Mitchell (102*). *Match drawn*

**Trent Bridge**, June 17, 19, 20: Yorkshire 244 & 108 (A.Jepson 6-27), Nottinghamshire 120 (W.E.Bowes 5-29) & 3-4. *Match drawn*

**Bradford**, June 21, 22: Glamorgan 168 (H.Verity 7-48) & 65 (H.Verity 7-20), Yorkshire 328 (L.Hutton 144, P.F.Judge 8-75). *Won by an innings and 95 runs*

**Sheffield**, June 24, 26, 27: Yorkshire 83 (G.H.Pope 6-44) & 310 (W.Barber 100), Derbyshire 20 (J.Smurthwaite 5-7) & 97 (T.F.Smailes 10-47). *Won by 276 runs*

**Bristol**, June 28, 29, 30: Yorkshire 176 (T.W.J.Goddard 6-61) & 105 (T.W.J.Goddard 7-38), Gloucestershire 168 (H.Verity 7-47) & 114-3. *Won by seven wickets*

**Headingley**, July 1, 3, 4: Yorkshire 406 (L.Hutton 151, E.A.Watts 5-70) & 199-6dec, Surrey 290 (F.R.Brown 119) & 138. *Won by 177 runs*

**Bradford**, July 8, 10, 11: Yorkshire 171 (C.I.J.Smith 5-48) & 172-5, Middlesex 292. *Match drawn*

**Northampton**, July 12, 13, 14: Northamptonshire 216 (W.E.Bowes 5-43) & 188 (H.Verity 6-58), Yorkshire 502-4dec (W.Barber 128*, H.Sutcliffe 107*). *Won by an innings and 98 runs*

**Chesterfield**, July 15, 17, 18: Derbyshire 208-6 v Yorkshire. *Match drawn*

**Scarborough**, July 19, 20, 21: Sussex 156 (W.E.Bowes 7-54) & 319, Yorkshire 386 (L.Hutton 177, J.K.Nye 5-100) & 90-0. *Won by ten wickets*

**Sheffield**, July 22, 24, 25: Nottinghamshire 200, Yorkshire 94-3. *Match drawn*

**Stourbridge**, July 26, 27: Worcestershire 102 & 118, Yorkshire 91 & 113 (R.T.D.Perks 5-50). *Lost by 16 runs*

**The Oval**, July 29, 31, August 1: Yorkshire 431 (W.Barber 141, M.Leyland 114), Surrey 219 & 227-3 (R.J.Gregory 108). *Match drawn*

**Cardiff**, August 2, 3, 4: Yorkshire 234 & 186-6dec (W.E.Jones 5-60), Glamorgan 194 (E.P.Robinson 5-60) & 140 (E.P.Robinson 5-59). *Won by 86 runs*

**Headingley**, August 5, 7, 8: Lancashire 217 (E.P.Robinson 5-80) & 92 (E.P.Robinson 8-35), Yorkshire 163 & 147-5 (L.Hutton 105*). *Won by five wickets*

**Leicester**, August 9, 10, 11: Yorkshire 155 (J.E.Walsh 5-56) & 134-3dec, Leicestershire 89 (E.P.Robinson 6-34) & 103 (J.Johnson 5-16). *Won by 97 runs*

**Bradford**, August 12, 14, 15: Yorkshire 171 (R.T.D.Perks 5-65) & 309 (L.Hutton 109), Worcestershire 194 & 197 (L.Hutton 5-58). *Won by 89 runs*

**Scarborough**, August 16, 17, 18: Yorkshire 403 (N.W.D.Yardley 108, C.W.Grove 5-102) & 171-4dec, Warwickshire 158 (H.Verity 7-35) & 310 (R.E.S.Wyatt 138, L.Hutton 5-70). *Won by 106 runs*

**Sheffield**, August 19, 21, 22: Essex 343 (H.Verity 5-40), Yorkshire 131 & 208. *Lost by an innings and 4 runs*

**Dover**, August 23, 24: Yorkshire 338 (L.Hutton 100, D.V.P.Wright 5-97), Kent 109 & 215 (F.G.H.Chalk 115*, H.Verity 5-48). *Won by an innings and 14 runs*
**Bournemouth**, August 26, 28: Hampshire 116 (H.Verity 6-22) & 116, Yorkshire 243 (T.A.Dean 5-58). *Won by an innings and 11 runs*
**Hove**, August 30, 31, September 1: Sussex 387 (G.Cox 198) & 33 (H.Verity 7-9), Yorkshire 392 (N.W.D.Yardley 108, L.Hutton 103) & 30-1. *Won by nine wickets*

## NOTES and HIGHLIGHTS

Yorkshire won the Championship for the third consecutive season and Middlesex were runners-up for the third consecutive time. Sellers became the third Yorkshire captain to lead a side to such a sequence, following Lord Hawke and Geoffrey Wilson.

Chasing 233 to win and being pinned back at three runs for four wickets was a far from ideal position for Nottinghamshire to be in on their home ground at Trent Bridge. However, despite Bowes having taken three of the four wickets for no runs in 3.6 eight-ball overs, the rain proved mightier and no play was possible in the final two sessions.

Sutcliffe and Hutton posted a first wicket stand of 315 against Hampshire at Sheffield. Sutcliffe's century in this partnership was his second in a run of four in consecutive innings, these being scored against four different opponents. Sutcliffe also shared a triple century stand with Leyland – 301 against Middlesex at Lord's for the third wicket. It was to be his final full season and he also marked it by scoring his 50,000th first-class run as well as making the first century of the season (against Oxford University at The Parks). Both he (eighth) and Hutton (third) were in the top ten of the national averages. Hutton's double-century against Hampshire at Sheffield was the highest score of his county career.

When Joe Johnson had figures of 5-16 in the away match against Leicestershire the 36-ball spell contained the only wickets that he ever took for the county. In the preceding five innings Ellis Robinson had taken at least five wickets on every occasion, his combined figures being 29 wickets for 268 runs at an average of 9.24. In helping to dismiss Derbyshire for a measly 20, at Sheffield, James Smurthwaite took five for seven in only the second game of his seven-match career. Although the visitors managed to reach 97 at their second attempt, Smailes became only the third Yorkshire bowler to take ten wickets in an innings, following Drake and Verity. Robinson's innings figures in the Roses match at Headingley were the best of his career.

Gloucestershire's Tom Goddard was influential in helping his team to a win at Bradford by having match figures of six wickets for 125 runs. He surpassed this on his own patch at Bristol with 13-99 but the sting in the tail was that he was this time on the losing side.

The end of the season had a most eerie feel to it. Several games were cancelled due to the onset of war and the final fixture against Sussex went ahead mainly because it was the Benefit Match for J.H.Parks. The game ended at 14.30, shortly after Verity had produced his final astounding bowling performance (6-1-9-7). He concluded his career by topping the national averages yet again (Bowes was third and Hutton, taking 37 wickets at 18.40 with his occasional leg-breaks, was also in the top ten). Wood's 66 dismissals placed him second in the list of wicket-keepers.

The war had a big impact on Yorkshire cricket, as it did in more important walks of life. Verity was tragically killed in Italy, Hutton suffered the consequences from an accident and Sutcliffe found it necessary to retire when hostilities did eventually cease.

Both Sutcliffe and Verity can be classed amongst the game's truly great players. Verity's feat of taking ten wickets in an innings twice remains unequalled for the county and his final career average for Yorkshire (13.70) is the lowest amongst the 20 bowlers who have taken at least 800 wickets (Verity's total is 1558).

# PLAYER of the SEASON

In scoring almost 800 runs more than his nearest Yorkshire rival in the averages Len Hutton was already emerging as the best English batsman of his generation. Such would his influence eventually be that he would open the batting, with Jack Hobbs, in most versions of an all-time England XI. Even as distinguished a coach as George Hirst claimed that he could not have taught the teenage prodigy anything about batting. Born in Pudsey in 1916, he made his county debut in 1934 and soon became the youngest Yorkshire player to score a century. He played in his first Test match three years later scoring a duck (as he had on his debut for both county first and second elevens) and was immortalised in the following season by making 364 against Australia at The Oval in an innings lasting over thirteen hours. It broke the Test record for the highest individual innings and was not surpassed for almost twenty years. Hutton became a national hero.

An oustanding batting technique was founded on an extremely solid defence and the ability to play all shots to perfection. His cover drive, in particular, is regarded as one of the most graceful and beautiful strokes ever seen on a cricket field. Hutton could succeed on the most treacherous of surfaces even when all around him fell. One of his best innings would be a score of 30 when England were all out for 52 against Australia at The Oval in 1948.

Hutton's fine season in 1939 confirmed him to be already at the peak of his powers but he was to lose the next six seasons of his career due to conflict. Not only that, he was to lose two inches of his right arm, this being the result of surgery following an accident in an army gymnasium. Despite this, and the consequent adjustment in technique, there was no apparent waning in his accumulation of runs. 1949 was to be his best-ever season producing 3429 runs, including 1294 in June to set an unbeaten record for any month anywhere in the world.

Thereafter, his batting seemed to bear a more responsible approach as both county and country relied on him more and more to play the anchor role. This was especially so after his appointment as England's first professional captain in 1952. The critics of this situation were appeased when the Ashes were won a year later and retained convincingly on the 1954/55 tour. The strain of these years affected Hutton's health, however, and he retired after the 1955 season, during which he played in about half of Yorkshire's matches and none for England.

His final record eventually showed 40,140 first-class runs (average 55.51), including 6971 (av. 56.67) in 79 Tests and his 1950 Benefit raised £9712 and a county record that stood for 23 years. On retirement he withdrew from the game that he loved, apart from two years as a Test selector in the 1970s, and died in Surrey in 1990 a few months after taking office as Yorkshire president.

Knighted in 1955 (the only Yorkshire player to be thus honoured), he probably remains the county's most admired cricketer of all time.

The Championship would resume again in 1946, after the War.

# Post-war and Surrey

*Yorkshire's Championship winning team of 1946. From left: back row – B.Heyhirst (masseur), E.P.Robinson, L.Hutton, A.Coxon, T.F.Smailes, W.Watson, H.Beaumont, A.Booth, H.Walker (scorer); front row – W.Barber, W.E.Bowes, A.B.Sellers (capt.), P.A.Gibb, M.Leyland. As in 1919, the county won the first post-War Championship.*

# 1946-1958

# Post-war and Surrey

For the 1946 season all of the teams would play the same number of matches as each other, as occurred in the period 1929 to 1932, except that the figure would this time be 26 instead of 28.

## 1946

### TOP FIVE COUNTIES

|  | Pld | W | L | D | Pts |
|---|---|---|---|---|---|
| Yorkshire | 26 | 16 | 1 | 9 | 216 |
| Middlesex | 26 | 16 | 5 | 5 | 204 |
| Lancashire | 26 | 15 | 4 | 7 | 200 |
| Somerset | 26 | 12 | 6 | 8 | 166 |
| Gloucestershire | 26 | 12 | 6 | 8 | 160 |

### LEADING YORKSHIRE AVERAGES

#### BATTING

|  | M | I | NO | Runs | HS | Avge | 100 | 50 |
|---|---|---|---|---|---|---|---|---|
| L.Hutton | 17 | 26 | 4 | 1112 | 171* | 50.54 | 3 | 5 |
| W.Barber | 22 | 36 | 3 | 1029 | 113 | 31.18 | 1 | 3 |
| A.B.Sellers | 22 | 30 | 6 | 709 | 85* | 29.54 | - | 7 |
| P.A.Gibb | 11 | 17 | 1 | 460 | 104 | 28.75 | 1 | 2 |

#### BOWLING

|  | O | M | R | W | Avge | 5WI | 10WM | BB |
|---|---|---|---|---|---|---|---|---|
| A.Booth | 740.1 | 351 | 1000 | 84 | 11.90 | 2 | - | 6-21 |
| W.E.Bowes | 459.2 | 150 | 778 | 56 | 13.89 | 4 | - | 5-17 |
| E.P.Robinson | 832.4 | 274 | 1810 | 129 | 14.03 | 13 | 2 | 8-78 |
| A.Coxon | 541 | 151 | 1154 | 63 | 18.31 | 3 | - | 8-31 |
| T.F.Smailes | 556.3 | 159 | 1203 | 64 | 18.79 | 4 | - | 6-40 |

## FIELDING and WICKET-KEEPING

27 (20 ct, 7 st) K.Fiddling
21 E.P.Robinson
19 A.Coxon
18 A.B.Sellers

# RESULTS

**Cardiff**, May 11, 13: Glamorgan 116 (E.P.Robinson 7-22) & 162, Yorkshire 195 (E.Davies 5-37) & 84-5. *Won by five wickets*
**Canterbury**, May 18, 20: Yorkshire 252 (D.V.P.Wright 5-89), Kent 69 (W.E.Bowes 5-32) & 92. *Won by an innings and 91 runs*
**Headingley**, May 25, 27, 28: Yorkshire 232 (L.Hutton 111) & 37-0, Leicestershire 203 (L.G.Berry 103, E.P.Robinson 5-31). *Match drawn*
**Bradford**, May 29, 30: Yorkshire 236 (J.W.Martin 5-59) & 175 (D.V.P.Wright 5-50), Kent 106 (W.E.Bowes 5-17) & 113 (E.P.Robinson 5-29). *Won by 192 runs*
**Bristol**, June 1, 3, 4: Gloucestershire 369 (W.R.Hammond 143), Yorkshire 336-6. *Match drawn*
**Sheffield**, June 8, 10, 11: Yorkshire 171-3dec, Lancashire 127-4. *Match drawn*
**Edgbaston**, June 12, 13, 14: Yorkshire 268-9dec (P.A.Gibb 104, M.P.Barker 7-68), Warwickshire 99 (A.Booth 6-21) & 91 (M.Leyland 7-36). *Won by an innings and 78 runs*
**Lord's**, June 15, 17, 18: Yorkshire 140 & 108 (J.Young 8-31), Middlesex 74 & 101 (E.P.Robinson 5-36). *Won by 73 runs*
**Bradford**, June 22, 24, 25: Yorkshire 417-9dec (N.W.D.Yardley 137), Nottinghamshire 209 & 159 (C.Turner 5-39). *Won by an innings and 49 runs*
**Sheffield**, June 26, 27, 28: Glamorgan 165 (E.P.Robinson 5-64) & 96 (A.Coxon 5-41, T.F.Smailes 5-45), Yorkshire 83 (E.Davies 6-31) & 179-4. *Won by six wickets*
**Chesterfield**, June 29, July 1: Derbyshire 182 (W.E.Bowes 5-66) & 78, Yorkshire 173 & 88-6 (T.R.Armstrong 5-32). *Won by four wickets*
**Headingley**, July 6, 8, 9: Surrey 167 (T.F.Smailes 6-40) & 191 (E.P.Robinson 6-33), Yorkshire 195 & 167-4. *Won by six wickets*
**Harrogate**, July 10, 11: Essex 170 & 256, Yorkshire 262 (F.H.Vigar 5-94) & 168-4. *Won by six wickets*

**Headingley**, July 20, 22: Worcestershire 119 (E.P.Robinson 7-41) & 121 (A.Coxon 8-31), Yorkshire 152 (P.F.Jackson 5-48) & 90-9. *Won by one wicket*

**Taunton**, July 24, 25, 26: Somerset 508 (G.R.Langdale 146), Yorkshire 312-7 (W.Barber 113). *Match drawn*

**The Oval**, July 27, 29, 30: Surrey 114 (E.P.Robinson 8-76) & 194 (E.P.Robinson 5-88), Yorkshire 197 (L.Hutton 101, A.R.Gover 7-66) & 113-2. *Won by eight wickets*

**Hull**, July 31, August 1, 2: Northamptonshire 183 & 138 (A.Coxon 5-33), Yorkshire 344-5dec (L.Hutton 171*). *Won by an innings and 23 runs*

**Old Trafford**, August 3, 5, 6: Yorkshire 180 (W.B.Roberts) & 220-5, Lancashire 396 (B.P.King 122, W.Place 107). *Match drawn*

**Leicester**, August 7, 8, 9: Yorkshire 308 (A.Riddington 5-34) & 106-1dec, Leicestershire 159 & 125-9. *Match drawn*

**Bradford**, August 10, 12, 13: Yorkshire 104-7dec, Warwickshire 56 (T.F.Smailes 5-16). *Won by 48 runs on first innings in game reduced to one day*

**Scarborough**, August 14, 15: Yorkshire 168 (O.W.Herman 7-77) & 69 (C.J.Knott 5-35), Hampshire 97 (E.P.Robinson 5-29) & 84 (E.P.Robinson 7-24). *Won by 56 runs*

**Sheffield**, August 17, 19, 20: Yorkshire 226 (G.O.Allen 5-26) & 202-8dec (W.Harrington 6-57), Middlesex 169 (W.E.Bowes 5-50) & 144-8. *Match drawn*

**Headingley**, August 21, 22: Gloucestershire 106 & 89 (E.P.Robinson 6-27), Yorkshire 188 & 8-1. *Won by nine wickets*

**Eastbourne**, August 24, 26: Sussex 91 (T.F.Smailes 5-16) & 105 (E.P.Robinson 6-37), Yorkshire 82 (C.Oakes 5-10) & 115-4. *Won by six wickets*

**Bournemouth**, August 28, 29, 30: Yorkshire 135 & 130 (O.W.Herman 5-48), Hampshire 204 & 64-0. *Lost by ten wickets*

**Trent Bridge**, August 31, September 2, 3: Yorkshire 301, Nottinghamshire 102 (A.Booth 5-50) & 161-5. *Match drawn*

# NOTES and HIGHLIGHTS

As in 1919 Yorkshire won the first post-war Championship and repeated the feat of the 1920s team in winning the title for a fourth consecutive season. Middlesex were runners-up for the fifth year running. The batting depended a great deal on Hutton but the bowling was based around an efficient and varied quintet.

It was a very wet season of low scores and early finishes. Yorkshire's crucial run of eight victories saw them dismiss their opponents five times for scores of fewer than 100 and three of these games lasted for less than two days. The final match of this sequence was a nail-biting affair against Worcestershire at Headingley when the home side, requiring a mere 88 to win, scrambled home by only one wicket.

After conceding a first innings lead of 82 against Glamorgan at Sheffield, Yorkshire needed to make the highest score of the match to win. They were steered home by Hutton, who was rewarded by being left stranded on 99 not out as victory came. Although Robinson took thirteen wickets in the game against Surrey at The Oval, Yorkshire's first innings was dominated by two batsmen (Hutton and Sellers – 58) who scored 88% of the runs that came from the bat. Hutton (seventh) was the only batsman in the top ten of the national averages.

Although Robinson achieved the highest wicket aggregate, the averages were led by Arthur Booth who played his first full season at the age of 42, his left-arm spin having been plied in the shadow of Verity since his 1931 debut. He topped the national averages with Bowes (fourth) and Robinson (fifth) also making the top ten. Alec Coxon's analysis against Worcestershire at Headingley was the best of his career.

With a total of 23 players used during the season, Yorkshire, as with all the other counties, were starting to rebuild after the war. The two most significant debutants were Johnny Wardle and Vic Wilson. The former was to continue in the fine tradition of Yorkshire and England left-arm spinners, but with more of the googly variety, while the latter became a fine left-handed batsman, outstanding short leg fielder and very successful captain.

Arthur Wood played in his last game during the 1946 season. His total of 855 victims remains the fourth-best for the county but it will be more for his energy and wit that he will be remembered.

## PLAYER of the SEASON

Yorkshire's leading wicket-taker for the season, Ellis Robinson was one of the relatively unsung heroes of Yorkshire cricket. Born in South Yorkshire in 1911, he first played for the county in 1934 and gradually established himself as Verity's spin partner but without the same results and subsequent accolade. Being an off-spinner he turned the ball the other way from Verity and developed so much that he took over 100 wickets in four consecutive seasons from 1938. In the final season before the War he claimed his best performance of 8-35 in the Roses match at Headingley.

Robinson's long fingers spun the ball so much that he spent a considerable part of his career bowling round the wicket, especially under Sellers's leadership. 1946 was the best season of his career bringing him 167 (average 14.95) wickets in all first-class matches and he played in a Test trial but that was as far as representative honours went. A brilliant close to the wicket fielder, he was part of a group that stood as close to the batsman as possible and the six catches that he took at Bradford in Leicestershire's first innings in 1938 remain a county record.

In 1949 Robinson would be given his cap, a testimonial and be released from his contract! Three seasons with Somerset followed before the conclusion of his playing days. He died in 1998 in Conisbrough. A career that produced just over 1000 wickets included 735 (average 20.60) for Yorkshire, many of these contributing vitally to Championship-winning campaigns.

## 1947 to 1958

| | Champion County | Yorkshire's position |
|---|---|---|
| 1947 | Middlesex | 8th |
| 1948 | Glamorgan | 4th |
| 1949 | Middlesex and Yorkshire – joint champions | |
| 1950 | Lancashire and Surrey | 3rd |
| 1951 | Warwickshire | 2nd |
| 1952 | Surrey | 2nd |
| 1953 | Surrey | 12th |
| 1954 | Surrey | 2nd |
| 1955 | Surrey | 2nd |
| 1956 | Surrey | 7th |
| 1957 | Surrey | 3rd |
| 1958 | Surrey | 11th |

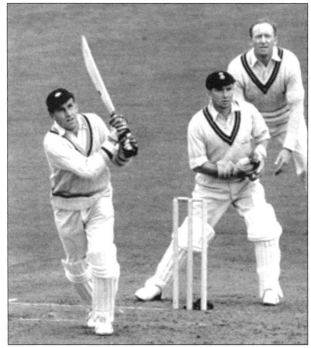

*Ted Lester hits out against Surrey in an innings of 142 at The Oval on July 3rd, 1954. Wicket-keeper Arthur McIntyre and skipper Stuart Surridge can only look on. Yorkshire won the game by 54 runs.*

From 1950 the number of games played by each team was increased to 28 and this remained in place throughout the rest of this period. Although the same basic points system was in operation, bonus points for performance in the first innings were added from 1957. The only new champions during this era were Glamorgan.

It was a frustrating time for Yorkshire, especially during the five consecutive seasons in which they were runners-up on four occasions. In 1949, when they were joint-champions, the county lost only two matches to Middlesex's three and would have been crowned champions in their own right in many other seasons. Their 1953 position was the lowest in their history up to that point.

The most significant individual performance was by Wardle who, with his left-arm spin, had match figures of 16-112 against Sussex at Hull in 1954. This remains the fourth-best performance for Yorkshire in all first-class cricket.

Surrey's seven-year domination of the title remains unprecedented yet Yorkshire consistently possessed a team that, on paper, often appeared as strong as that of the southern county. Yorkshire was probably at its strongest during the middle part of the decade and no less than 13 England players, past, present or future, represented Yorkshire during the 1955 season. These were:-

Batsmen – Len Hutton, Frank Lowson, Doug Padgett, Ken Taylor, Willie Watson

Bowlers – Bob Appleyard, Eddie Leadbeater, Fred Trueman, Johnny Wardle

All-rounders – Brian Close, Ray Illingworth, Norman Yardley
Wicket-keeper – Jimmy Binks

Significant roles were also played by batsmen Ted Lester, Billy Sutcliffe, and Vic Wilson.

The team was led by Yardley who was in charge for the last of his eight seasons. He was the first Yorkshire captain to lead the side for such a long period without winning the title outright. He was succeeded by Sutcliffe, who was captain for two seasons. Yorkshire had some very strong personalities in the team during this era and it was often felt that neither man could weld the talent at his disposal into a cohesive unit. Yardley was a real gentleman and Sutcliffe lacked the necessary presence to instill the desired discipline. The latter was son of the great Herbert and, naturally and sadly, suffered by comparison.

Despite the county's drop of eight places in 1958 the new skipper, Ronnie Burnet, who had never before played for Yorkshire, set about restoring pride and instilling a sense of discipline. His most famous act was to sack Wardle, the brilliant slow left-arm bowler. That Burnett's attitude and actions bred success was soon to be seen.

*Yorkshire's 30 Championships*

# A Fourth Great Side

*Happy scenes in the Yorkshire dressing room at Hove on September 1ˢᵗ, 1959 after the county had scored 218 in 95 minutes to claim their first outright title for 13 years. Skipper Ronnie Burnet is on the front row, second from right.*

# 1959-1968

# A Fourth Great Side

## 1959

### TOP FIVE COUNTIES

|  | Pld | W | L | D | Pts |
|---|---|---|---|---|---|
| Yorkshire | 28 | 14 | 7 | 7 | 204 |
| Gloucestershire | 28 | 12 | 11 | 5 | 186 |
| Surrey | 28 | 12 | 5 | 11 | 186 |
| Warwickshire | 28 | 13 | 10 | 5 | 184 |
| Lancashire | 28 | 12 | 7 | 9 | 184 |

*NOTE: Gloucestershire's total of five drawn games includes one tied match.*

## LEADING YORKSHIRE AVERAGES

### BATTING

|  | M | I | NO | Runs | HS | Avge | 100 | 50 |
|---|---|---|---|---|---|---|---|---|
| D.E.V.Padgett | 28 | 48 | 7 | 1787 | 139* | 43.58 | 3 | 10 |
| R.Illingworth | 21 | 34 | 10 | 1036 | 150 | 43.16 | 2 | 4 |
| W.B.Stott | 26 | 45 | 2 | 1628 | 144* | 37.86 | 2 | 10 |
| D.B.Close | 25 | 44 | 1 | 1197 | 154 | 27.83 | 3 | 5 |
| K.Taylor | 23 | 42 | 1 | 1126 | 144 | 27.46 | 2 | 6 |

### BOWLING

|  | O | M | R | W | Avge | 5WI | 10WM | BB |
|---|---|---|---|---|---|---|---|---|
| F.S.Trueman | 676.3 | 167 | 1712 | 92 | 18.60 | 6 | - | 7-57 |
| R.Illingworth | 683.3 | 232 | 1514 | 76 | 19.92 | 2 | - | 5-35 |
| R.K.Platt | 829.2 | 258 | 1909 | 82 | 23.28 | 4 | 1 | 6-72 |
| D.B.Close | 656.4 | 193 | 1747 | 69 | 25.31 | 4 | - | 8-41 |
| D.Wilson | 585.2 | 182 | 1484 | 51 | 29.09 | 3 | - | 5-57 |

## FIELDING and WICKET-KEEPING

56 (40 ct, 16 st) J.G.Binks
26 D.B.Close
22 P.J.Sharpe
18 D.Wilson

## RESULTS

**Middlesbrough**, May 9, 11, 12: Yorkshire 238 & 237-4dec (K.Taylor 103), Nottinghamshire 153 (F.S.Trueman 7-57) & 128. *Won by 194 runs*

**Old Trafford**, May 16, 18, 19: Lancashire 282-9dec & 230-5dec (G.Pullar 105), Yorkshire 188 (D.E.V.Padgett 100) & 145. *Lost by 179 runs*

**Edgbaston**, May 20, 21, 22: Warwickshire 162 (F.S.Trueman 5-72), Yorkshire 164-4. *Match drawn*

**Bradford**, Glamorgan 137 (F.S.Trueman 5-56) & 233 (J.Birkenshaw 5-54), Yorkshire 405-8dec (H.D.Bird 181*). *Won by an innings and 35 runs*

**Harrogate**, May 27, 28, 29: Somerset 339 & 273-8, Yorkshire 341-8dec (D.E.V.Padgett 122, B.Lobb 5-59). *Match drawn*

**Headingley**, May 30, June 1, 2: Northamptonshire 241 & 201-7dec (R.Subba Row 126*), Yorkshire 172 & 156-3. *Match drawn*

**Sheffield**, June 6, 8, 9: Yorkshire 232 (H.L.Jackson 5-70) & 248-2, Derbyshire 226 (R.K.Platt 6-72). *Match drawn*

**Hull**, June 10, 11, 12: Hampshire 203 (F.S.Trueman 5-77) & 209, Yorkshire 215 (V.H.D.Cannings 5-68) & 200-6 (W.B.Stott 130*). *Won by four wickets*

**The Oval**, June 13, 15, 16: Surrey 277-9dec (R.K.Platt 5-56) & 87 (R.K.Platt 5-31, F.S.Trueman 5-51), Yorkshire 145 & 133. *Lost by 86 runs*

**Trent Bridge**, June 17, 18, 19: Yorkshire 418-3dec (D.B.Close 154, D.E.V.Padgett 139*), Nottinghamshire 151 (M.Ryan 5-45) & 460-6 (N.Hill 167, J.D.Clay 137, D.Wilson 5-129). *Match drawn*

**Bradford**, June 20, 22: Sussex 161 & 103 (R.K.Platt 5-26), Yorkshire 304. *Won by an innings and 40 runs*

**Sheffield**, June 24, 25, 26: Warwickshire 77 (D.B.Close 5-12) & 159, Yorkshire 190 (T.W.Cartwright 6-69) & 48-4. *Won by six wickets*

**Colchester**, June 27, 29, 30: Essex 189 & 225 (F.S.Trueman 5-65), Yorkshire 329 (R.Illingworth 150, T.E.Bailey 6-105) & 86-3. *Won by seven wickets*

**Bournemouth**, July 1, 2, 3: Hampshire 279 & 233-5dec (R.E.Marshall 143), Yorkshire 215-9dec & 269 (M.Heath 6-66). *Lost by 28 runs*
**Chesterfield**, July 4, 6, 7: Derbyshire 351-8dec & 224-5dec, Yorkshire 275 & 304-4 (K.Taylor 144). *Won by six wickets*
**Scarborough**, July 8, 9, 10: Yorkshire 376-6dec & 150, Essex 248 & 209. *Won by 69 runs*
**Headingley,** July 15, 16, 17: Gloucestershire 339 (D.M.Young 148) & 42-0, Yorkshire 223. *Match drawn*
**Bradford**, July 18, 20, 21: Surrey 153 (R.Illingworth 5-38) & 159, Yorkshire 91 (P.J.Loader 6-42) & 173 (P.J.Loader 6-57). *Lost by 48 runs*
**Northampton**, July 25, 27, 28: Northamptonshire 375-8dec (R.Subba Row 183*), Yorkshire 167 & 64 (A.Lightfoot 6-31). *Lost by an innings and 144 runs*
**Leicester**, July 29, 30, 31: Yorkshire 218 & 222-3dec, Leicestershire 132 & 230. *Won by 78 runs*
**Sheffield**, August 1, 3, 4: Lancashire 343 (G.Pullar 109) & 102-4, Yorkshire 361 (D.B.Close 128, K.Higgs 6-85). *Match drawn*
**Scarborough**, August 5, 6, 7: Middlesex 144 (R.Illingworth 5-35) & 164 (D.B.Close 5-75), Yorkshire 84 (F.J.Titmus 5-21, D.Bick 5-22) & 225-6. *Won by four wickets*
**Headingley**, August 8, 10, 11: Kent 365 (M.C.Cowdrey 108, D.Wilson 5-67) & 109 (D.B.Close 8-41), Yorkshire 231-5dec & 247-8. *Won by two wickets*
**Lord's**, August 15, 17, 18: Yorkshire 298-9dec & 83-4, Middlesex 137 & 241. *Won by six wickets*
**Bath**, August 19, 20, 21: Somerset 342-5dec (D.Wilson 5-57) & 187 (D.B.Close 6-87), Yorkshire 275 (D.B.Close 128) & 238 (B.A.Langford 6-85). *Lost by 16 runs*
**Bristol**, August 22, 24, 25: Gloucestershire 294-8dec, Yorkshire 35 (A.Brown 7-11) & 182. *Lost by an innings and 77 runs*
**Worcester**, August 26, 27, 28: Worcestershire 120 & 301 (D.Kenyon 122), Yorkshire 262 (W.B.Stott 144*, L.J.Coldwell 6-66) & 163-4. *Won by six wickets*
**Hove**, August 29, 30, September 1: Sussex 210 & 311, Yorkshire 307 (R.Illingworth 122) & 218-5. *Won by five wickets*

# NOTES and HIGHLIGHTS

Yorkshire's first outright title for 13 years ended their longest barren sequence thus far since the formation of the official Championship in 1890. The pulsating nature of the season is reflected in the fact that ten of the 14 victories were not completed until the final session of play. Nine games were won by having to bat in the fourth innings of the match and none of these came as a result of a declaration by Yorkshire's opponents. The final game reflected the frenetic pace of the season when the victory came as a result of the winning total of 218 being scored in only 95 minutes from fewer than 29 overs. The vital third-wicket stand of 141 put together by Bryan Stott and Padgett came in just over an hour's play.

However it was never plain sailing: in losing seven matches, Yorkshire were defeated on more occasions than in any championship-winning season in their history. With only three games to go the team was dismissed for 35 - their lowest total for 24 years – suffered a heavy defeat and stood only third in the table.

The success was a real team effort; there were no outstanding individuals and only Trueman (ninth) featured in the top ten of the national averages for either batting or bowling. In the match against Hampshire at Hull, Stott (94 and 103 not out) scored 54% of Yorkshire's runs. The next highest aggregate was the 43 (10%) scored by Illingworth. With Trueman taking nine of the opposition's twenty wickets the four-wicket victory was almost a two-man show.

Having led Yorkshire to something resembling its former glories, Ronnie Burnet retired. He had captained the county for two seasons, having had no previous experience of first-class cricket. He was instrumental in clinching the sacking of Wardle in 1958 and welded a winning side of young players of whom only Vic Wilson and Burnet himself were aged over 30. They achieved something that was beyond the more talented team of the early 1950s, a side beset with disharmony and bitter personal rivalry.

Brian Close's figures against Kent at Headingley were the best of his career. H.D. 'Dickie' Bird, later to become a celebrated international umpire, played the last of his four seasons with Yorkshire. Despite compiling 316 runs at an average of just below 40, his contract was not renewed. After scoring 181 not out against Glamorgan at Bradford he was dropped for the next match to make way for the returning Taylor!

Padgett and Binks played in all 28 games of the campaign. The summer was an excellent one from the point of view of the weather, very little play being lost, and it was the third sunniest in the entire century.

## PLAYER of the SEASON

Fred Trueman was Yorkshire's leading wicket-taker for the season and also led the bowling averages. He was just beginning what was probably the five-year peak period of his career. He would eventually be revered as probably Yorkshire's greatest fast bowler (only George Freeman being a possible contender) and England's, too. He would become the first bowler from any country to take 300 Test wickets and the moment that this was achieved (at The Oval against Australia in 1964) remains one of the bowler's proudest. This ranks alongside his achievement of leading Yorkshire to victory over the same opponents by an innings four years later at Sheffield.

From Maltby mining stock, Trueman made his county debut in 1949 at the age of 18. His hostility and sheer pace were almost frightening and he was probably at his fastest in 1952 when he helped reduce India to 0-4 on his Test debut at Headingley. He took eight for 31 at Old Trafford and these remained his best Test figures. Without doubt 'Fiery Fred' was a suitable nickname in those early years, especially as his forthright comments did not endear him to everyone and may have contributed to him missing two significant tours and around thirty Test matches.

As Trueman mellowed, however, so did his bowling and gradually came the complete mastery of all that the fast bowler possessed in his armoury. He varied the line of attack, yorkers and bouncers being interspersed with good-length deliveries and when he cut down on pace, often deliberately so, swing and the more pronounced use of the seam, came into action. This was especially so against the 1963 West Indies when he took 34 wickets in a pulsating series.

Trueman's 307 Test wickets (average 21.57) came in 67 matches and this England record would stand for almost twenty years after his final game in 1965. His first-class career tally of 2304 victims (av. 18.30) included 1745 (at 17.12) for Yorkshire and is exceptional for a fast bowler. His best season would be 1960 when he took 175 wickets at only 13.98. His final match was in 1968 and afterwards he continued to serve the game as a commentator. His views are still always sought, particularly on any of Yorkshire's controversial issues, and his colourful personality comes through as strongly as it did in the days of his pomp.

For the following season, each county could play 28 or 32 matches and it was thus necessary to re-introduce the average to determine the final ranking.

## 1960

## TOP FIVE COUNTIES

|  | Pld | W | L | D | Pts | Avge |
|---|---|---|---|---|---|---|
| Yorkshire | 32 | 17 | 6 | 9 | 246 | 7.68 |
| Lancashire | 32 | 13 | 8 | 11 | 214 | 6.68 |
| Middlesex | 28 | 12 | 4 | 12 | 186 | 6.64 |
| Sussex | 32 | 12 | 6 | 14 | 188 | 5.87 |
| Derbyshire | 28 | 10 | 7 | 11 | 152 | 5.42 |

## LEADING YORKSHIRE AVERAGES

### BATTING

|  | M | I | NO | Runs | HS | Avge | 100 | 50 |
|---|---|---|---|---|---|---|---|---|
| D.E.V.Padgett | 25 | 36 | 2 | 1387 | 146 | 40.79 | 5 | 5 |
| D.B.Close | 32 | 45 | 3 | 1573 | 198 | 37.45 | 3 | 7 |
| W.B.Stott | 28 | 46 | 4 | 1548 | 186 | 36.85 | 4 | 6 |
| K.Taylor | 24 | 37 | 5 | 994 | 130* | 31.06 | 1 | 6 |
| J.B.Bolus | 25 | 38 | 5 | 885 | 146* | 26.81 | 1 | 4 |
| J.V.Wilson | 31 | 40 | 7 | 855 | 84* | 25.90 | - | 7 |

## BOWLING

| | O | M | R | W | Avge | 5WI | 10WM | BB |
|---|---|---|---|---|---|---|---|---|
| F.S.Trueman | 779.5 | 217 | 1689 | 132 | 12.79 | 10 | 4 | 7-41 |
| R.Illingworth | 716.3 | 309 | 1350 | 75 | 18.00 | 5 | 1 | 8-70 |
| D.Wilson | 906.1 | 412 | 1597 | 72 | 22.18 | 4 | 1 | 6-34 |
| M.J.Cowan | 718.4 | 180 | 1502 | 66 | 22.75 | 3 | 1 | 9-43 |
| D.B.Close | 575.3 | 190 | 1434 | 63 | 22.76 | 3 | - | 8-43 |

## FIELDING and WICKET-KEEPING

83 (77 ct, 8st) J.G.Binks
40 D.B.Close
31 P.J.Sharpe
26 J.V.Wilson
22 D.Wilson

# RESULTS

**Hove**, May 7, 9, 10: Sussex 280 (F.S.Trueman 5-53) & 250-2dec, Yorkshire 281-0dec (W.B.Stott 138*, K.Taylor 130*) & 217. *Lost by 32 runs*
**Bradford**, May 14, 16: Gloucestershire 149 & 175 (D.Wilson 5-44), Yorkshire 179 (D.A.Allen 8-41) & 147-7dec. *Won by three wickets*
**Hull**, May 18, 19, 20: Yorkshire 339 (D.E.V.Padgett 130) & 35-0, Somerset 178 & 195. *Won by ten wickets*
**Portsmouth**, May 21, 23, 24: Yorkshire 399-7dec (J.B.Bolus 146*, D.B.Close 102), Hampshire 191 (F.S.Trueman 6-34) & 147 (F.S.Trueman 6-28). *Won by an innings and 61 runs*
**Gravesend**, May 25, 26: Yorkshire 436-9dec (W.B.Stott 116), Kent 194 & 128. *Won by an innings and 114 runs*
**Sheffield**, May 28, 30, 31: Northamptonshire 169 (F.S.Trueman 7-60) & 233 (F.S.Trueman 7-65), Yorkshire 205 (F.H.Tyson 6-57) & 198-4. *Won by six wickets*
**Middlesbrough**, June 1, 2, 3: Yorkshire 381 (D.E.V.Padgett 146) & 4-0, Sussex 200 (D.B.Close 5-64) & 181. *Won by ten wickets*
**Headingley**, June 4, 6: Yorkshire 96 & 117, Lancashire 210 (G.Pullar 121, D.Wilson 5-49, R.Illingworth 5-55) & 5-0. *Lost by ten wickets*

**Hull**, June 8, 9, 10: Yorkshire 117 (D.C.Morgan 7-38) & 353-8dec, Derbyshire 138 (D.Wilson 6-34) & 91. *Won by 241 runs*

**Lord's**, June 11, 13, 14: Middlesex 147 (R.K.Platt 6-33) & 161, Yorkshire 102 & 15-1. *Match drawn*

**Worksop**, June 15, 16, 17: Nottinghamshire 157 (M.J.Cowan 5-38) & 155, Yorkshire 367-7dec. *Won by an innings and 55 runs*

**The Oval**, June 18, 20, 21: Surrey 123 (F.S.Trueman 7-41) & 312 (F.S.Trueman 7-82), Yorkshire 434-4dec (D.B.Close 198, D.E.V.Padgett 117) & 4-1. *Won by nine wickets*

**Headingley**, June 22, 23, 24: Middlesex 270 (J.Birkenshaw 7-76) & 214-6dec, Yorkshire 264 & 116-5. *Match drawn*

**Chesterfield**, June 25, 27, 28: Yorkshire 168 & 172, Derbyshire 154 (D.B.Close 6-59) & 128 (D.Wilson 5-30). *Won by 58 runs*

**Northampton**, June 29, 30, July 1: Yorkshire 377-7dec (D.E.V.Padgett 120) & 139-7dec, Northamptonshire 231 & 287-4 (R.Subba Row 135*). *Lost by six wickets*

**Bradford**, July 2, 4, 5: Yorkshire 304-9dec (D.E.V.Padgett 113, O.S.Wheatley 7-109), Warwickshire 142 & 92 (F.S.Trueman 7-42). *Won by an innings and 70 runs*

**Sheffield**, July 6, 7, 8: Yorkshire 315 (P.J.Sharpe 152), Kent 263-3 (A.H.Phebey 122*). *Match drawn*

**Gloucester**, July 9, 11, 12: Yorkshire 253 (D.G.A'Court 6-69), Gloucestershire 77 (M.Ryan 6-40) & 239-4. *Match drawn*

**Colchester**, July 13, 14, 15: Essex 242-9dec (R.Illingworth 5-77) & 152-7dec, Yorkshire 135 & 136-4. *Match drawn*

**Sheffield**, July 16, 18, 19: Surrey 283-8dec (D.G.W.Fletcher 103) & 157-2 (J.H.Edrich 103*), Yorkshire 196-9dec & 82-3. *Match drawn*

**Bradford**, July 20, 21, 22: Yorkshire 282 (W.B.Stott 124), Hampshire 113. *Match drawn*

**Headingley**, July 23, 25, 26: Essex 180 & 200 (D.B.Close 8-43), Yorkshire 86 (T.E.Bailey 7-40) & 237 (T.E.Bailey 5-61) *Lost by 57 runs*

**Leicester**, July 27, 28, 29: Leicestershire 172 (R.Illingworth 5-45) & 141 (F.S.Trueman 5-41), Yorkshire 318. *Won by an innings and 5 runs*

**Old Trafford**, July 30, August 1, 2: Yorkshire 154 (J.B.Statham 5-43) & 149, Lancashire 226 & 81-8 (M.Ryan 5-50). *Lost by two wickets*

**Scarborough**, August 3, 4, 5: Yorkshire 408-4dec (D.B.Close 184), Nottinghamshire 238 (F.S.Trueman 6-39) & 113. *Won by an innings and 57 runs*

**Bradford**, August 10, 11, 12: Glamorgan 194 & 207 (M.J.Cowan 5-57), Yorkshire 229 (P.M.Walker 5-63) & 175-9. *Won by one wicket*
**Headingley**, August 13, 15, 16: Yorkshire 293 & 9-0, Leicestershire 110 & 189. *Won by ten wickets*
**Swansea**, August 17, 18, 19: Glamorgan 206 (R.Illingworth 8-70) & 202 (R.Illingworth 7-53), Yorkshire 177 (D.J.Shepherd 5-52 & 144 (D.Ward 5-43). *Lost by 87 runs*
**Edgbaston**, August 20, 22, 23: Warwickshire 173 & 162 (M.J.Cowan 9-43), Yorkshire 295 (W.B.Stott 186) & 41-1. *Won by nine wickets*
**Bristol**, August 24, 25, 26: Yorkshire 184 (K.D.Biddulph 6-56), Somerset 113-5. *Match drawn*
**Harrogate**, August 27, 29, 30: Worcestershire 139 & 148, Yorkshire 243 & 48-1. *Won by nine wickets*
**Worcester**, September 3, 5, 6: Yorkshire 125, Worcestershire 81-4. *Match drawn*

## NOTES and HIGHLIGHTS

Other than in the feats of the outstanding Trueman, Yorkshire's Championship win was very much a team effort. The fielding and catching were the main feature of the county's success and this put persistent pressure on the opposition in what were often low-scoring games.

Despite scoring 281 without losing a single wicket in their first innings of the season, Yorkshire lost the match to Sussex at Hove by 32 runs. This was followed, however, by six consecutive victories and the county rarely looked back after that point, excepting for two defeats by Lancashire!

Close's 198 at The Oval against Surrey was the highest score of his career and this also applies to Stott's innings in the away game against Warwickshire. No Yorkshire batsman came in the top ten of the national averages although a total of eight passed the 1000-run target in all county matches. Illingworth scored 661 runs at 27.54 in the Championship.

Illingworth's match figures of 15-123 against Glamorgan at Swansea were the best for the whole season but were achieved in a losing cause! They remain the best figures by an off-spinner in Yorkshire's entire history.

Trueman had the best season of his career and finished third in the national averages. Ryan (37 wickets at 22.54 and Platt (24, 24.01) also contributed well when needed.

The campaign was the first season under the leadership of Vic Wilson. A momentous break with tradition occurred when he was appointed to be the first professional captain since 1883 but the move was very much in the spirit of the times and the amateur/professional distinction would be abolished after the 1962 season.

Binks and Close played in every match of the campaign, the former having the best season of his career. He set a record for most catches (96) in a season of first-class cricket and this still stands.

## PLAYER of the SEASON

In making the highest score of his career and having Yorkshire's highest run aggregate for the season, Brian Close showed that he was to be ranked among the best of the county's left-handed batsmen. A total of 22 Test caps spread out over no less than 28 years would be scant reward for his prodigious talents. In 1949, at the age of 18, he had completed the 'double' and made his Test debut in his first season of first-class cricket. He remains England's youngest Test player. A natural games player, from Rawdon, Close played professional soccer before a knee injury ended his career.

His second 'double' came in his second full season (1952) - after National Service - but his batting became more prominent thereafter and never again did he take 100 wickets in a season. Character was the most important aspect of his play, however, and his courage and bravery were reflected in his batting, when taking body-blows from hostile West Indians, even at the age of 45, and when fielding in astonishingly suicidal positions. He was the natural successor to the Yorkshire captaincy in 1963 and he set an example at all times in all three skills of the game. He always batted according to the situation, put himself on to bowl when others were not breaking through and set an outstanding example in the field.

Yorkshire won the title in his first season in charge and he led them to three more Championships as well as two Gillette Cup victories. Despite this success he would be sacked after the 1970 season and move to Somerset, whom he led for six summers laying the foundations of their subsequent first-ever trophies. Meanwhile, he had become captain of England for the last Test of 1966 and continued in that capacity for six Tests in 1967. He was fully expected to lead England on tour but the use of time-wasting tactics for Yorkshire on an infamous occasion against Warwickshire at Edgbaston led to a severe censure and a complete fall from grace. Nevertheless his record as England captain reads six wins, one draw and no defeats.

Close's tremendously varied career in first-class cricket lasted 37 years and ended with a Scarborough festival match in 1986. He returned to the Yorkshire Club later in life and became chairman of the cricket committee. His playing record of 34,994 runs, 1171 wickets and 813 catches pay testimony to a tenacious and immensley committed player. His best bowling analysis was in 1959.

Perhaps the final word could rest with Ian Botham who, as a young player, came under Close's wing at Somerset. Writing in his autobiography many years later, he still regarded Close as 'the toughest man I ever played sport with or against'.

# 1961

Hampshire were champions for the first time in their history with Yorkshire taking the runners-up spot.

*Skipper Vic Wilson and Fred Trueman arrive for net practice at Headingley in April, 1962.*

# 1962

## TOP FIVE COUNTIES

|  | Pld | W | L | D | Pts | Avge |
|---|---|---|---|---|---|---|
| Yorkshire | 32 | 14 | 4 | 14 | 224 | 7.00 |
| Worcestershire | 32 | 14 | 3 | 15 | 220 | 6.87 |
| Warwickshire | 32 | 12 | 5 | 15 | 202 | 6.31 |
| Gloucestershire | 28 | 11 | 11 | 6 | 174 | 6.21 |
| Surrey | 28 | 10 | 3 | 15 | 174 | 6.21 |

## LEADING YORKSHIRE AVERAGES

### BATTING

|  | M | I | NO | Runs | HS | Avge | 100 | 50 |
|---|---|---|---|---|---|---|---|---|
| P.J.Sharpe | 31 | 54 | 5 | 1872 | 138 | 38.20 | 6 | 6 |
| D.B.Close | 25 | 41 | 5 | 1356 | 142* | 37.66 | 3 | 7 |
| R.Illingworth | 30 | 48 | 7 | 1468 | 127 | 35.80 | 3 | 7 |
| D.E.V.Padgett | 30 | 50 | 2 | 1404 | 125* | 29.25 | 2 | 9 |
| K.Taylor | 22 | 36 | 0 | 986 | 163 | 27.38 | 1 | 7 |
| J.V.Wilson | 32 | 48 | 2 | 1135 | 134 | 24.67 | 2 | 5 |

### BOWLING

|  | O | M | R | W | Avge | 5WI | 10WM | BB |
|---|---|---|---|---|---|---|---|---|
| F.S.Trueman | 802 | 193 | 1889 | 106 | 17.82 | 4 | 1 | 8-84 |
| R.Ilingworth | 914 | 363 | 1871 | 102 | 18.34 | 8 | - | 7-40 |
| M.Ryan | 627.1 | 151 | 1607 | 74 | 21.71 | 2 | - | 6-33 |
| D.Wilson | 873.4 | 330 | 1847 | 83 | 22.25 | 3 | 1 | 6-24 |

### FIELDING and WICKET-KEEPING

71 (59 ct, 12 st) J.G.Binks
65 P.J.Sharpe
27 D.B.Close
26 J.V.Wilson
24 R.Illingworth
21 D.Wilson

# RESULTS

**Hull**, May 9, 10, 11: Somerset 105 (D.Wilson 5-23) & 128 (F.S.Trueman 6-45), Yorkshire 246 (B.A.Langford 5-75). *Won by an innings and 13 runs*
**Bradford**, May 12, 14, 15: Yorkshire 259 & 166-9dec (D.R.Smith 5-63), Gloucestershire 95 (R.Illingworth 5-31) & 134. *Won by 196 runs*
**Edgbaston,** May 16, 17, 18: Warwickshire 108 & 171, Yorkshire 386 (D.Wilson 134, D.J.Brown 5-106). *Won by an innings and 107 runs*
**Middlesbrough,** May 19, 21, 22: Middlesex 280-7dec (P.H.Parfitt 132) & 11-0, Yorkshire 283 (F.J.Titmus 6-73). *Match drawn*
**Worcester**, May 23, 24, 25: Worcestershire 292 (R.K.Platt 6-67) & 162, Yorkshire 226 (L.J.Coldwell 5-58) & 103-7. *Match drawn*
**Hove**, May 26, 28, 29: Sussex 179 & 295-4dec, Yorkshire 173 & 168-4. *Match drawn*
**Sheffield**, May 30, 31, June 1: Warwickshire 301-7dec & 198 (R.Illingworth 5-64), Yorkshire 302-6dec (D.B.Close 140*, R.Illingworth 107) & 148 (R.Miller 5-31). *Lost by 49 runs*
**Lord's**, June 2, 4, 5: Yorkshire 297-9dec (R.W.Hooker 5-55) & 148, Middlesex 300-9dec (R.A.Gale 133) & 147-4. *Lost by six wickets*
**Cardiff**, June 6, 7, 8: Yorkshire 276 (O.S.Wheatley 5-68) & 278-7dec, Glamorgan 334 (P.M.Walker 100) & 224-5. *Lost by five wickets*
**Headingley**, June 9, 11, 12: Lancashire 308-6dec (J.D.Bond 144) & 112 (F.S.Trueman 5-29), Yorkshire 294 (P.J.Sharpe 108*, T.Greenhough 5-93) & 127-3. *Won by seven wickets*
**Hull**, June 13, 14, 15: Derbyshire 232 & 114, Yorkshire 377 (W.B.Stott 145). *Won by an innings and 31 runs*
**Northampton**, June 20, 21, 22: Yorkshire 157 & 193, Northamptonshire 201 (R.Illingworth 7-40) & 152-4. *Lost by six wickets*
**Chesterfield**, June 23, 25, 26: Derbyshire 309 & 214-5dec, Yorkshire 279 (E.Smith 5-39) & 61-2. *Match drawn*
**Bradford**, June 27, 28, 29: Yorkshire 151 (D.Shackleton 7-78) & 176 (D.Shackleton 5-67), Hampshire 165 (F.S.Trueman 5-34) & 157 (R.Illingworth 5-33). *Won by 5 runs*
**Sheffield**, June 30, July 2, 3: Surrey 218 & 333-7 (J.H.Edrich 154), Yorkshire 317-4dec (P.J.Sharpe 132, D.E.V.Padgett 125*). *Match drawn*
**Westcliff-on-Sea**, July 7, 9, 10: Yorkshire 229 (K.C.Preston 5-63) & 185 (T.E.Bailey 5-55), Essex 202 & 60-1. *Match drawn*

**Worksop**, July 11, 12, 13: Yorkshire 258 (P.J.Sharpe 104) & 217-6dec, Nottinghamshire 126 (F.S.Trueman 8-84) & 169. *Won by 180 runs*
**Sheffield**, July 14, 16, 17: Northamptonshire 255-7dec & 119-2, Yorkshire 281 (P.J.Sharpe 110). *Match drawn*
**Headingley**, July 18, 19, 20: Nottinghamshire 245 & 351-6 (M.Hill 118*), Yorkshire 441-9dec (K.Taylor 163, J.V.Wilson 134). *Match drawn*
**Taunton**, July 21, 23, 24: Yorkshire 323 (P.J.Sharpe 138, M.Latham 5-61) & 239-6 (D.B.Close 121*), Somerset 497 (P.B.Wight 215, M.J.Cowan 5-135). *Match drawn*
**Bristol**, July 25, 26, 27: Yorkshire 230 (D.E.V.Padgett 115*, J.B.Mortimore 5-56) & 222-8dec, Gloucestershire 249 (R.Illingworth 5-63) & 134. *Won by 69 runs*
**Sheffield**, July 28, 30, 31: Essex 207 & 112 (R.Illingworth 6-26), Yorkshire 363-9dec (D.B.Close 142*, P.J.Phelan 5-103). *Won by an innings and 44 runs*
**Middlesbrough**, August 1, 2, 3: Kent 344-7dec (P.E.Richardson 162) & 136 (R.Illingworth 5-52), Yorkshire 251 (D.J.Halfyard 5-86) & 230-7. *Won by three wickets*
**Old Trafford**, August 4, 6, 7: Yorkshire 235 (P.J.Sharpe 112, J.B.Statham 6-68) & 149-1dec, Lancashire 202 (J.D.Bond 109) & 50-1. *Match drawn*
**Scarborough**, August 8, 9, 10: Yorkshire 148 (E.R.Dexter 5-44) & 238-8dec, Sussex 194 & 99 (R.Illingworth 5-10). *Won by 93 runs*
**Headingley**, August 11, 13, 14: Yorkshire 321 (L.J.Coldwell 5-92), Worcestershire 214 (D.W.Richardson 102). *Match drawn*
**Bradford**, August 15, 16, 17: Yorkshire 193 & 125-8dec, Leicestershire 132 & 70 (M.Ryan 6-33). *Won by 116 runs*
**Gillingham**, August 18, 20, 21: Kent 65 & 277, Yorkshire 257 (A.Brown 5-71) & 89-3. *Won by seven wickets*
**Bournemouth**, August 22, 23, 24: Yorkshire 346 (R.Illingworth 115) & 125-9dec, Hampshire 233 (D.Wilson 6-70) & 187-9. *Match drawn*
**The Oval**, August 25, 27, 28: Yorkshire 416 (R.Illingworth 127) & 113-4dec, Surrey 172 & 61-7. *Match drawn*
**Leicester**, August 29, 30, 31: Yorkshire 197 (R.L.Pratt 7-53) & 200, Leicestershire 271 (M.R.Hallam 129, M.Ryan 5-53) & 79-4. *Match drawn*
**Harrogate**, September 5, 6, 7: Glamorgan 65 (D.Wilson 6-24) & 101, Yorkshire 101 & 66-3. *Won by seven wickets*

# NOTES and HIGHLIGHTS

The title was not won as convincingly as some, there being a very narrow point gap between Yorkshire and runners-up Worcestershire. Three victories in the first three matches were soon offset by three defeats at the beginning of June. However, no more games were lost after June 22nd but Yorkshire still needed to win their last game. This was not entirely straightforward with the middle day being completely washed out but victory occurred shortly after 4.00pm on the last day of the season.

A pulsating game took place against Hampshire, the reigning champions, at Bradford. Vic Wilson led from the front and made the top scores (51 and 45) in each innings but only two other players passed fifty in the entire game. Derek Shackleton had put the visitors in a winning position with twelve wickets for 145 especially when his team reached 156-5 requiring 163 for victory. However the remaining five wickets fell for the addition of only one run, thanks to Illingworth, and the home side were victorious by a mere five runs.

The batting was, as in 1960, consistent with no one appearing in the top ten of the national averages. Sharpe had a golden run of form at the beginning of July, scoring a total of 593 runs at an average of 74.13 including four centuries in seven consecutive innings. It was the best season of his career and this also applies to his aggregate of catches. Jack Bond (Lancashire) scored a century in each of the Roses matches.

Trueman (third) and Illingworth (fifth) were both in the top ten of the national bowling averages. The latter's full analysis against Sussex at Scarborough was a remarkable 12.4-8-10-5. He completed the double of 1000 runs and 100 wickets in Championship matches alone.

Binks and Vic Wilson played in every match of the campaign and the county came to the end of its busiest period in its history having played 114 first-class matches in three seasons.

Three significant debuts took place in 1962. Geoff Boycott was to become England's most reliable batsman during his 18 years as a Test cricketer and his totals of 32,570 runs and 103 centuries would eventually place him in third and second positions, respectively, in Yorkshire's all-time records. However, controversy followed him everywhere and he was Yorkshire's captain for eight years in the 1970s when nothing was won and he was very much at the centre of the county's troubles in the 1980s.

Richard Hutton suffered, in the eyes of many Yorkshire supporters, from having a famous father but he forced his way into the England side as an all-rounder. He left the county at the end of 1974, disillusioned and with promise unfulfilled. Tony Nicholson quickly became the most reliable of Trueman's partners and developed into an excellent seam bowler who ended his Yorkshire career with 876 wickets at an impressive average of 19.74.

Having led the county to the Championship twice in the three seasons for which he was in charge (and being runners-up in the other) Vic Wilson retired from the game. He scored over 20,000 runs for Yorkshire and his 520 catches place him fifth on the county's all-time list.

## PLAYER of the SEASON

Already one of the country's leading all-rounders Ray Illingworth was fast developing into one of the game's most astute thinkers. Another Pudsey product, his birth being in 1932, he donned the Yorkshire sweater for the first time in 1951. By the time of his first 100-wicket haul, five years later, he had developed into a very nagging off-spinner with accurate line and length and more than useful turn.

With the bat Illingworth settled into the number six position from which he was able to guide the course of the remainder of the innings. He could play very much according to the needs of the side, being capable of flamboyant stroke-play as well as solid defence. Added to this was his excellent close fielding, especially in the gully, and the picture is one of the complete cricketer.

Illingworth played the first of his eventual total of 61 Tests in 1958 but for the first decade of his international career his appearances were spasmodic. The dramatic change in this sequence of appearances came about as a direct result of his sacking by Yorkshire! At the end of the 1968 season his request for a three-year contract would be declined and so he moved to Leicestershire and was promptly made captain. Within weeks, because of an injury to Colin Cowdrey, he was asked to lead England and did so for five years with only five of the 31 Tests for which he was in charge being lost.

The highlight of Illingworth's career was the winning of the Ashes in Australia in 1970/71 and he is still regarded as one of England's best four leaders over the last fifty years. Both his batting and bowling averages improved on being promoted to the captaincy and his ability to bring out the best in all types of players also resulted in success for his adopted county as they won the first trophies in their history, including the Championship in 1975.

Illingworth would return to Yorkshire in 1979 as the Club's first-ever manager and this proved to be a most inauspicious appointment that concluded with him taking over the captaincy. He later became a commentator and followed this with a second unsuccessful period as a manager – this time for England – that culminated in a disastrous showing in the 1996 World Cup.

Illingworth is one of only three post-1946 players to score 20,000 runs and take 2000 wickets in first-class cricket. For Yorkshire his figures were 14,986 runs (average 27.90) and 1431 wickets (at 18.73). Still a forthright columnist, it is a great pity that his wisdom was not allowed to be put to the use of Yorkshire's young players in the 1970s as he would have been the ideal successor to Close.

For the 1963 season there would be ten points for a win and two points for first innings lead in a drawn match. Every county would once more play 28 matches so that the average column was removed. One of the reasons for this was that the counties, for the first time ever, would be competing for two trophies. The Gillette Cup would be run on a knock-out basis with a final at Lord's near the end of the season.

## 1963

## TOP FIVE COUNTIES

|  | Pld | W | L | D | Pts |
|---|---|---|---|---|---|
| Yorkshire | 28 | 13 | 3 | 12 | 144 |
| Glamorgan | 28 | 11 | 8 | 9 | 124 |
| Somerset | 28 | 10 | 6 | 12 | 118 |
| Sussex | 28 | 10 | 6 | 12 | 116 |
| Warwickshire | 28 | 10 | 3 | 15 | 116 |

## LEADING YORKSHIRE AVERAGES

### BATTING

|  | M | I | NO | Runs | HS | Avge | 100 | 50 |
|---|---|---|---|---|---|---|---|---|
| G.Boycott | 25 | 38 | 7 | 1446 | 165* | 46.64 | 3 | 9 |
| D.B.Close | 19 | 28 | 2 | 915 | 161 | 35.19 | 1 | 6 |
| P.J Sharpe | 21 | 33 | 5 | 766 | 138* | 27.35 | 2 | 3 |
| J.H.Hampshire | 27 | 42 | 4 | 995 | 120 | 26.18 | 1 | 5 |
| D.E.V.Padgett | 22 | 33 | 1 | 811 | 142 | 25.34 | 2 | 1 |

### BOWLING

|  | O | M | R | W | Avge | 5WI | 10WM | BB |
|---|---|---|---|---|---|---|---|---|
| F.S.Trueman | 472.2 | 128 | 976 | 76 | 12.84 | 4 | 2 | 8-45 |
| A.G.Nicholson | 527.1 | 162 | 1056 | 65 | 16.24 | 4 | - | 6-36 |
| D.Wilson | 714.1 | 277 | 1552 | 82 | 18.92 | 4 | - | 6-22 |
| M.Ryan | 604.2 | 163 | 1309 | 57 | 22.96 | - | - | 4-13 |

## FIELDING and WICKET-KEEPING

80 (73 ct, 7 st) J.G.Binks
34 P.J.Sharpe
19 D.B.Close
16 D.E.V.Padgett

# RESULTS

**Northampton**, May 4, 6, 7: Yorkshire 339 (D.B.Close 161, F.S.Trueman 104, J.D.F.Larter 6-61) & 105-3, Northamptonshire 137 & 303 (C.Milburn 123). *Won by seven wickets*
**Hull**, May 8, 9, 10: Yorkshire 214 (D.E.V.Padgett 101) & 107-2, Kent 184. *Match drawn*
**Edgbaston**, May 11, 13: Yorkshire 261 (R.Illingworth 107*), Warwickshire 35 & 55 (F.S.Trueman 6-18). *Won by an innings and 171 runs*
**Bradford**, May 18, 20, 21: Gloucestershire 80 (F.S.Trueman 8-45) & 54-5, Yorkshire 187. *Match drawn*
**Headingley**, May 25, 27, 28: Hampshire 260 & 203-6dec, Yorkshire 189 (P.J.Sainsbury 7-77) & 144. *Lost by 130 runs*
**Gravesend**, May 29, 30, 31: Yorkshire 263 & 187-9dec (A.L.Dixon 5-60), Kent 199 & 229. *Won by 22 runs*
**Sheffield**, June 1, 3, 4: Lancashire 151 & 123 (D.Wilson 5-57), Yorkshire 384-6dec (G.Boycott 145, W.B.Stott 143). *Won by an innings and 110 runs*
**Harrogate**, June 5, 6, 7: Somerset 202 & 111, Yorkshire 352. *Won by an innings and 39 runs*
**Chesterfield**, June 8, 10, 11: Derbyshire 238 (A.G.Nicholson 6-36) & 110, Yorkshire 404-4dec (D.E.V.Padgett 142, P.J.Sharpe 138*). *Won by an innings and 56 runs*
**Taunton**, June 15, 17, 18: Yorkshire 222 & 241, Somerset 271-8dec & 13-1. *Match drawn*
**Bristol**, June 19, 20, 21: Gloucestershire 126-2dec & 154-4dec, Yorkshire 63-2dec & 173-7. *Match drawn*
**Bradford**, June 22, 24, 25: Worcestershire 307 (J.Waring 5-49), Yorkshire 213-9. *Match drawn*
**Sheffield**, June 26, 27, 28: Glamorgan 185 (D.B.Close 6-55) & 95, Yorkshire 218 (O.S.Wheatley 6-73) & 63-0. *Won by ten wickets*

**Trent Bridge**, June 29, July 1, 2: Nottinghamshire 267 (F.S.Trueman 6-51) & 8-0, Yorkshire 126. *Match drawn*

**Headingley**, July 6, 8, 9: Yorkshire 147 & 147-7dec, Middlesex 47 (A.G.Nicholson 5-7) & 251-4. *Lost by six wickets*

**The Oval**, July 13, 15, 16: Yorkshire 149 (D.Gibson 6-40) & 180-6dec, Surrey 168-4dec. *Match drawn*

**Bradford**, July 17, 18, 19: Sussex 103 (A.G.Nicholson 5-26) & 112 (D.Wilson 6-22), Yorkshire 188 (N.I.Thomson 5-39) & 28-0. *Won by ten wickets*

**Sheffield**, July 20, 22, 23: Surrey 225 & 230-3dec (M.D.Willett 109*), Yorkshire 246 (J.H.Hampshire 120) & 21-4. *Match drawn*

**Cardiff**, July 24, 25, 26: Yorkshire 332-7dec, Glamorgan 88 (D.Wilson 5-33) & 178 (J.H.Hampshire 7-52). *Won by an innings and 66 runs*

**Worcester**, July 27, 29, 30: Worcestershire 352-7dec, Yorkshire 166 (D.N.F.Slade 6-48) & 129. *Lost by an innings and 57 runs*

**Scarborough**, July 31, August 1, 2: Yorkshire 301 & 172, Warwickshire 269 & 112 (R.Illingworth 5-35). *Won by 92 runs*

**Old Trafford**, August 3, 5, 6: Yorkshire 345-8dec (G.Boycott 113, P.J.Sharpe 106), & 63-1, Lancashire 237 (F.S.Trueman 5-50). *Match drawn*

**Headingley**, August 7, 8: Derbyshire 123 & 85, Yorkshire 152 & 60-3, *Won by seven wickets*

**Bradford**, August 14, 15, 16: Nottinghamshire 55 & 214 (J.B.Bolus 114), Yorkshire 176-9dec (B.D.Wells 5-22) & 20-0. *Match drawn*

**Lord's**, August 17, 19, 20: Yorkshire 144, Middlesex 145-8 (A.G.Nicholson 5-43). *Match drawn*

**Clacton**, August 21, 22, 23: Yorkshire 160 & 125-8dec, Essex 83 & 151-7. *Match drawn*

**Scarborough**, August 24, 26, 27: Leicestershire 124 & 102 (R.Illingworth 5-13), Yorkshire 337-5dec (G.Boycott 165*). *Won by an innings and 111 runs*

**Leicester**, August 28, 29, 30: Yorkshire 250 & 221-5dec, Leicestershire 133 (D.Wilson 5-44) & 69 (R.Illingworth 6-13). *Won by 269 runs*

## NOTES and HIGHLIGHTS

Although Sussex led the table for much of the season, Yorkshire's winning of the title was eventually achieved with some comfort and the result of the last game was immaterial. Three consecutive innings victories at the start of June showed what the team was made of. Despite Close, Sharpe and Trueman all being needed regularly by England and Illingworth missing half the season through injury the uncapped trio of Boycott, John Hampshire and Nicholson were amongst the most prominent performers.

Warwickshire were completely humiliated at Edgbaston, being dismissed for 35 and 55, Trueman having match figures of ten for 36. He followed this with 10-65 in the very next game, against Gloucestershire at Bradford. An exciting game at Gravesend see-sawed throughout and Kent, needing 252 to win, seemed well-placed at 205-5. However Don Wilson, who had been severely punished, had other ideas and took four of the last five wickets to finish with an analysis of 8.4-0-72-4!

Boycott's outstanding season, which saw him finish second in the national batting averages, included him scoring centuries in each of the Roses matches – his first two such games. Other batsmen who contributed valuably included Illingworth (508 runs at 29.88) and Stott (655, 27.29).

Economical analyses were achieved by Wilson (27-15-22-6 against Sussex at Bradford) and Illingworth (20.5-13-13-5 against Leicestershire at Scarborough). Trueman came top of the national bowling averages with Nicholson and Illingworth (48 wickets at 16.37) also being in the top ten. Binks, the only player not to miss a match, was the leading wicket-keeper, equal with David Evans of Glamorgan.

Close led the county to the Championship in his first season as leader. Stott retired at the end of the campaign despite being only 29. He scored over 9000 runs for Yorkshire and is best remembered for the exciting opening partnership that he formed with Taylor.

## PLAYER of the SEASON

Yorkshire cricketers from the western fringes of the county are rare but Settle is where Don Wilson first saw the light of day in 1937. He was to become the latest in Yorkshire's long line of left-arm spinners and the last to represent his country. His county debut in 1957 began a brief apprenticeship because when Wardle was sacked in 1958 he suddenly became the senior bowler of his type.

However nothing was too much for this most enthusiastic of players. Wilson varied the flight of the ball intelligently, maintained a teasing length and expected to take a wicket with every ball. He would eventually take 1104 wickets (average 20.49) for his county, including two hat-tricks in 1966, but played in only six Tests, all on two tours.

After Wilson's last game in 1974 his sheer enthusiasm for the game took him into coaching, firstly in South Africa and then as Head Coach at Lord's for 13 years until 1990. Young boys found his love for the game infectious and he was also able to assist seasoned Test players with the same approach albeit on a more advanced technical level. For the last ten years he has worked at Ampleforth College putting back into the game the obvious pleasure that it gave to him.

## 1964 and 1965

Worcestershire, who had never previously won the Championship, did so in both of these two seasons, Yorkshire finishing in fifth and fourth places, respectively. Compensation was gained, however, in 1965 when Yorkshire won the Gillette Cup by defeating Surrey in the final.

For the following season the points gained for first innings lead were to be retained whatever the result. The first innings of the first 102 matches (out of 238) were restricted to 65 overs.

## 1966

## TOP FIVE COUNTIES

|  | Pld | W | L | D | Pts |
|---|---|---|---|---|---|
| Yorkshire | 28 | 15 | 5 | 8 | 184 |
| Worcestershire | 28 | 13 | 5 | 10 | 166 |
| Somerset | 28 | 13 | 7 | 8 | 156 |
| Kent | 28 | 11 | 8 | 9 | 144 |
| Northamptonshire | 28 | 10 | 9 | 9 | 130 |

# LEADING YORKSHIRE AVERAGES

## BATTING

|  | M | I | NO | Runs | HS | Avge | 100 | 50 |
|---|---|---|---|---|---|---|---|---|
| G.Boycott | 18 | 31 | 3 | 1097 | 164 | 39.17 | 4 | 5 |
| D.B.Close | 26 | 43 | 8 | 1060 | 115* | 30.28 | 2 | 6 |
| D.E.V.Padgett | 27 | 45 | 4 | 1054 | 79 | 25.70 | - | 6 |
| J.H.Hampshire | 26 | 44 | 4 | 988 | 78 | 24.70 | - | 5 |
| K.Taylor | 23 | 41 | 2 | 881 | 87 | 22.58 | - | 5 |
| P.J.Sharpe | 28 | 43 | 3 | 875 | 72 | 21.87 | - | 2 |

## BOWLING

|  | O | M | R | W | Avge | 5WI | 10WM | BB |
|---|---|---|---|---|---|---|---|---|
| R.Illingworth | 631.4 | 240 | 1234 | 85 | 14.51 | 8 | 1 | 6-30 |
| A.G.Nicholson | 822.3 | 282 | 1581 | 105 | 15.05 | 5 | - | 6-32 |
| D.Wilson | 733 | 289 | 1443 | 87 | 16.58 | 4 | - | 6-15 |
| F.S.Trueman | 756.1 | 182 | 1732 | 101 | 17.14 | 2 | 1 | 8-37 |

## FIELDING and WICKET-KEEPING

55 (47 ct, 8 st) J.G.Binks
41 D.B.Close, P.J.Sharpe
22 F.S.Trueman
20 J.H.Hampshire

# RESULTS

**Middlesbrough**, May 7, 9: Gloucestershire 135 & 69 (D.Wilson 6-15), Yorkshire 171 (D.A.Allen 6-70) & 34-3. *Won by seven wickets*
**Taunton**, May 11, 12, 13: Somerset 178-6 & 70 (D.Wilson 5-40), Yorkshire 214-5dec & 36-2. *Won by eight wickets*
**Bristol**, May 14, 16, 17: Yorkshire 190 (D.B.Close 105) & 274-9, Gloucestershire 272 (R.Illingworth 5-75). *Match drawn*
**Headingley**, May 28, 30: Lancashire 57 (F.S.Trueman 5-18) & 144 (J.Waring 7-40), Yorkshire 196-9 & 6-0. *Won by ten wickets*

**Leicester**, June 1, 2, 3: Leicestershire 253 (R.Illingworth 5-96) & 100 (R.Illingworth 6-30), Yorkshire 300 & 54-3. *Won by seven wickets*
**Lord's**, June 4, 6, 7: Middlesex 190 & 234-7dec (P.H.Parfitt 114*), Yorkshire 175 & 195-6. *Match drawn*
**Edgbaston**, June 8, 9, 10: Warwickshire 223-6 & 148 (R.Illingworth 6-66), Yorkshire 242-2 (G.Boycott 136*) & 130-2. *Won by eight wickets*
**Chesterfield**, June 11, 13: Yorkshire 258-6, Derbyshire 89 & 154. *Won by an innings and 15 runs*
**Bradford**, June 15, 16, 17: Hampshire 151-8 & 75-4, Yorkshire 104. *Match drawn*
**Headingley**, June 18, 20: Sussex 231-4 & 121 (R.Illingworth 5-42), Yorkshire 202 (J.A.Snow 5-79) & 128 (J.A.Snow 5-41). *Lost by 22 runs*
**Sheffield**, June 25, 27, 28: Derbyshire 85 (A.G.Nicholson 5-12) & 65, Yorkshire 149 & 2-0. *Won by ten wickets*
**Worcester**, June 29, 30, July 1: Worcestershire 302 (R.G.A.Headley 137, A.G.Nicholson 5-60) & 172-4dec, Yorkshire 180 (L.J.Coldwell 5-57) & 148-3. *Match drawn*
**Sheffield**, July 2, 4, 5: Yorkshire 267 & 104 (C.R.M.Atkinson 5-51), Somerset 168 & 154. *Won by 49 runs*
**Bradford**, July 6, 7, 8: Yorkshire 263-8 & 123-3dec, Essex 125 (F.S.Trueman 8-37) & 122 (A.G.Nicholson 6-32). *Won by 139 runs*
**Hove**, July 9, 11, 12: Sussex 276-9dec & 223-4, Yorkshire 383-8dec (G.Boycott 164). *Match drawn*
**Headingley**, July 13, 14, 15: Northamptonshire 174 & 190, Yorkshire 175 (A.Lightfoot 7-25) & 123. *Lost by 66 runs*
**Sheffield**, July 16, 18, 19: Yorkshire 234-9 (G.Boycott 103, C.Forbes 5-85) & 243-4dec (G.Boycott 105), Nottinghamshire 163-8 & 85. *Won by 229 runs*
**Sheffield**, July 23, 25, 26: Yorkshire 214 (F.J.Titmus 5-63) & 240 (J.S.E.Price 5-76), Middlesex 220 & 114 (D.Wilson 6-22). *Won by 120 runs*
**Worksop**, July 27, 28, 29: Nottinghamshire 204 & 124 (D.Wilson 5-46, R.Illingworth 5-54), Yorkshire 332-8dec (D.B.Close 115*). *Won by ten wickets*
**Old Trafford**, July 30, August 1, 2: Yorkshire 146-7dec & inns forfeited, Lancashire 1-0dec & 133 (R.Illingworth 5-33). *Won by 12 runs*
**Portsmouth**, August 3, 4, 5: Yorkshire 280-9dec, Hampshire 64 & 119-4. *Match drawn*

**Leyton**, August 6, 8, 9: Essex 187 (D.Wilson 5-59) & 149-9dec, Yorkshire 181 & 130-4 *Match drawn*
**Bradford**, August 13, 15, 16: Surrey 189-9 (D.B.Close 6-47) & 98, Yorkshire 115 (R.I.Jefferson 5-51) & 151 (R.I.Jefferson 6-49). *Lost by 21 runs*
**Scarborough**, August 17, 18: Glamorgan 137 & 91, Yorkshire 124 (D.J.Shepherd 5-35) & 105-8. *Won by two wickets*
**Northampton**, August 20, 22, 23: Northamptonshire 300-8dec (R.M.Prideaux 109, A.G.Nicholson 5-83) & 186-5dec, Yorkshire 219 & 233. *Lost by 34 runs*
**Hull**, August 24, 25, 26: Yorkshire 197 & 101 (J.D.Bannister 5-38), Warwickshire 193 & 109-7. *Lost by three wickets*
**The Oval**, August 27, 29, 30: Yorkshire 143 (G.G.Arnold 6-33) & 108-5, Surrey 150 (D.B.Close 6-27). *Match drawn*
**Harrogate**, August 31, September 1, 2: Yorkshire 210 (A.Brown 5-30) & 109 (D.L.Underwood 7-30), Kent 119 & 176 (R.Illingworth 5-55). *Won by 24 runs*

## NOTES and HIGHLIGHTS

Yorkshire began the season most impressively in winning six of their first eight games and had an almost unassailable lead of 40 points soon after the beginning of August. However, rain and Test calls (which partly resulted in three defeats in the final month) reduced the deficit to a mere six points before the last match. In this game Yorkshire secured a first innings lead of 91 over Kent at Harrogate but the visitors fought back, mainly due to Derek Underwood's seven for 30, and were well-placed at 143-3 chasing 202 to win. However Illingworth had other ideas and took five of the final seven wickets to bring the title back to the Broad Acres.

The Championship was won mainly because of the bowling. The four main bowlers all took 100 wickets in all first-class matches for Yorkshire and Close (48 wickets at 20.39 in the Championship) provided excellent support. The fielding and close catching were outstanding with the trio of Binks, Sharpe and Close being particularly magnificent. The last-named led from the front, fielding fearlessly and making runs and taking wickets when others failed. He was rewarded with the England captaincy, despite not having been a member of the Test side for three years.

Only Boycott (eighth) appeared in the top ten of the national batting averages but three bowlers – Illingworth (fourth), Nicholson (fifth) and Wilson (eighth) – showed the true strength of the side. Particularly economical innings figures were achieved by Wilson (19-12-15-6 v Gloucestershire at Middlesbrough - 31-18-30-9 in the match) and Nicholson (21-12-12-5 v Derbyshire at Sheffield - 38.4-23-24-9 in the match). Binks, Sharpe, Trueman did not miss a single game of the entire campaign.

The county gave debuts to two players who were to go on to play Test cricket: Geoff Cope was an off-spinner whose career was dogged by controversy over his action but he would take over 600 wickets for the county and was very effective when conditions suited. Chris Old was a fast-medium bowler with a classical action who, in due course, took 143 Test wickets but who often had minor injuries. Memorably described by Mike Brearley as being 'a displaced gene away from greatness' he was also a batsman good enough to score over 4500 runs for Yorkshire and led the county during controversial times for one-and-a-half seasons in the early 1980s.

## PLAYER of the SEASON

Although Geoff Boycott did not have one of his better seasons, he was still good enough to lead the county's batting averages. He was already dedicated to run-making and would become one of the players more absorbed in this aspect of the game than possibly any other, in any era. He would eventually end his career with the highest first-class average (56.83) amongst all of the 61 batsmen to have scored over 30,000 runs. For 690 days in the early 1980s he would hold the world record for having scored most Test runs. But contrast this with his outspokenness and inability to avoid controversy and this is the player probably with a more paradoxical character than any other Yorkshire cricketer.

From his mining roots in Fitzwilliam in 1940 Boycott was subsumed by the need to prove himself via his batting. He first played for Yorkshire in 1962 and success and honours came one year later with the first of his Test caps arriving in 1964. In time his wicket became the prized one that bowlers strove for and both Yorkshire and England became very dependent on his stickability at the crease. This led to an introspective attitude on Boycott's part as his attacking strokes were gradually reduced in usage. Twice, however, and memorably, did he bat with particular freedom. In the Gillette Cup final of 1965 he produced a brilliant 146 not out and on the tour of Australia in 1979/80 he top-scored in five out of six one-day internationals with forthright innings against the might of the bowling attacks of Australia and the West Indies.

Boycott would succeed to the Yorkshire captaincy in 1971 and hold the post for eight years during which time Yorkshire won nothing, albeit with a largely inexperienced squad. He was tactlessly sacked two days after the death of his mother and his supporters had a field day. Further mis-handling of this enigmatic player came in 1983 when he was, almost simultaneously, awarded a testimonial and the non-renewal of his contract!

Boycott's playing days would end in 1986 and his Yorkshire record conclude with 32,570 runs (average 57.85) and 103 centuries. His highest score of 260 not out came against Essex at Colchester in 1970 and twice he averaged over 100 for a season. He became a lively and energetic commentator working for several media organisations. Despite his apparent lack of friends from within the game his batting remains legendary.

For 1967 eight points would be awarded for a win with two for a draw. Four points would be awarded for first innings lead.

## 1967

## TOP FIVE COUNTIES

|  | Pld | W | L | D | Pts |
|---|---|---|---|---|---|
| Yorkshire | 28 | 12 | 5 | 11 | 186 |
| Kent | 28 | 11 | 3 | 14 | 176 |
| Leicestershire | 28 | 10 | 3 | 15 | 176 |
| Surrey | 28 | 8 | 4 | 16 | 148 |
| Worcestershire | 28 | 6 | 6 | 16 | 132 |

# LEADING YORKSHIRE AVERAGES

## BATTING

|  | M | I | NO | Runs | HS | Avge | 100 | 50 |
|---|---|---|---|---|---|---|---|---|
| G.Boycott | 17 | 28 | 2 | 1260 | 220* | 48.46 | 2 | 11 |
| D.E.V.Padgett | 25 | 40 | 5 | 1103 | 139 | 31.51 | 2 | 4 |
| P.J.Sharpe | 24 | 39 | 5 | 1012 | 93 | 29.76 | - | 9 |
| J.H.Hampshire | 25 | 39 | 5 | 922 | 102 | 27.11 | 1 | 6 |

## BOWLING

|  | O | M | R | W | Avge | 5WI | 10WM | BB |
|---|---|---|---|---|---|---|---|---|
| A.G.Nicholson | 663.3 | 187 | 1511 | 90 | 16.78 | 6 | 1 | 9-62 |
| R.Illingworth | 555.1 | 219 | 1075 | 63 | 17.06 | 5 | 2 | 7- 6 |
| D.Wilson | 612.2 | 260 | 1128 | 63 | 17.90 | 3 | 2 | 7-21 |
| F.S.Trueman | 476.1 | 107 | 1296 | 57 | 22.73 | 1 | - | 5-39 |

## FIELDING and WICKET-KEEPING

40 (31 ct, 9 st) J.G.Binks
33 P.J.Sharpe
29 F.S.Trueman
20 D.B.Close

# RESULTS

**Harrogate**, May 3, 4, 5: Glamorgan 130 (F.S.Trueman 5-39) & 41-2, Yorkshire 217-5dec (G.Boycott 102). *Match drawn*
**Bradford**, May 6, 8, 9: Yorkshire 40 (J.N.Graham 6-14) & 13-2, Kent 94-4dec. *Match drawn*
**Hull**, May 10, 11, 12: Worcestershire 187 & 74 (R.Illingworth 6-34), Yorkshire 225 & 37-5. *Won by five wickets*
**Headingley**, May 17, 18, 19: Yorkshire v Leicestershire. *Match abandoned*
**Bradford**, May 20, 22, 23: Nottinghamshire 159-5dec & 52-0dec, Yorkshire 62-3dec & 150-5. *Won by five wickets*
**Old Trafford**, May 27, 29, 30: Lancashire v Yorkshire. *Match abandoned*
**Kidderminster**, May 31, June 1, 2: Worcestershire 119 & 197, Yorkshire 318-4dec (K.Taylor 162). *Won by an innings and 2 runs*

**Lord's**, June 3, 5, 6: Middlesex 367-7dec (P.H.Parfitt 134), Yorkshire 163 (F.J.Titmus 7-64) & 146. *Lost by an innings and 58 runs*

**Bath**, June 7, 8, 9: Somerset 273 & 148-9dec (D.Wilson 7-50), Yorkshire 124 (B.A.Langford 5-14) & 217. *Lost by 80 runs*

**Swansea**, June 10, 12, 13: Glamorgan 141 & 273, Yorkshire 389 (I.J.Jones 5-76) & 27-0. *Won by ten wickets*

**Bristol**, June 17, 19, 20: Gloucestershire 356-8dec (D.Shepherd 123) & 63-1dec, Yorkshire 227-7dec & 193-1. *Won by nine wickets*

**Sheffield**, June 21, 22, 23: Northamptonshire 173 & 99, Yorkshire 388-5dec (G.Boycott 220*). *Won by an innings and 116 runs*

**Headingley**, June 24, 26, 27: Yorkshire 300 (R.D.Jackman 7-98), Surrey 118 & 90 (G.A.Cope 5-23). *Won by an innings and 92 runs*

**Leicester**, July 5, 6: Leicestershire 161 (R.Illingworth 6-52) & 96 (R.Illingworth 5-27), Yorkshire 380. *Won by an innings and 123 runs*

**Chesterfield**, July 8, 10, 11: Derbyshire 346-7dec & 125-5, Yorkshire 310 (H.J.Rhodes 5-57). *Match drawn*

**Sheffield**, July 12, 13, 14: Middlesex 261, Yorkshire 354 (D.E.V.Padgett 111, R.Herman 5-99). *Match drawn*

**The Oval**, July 22, 24, 25: Surrey 395-8dec (K.F.Barrington 158*), Yorkshire 178 (K.F.Barrington 5-51) & 209 (P.I.Pocock 7-73). *Lost by an innings and eight runs*

**Bradford**, July 26, 27, 28: Yorkshire 182 (W.E.Alley 6-63) & 156-6dec, Somerset 110 (A.G.Nicholson 6-34) & 126-3. *Match drawn*

**Bournemouth**, July 29, 31, August 1: Yorkshire 179 (D.White 6-32) & 39-4dec, Hampshire 90-5dec & 129-4. *Lost by four wickets*

**Sheffield**, August 5, 7, 8: Lancashire 183 (G.Pullar 104) & 206-6dec, Yorkshire 207 (J.B.Statham 5-82) & 75-4. *Match drawn*

**Canterbury**, August 9, 10, 11: Kent 223 & 100 (A.G.Nicholson 5-37), Yorkshire 225 (A.L.Dixon 7-93) & 99-3. *Won by seven wickets*

**Bradford**, August 12, 14, 15: Yorkshire 144-4dec, Derbyshire 117 (A.G.Nicholson 5-24). *Match drawn*

**Edgbaston**, August 16, 17, 18: Yorkshire 238 (J.H.Hampshire 102) & 145, Warwickshire 242 (A.G.Nicholson 6-50) & 133-5. *Match drawn*

**Scarborough**, August 19, 21, 22: Essex 87 & 245 (A.G.Nicholson 5-30), Yorkshire 214 & 109 (D.L.Acfield 5-32). *Lost by 9 runs*

**Eastbourne**, August 23, 24, 25: Yorkshire 210 (M.A.Buss 5-54) & 281-9dec, Sussex 142 (A.G.Nicholson 9-62) & 266. *Won by 83 runs*

**Trent Bridge**, August 26, 28, 29: Yorkshire 332 (D.E.V.Padgett 139) & 135-5dec, Nottinghamshire 197-7dec & 217-6. *Match drawn*
**Middlesbrough**, August 30, 31, September 1: Yorkshire 250 (T.W.Cartwright 6-95) & 197-5dec, Warwickshire 148 (D.Wilson 6-31) & 70 (D.Wilson 7-21). *Won by 229 runs*
**Harrogate**, September 6, 7: Yorkshire 309, Gloucestershire 134 (R.Illingworth 7-58) & 99 (R.Illingworth 7-6). *Won by an innings and 76 runs*

## NOTES and HIGHLIGHTS

That Yorkshire got off to a slow start was mainly due to the weather. Of the six games played in May two were won (including one with three declarations), two were drawn and two were abandoned without a single ball being bowled. Five consecutive convincing wins, including three in a row by an innings, took the county to the top of the table, however, and they were always in the hunt thereafter. Only two points (for first innings lead) were required to win the title when the final game began. Illingworth's bowling was the main factor in this being achieved but he then went on to win the game with second innings figures of 13-9-6-7 resulting in a match analysis of 14-64.

A controversial blot on the campaign was provided by events in the closing overs in the match against Warwickshire at Edgbaston. Close's time-wasting tactics ensured a draw, to Yorkshire's point-gaining advantage, but his exploits lost him the England captaincy. He made his point with an innings of 98 in the return match at Middlesbrough as the home side won by 229 runs but the whole episode damaged the county's image considerably.

The batting was more consistent than in the previous season with Padgett scoring his first century for three years and Close (585 runs at 34.41) and Illingworth (537, 29.83) also contributing well. Boycott was in fourth place in the national averages.

The attack was led by the same four bowlers as in 1966 with Nicholson having the best figures of his career against Sussex at Eastbourne, this being the best analysis for the whole season. He took five wickets in an innings in five consecutive matches in August, including in three innings in succession and his combined figures for these games produced 36 wickets at 10.14. One of the support bowlers was Cope and so well did he take his opportunities that his 32 wickets at 12.78 placed him in second position in the national averages.

No player appeared in every game, the most being 26 by Binks.

## PLAYER of the SEASON

*Tony Nicholson, who helped Yorkshire win four of the 1960s titles with his accurate fast-medium bowling.*

In topping Yorkshire's bowling averages and aggregate of wickets, as well as achieving a career-best performance, Tony Nicholson was continuing to show that he was one of the best seam and swing bowlers in the country during the latter part of this decade. The only regular member of Close's team not to gain a Test cap, he came relatively late into the game, making his debut in 1962, having been born in Dewsbury in 1938. He soon impressed with his work ethic and acted as an ideal foil for Trueman, being the best of his many partners. Although he bowled at a pace below fast-medium he operated with so much control and variety that he took wickets at a very economical rate.

Nicholson's best season – 1966 – brought him 115 wickets at 15.50 and his full county career eventually brought him 876 wickets at an average just below twenty. The closest he came to international honours was in 1964 when he was selected for the winter's tour to South Africa but had to withdraw owing to injury. He would retire in 1975 but die only ten years later. He left his reputation as being one of the most important members of the great 1960s side completely intact.

Further changes to the points system meant that from 1968 ten points were to be awarded for a win with bonuses for runs scored and wickets taken applying in the first 85 overs of the first innings.

## 1968

## TOP FIVE COUNTIES

|  | Pld | W | L | D | Pts |
|---|---|---|---|---|---|
| Yorkshire | 28 | 11 | 4 | 13 | 270 |
| Kent | 28 | 12 | 5 | 11 | 256 |
| Glamorgan | 28 | 11 | 6 | 11 | 237 |
| Nottinghamshire | 28 | 7 | 3 | 18 | 222 |
| Hampshire | 28 | 8 | 5 | 15 | 215 |

# LEADING YORKSHIRE AVERAGES

## BATTING

|  | M | I | NO | Runs | HS | Avge | 100 | 50 |
|---|---|---|---|---|---|---|---|---|
| G.Boycott | 10 | 15 | 5 | 774 | 180* | 77.40 | 5 | 1 |
| P.J.Sharpe | 26 | 42 | 8 | 1102 | 143* | 32.41 | 3 | 3 |
| J.H.Hampshire | 28 | 39 | 5 | 952 | 100 | 28.00 | 1 | 6 |
| D.E.V.Padgett | 28 | 39 | 2 | 984 | 136* | 26.59 | 2 | 5 |

## BOWLING

|  | O | M | R | W | Avge | 5WI | 10WM | BB |
|---|---|---|---|---|---|---|---|---|
| D.Wilson | 719.4 | 299 | 1275 | 102 | 12.50 | 3 | 2 | 7-36 |
| R.Illingworth | 585.5 | 208 | 1178 | 86 | 13.69 | 4 | 2 | 6-42 |
| A.G.Nicholson | 614 | 211 | 1269 | 79 | 16.06 | 4 | 1 | 8-22 |

## FIELDING and WICKET-KEEPING

60 (47 ct, 13 st) J.G.Binks
29 D.B.Close
27 J.H.Hampshire
23 P.J.Sharpe
21 D.Wilson

# RESULTS

**Harrogate**, May 4, 6, 7: Hampshire 122, Yorkshire 41-2. *Match drawn*
**Taunton**, May 8, 9, 10: Somerset 67-3dec & 107-4dec, Yorkshire 0-0dec & 2-0. *Match drawn*
**Bradford**, May 11, 13, 14: Yorkshire 242-5dec (G.Boycott 100), Sussex 96-7. *Match drawn*
**Leicester**, May 15, 16, 17: Leicestershire 128 (D.Wilson 7-50) & 146, Yorkshire 288-8dec (G.Boycott 132, P.Marner 6-84). *Won by an innings and 14 runs*
**Headingley**, May 18, 20, 21: Yorkshire 119 & 238 (R.White 5-71), Nottinghamshire 203-7dec & 17-2. *Match drawn*

**Middlesbrough**, May 22, 23, 24: Warwickshire 129 & 137 (R.Illingworth 6-44), Yorkshire 308-4dec (G.Boycott 180*). *Won by an innings and 42 runs*
**Bristol**, May 29, 30, 31: Gloucestershire 163 & 238, Yorkshire 266 (G.Boycott 125) & 93-9 (M.J.Procter 5-24). *Match drawn*
**Headingley**, June 1, 3, 4: Lancashire 176 (F.S.Trueman 5-45) & 116, Yorkshire 348 (D.E.V.Padgett 105). *Won by an innings and 56 runs*
**Edgbaston**, June 8, 10, 11: Warwickshire 273-9dec (R.B.Kanhai 111) & 158-1dec (W.J.Stewart 101*), Yorkshire 125-9dec (T.W.Cartwright 7-36) & 141. *Lost by 165 runs*
**Sheffield**, June 15, 17, 18: Yorkshire 297 (G.Boycott 114*, B.R.Knight 8-82) & 228-5dec (R.Illingworth 100*), Leicestershire 239 & 143 (F.S.Trueman 6-20). *Won by 143 runs*
**Headingley**, June 19, 20: Yorkshire 358-7dec (D.E.V.Padgett 136*), Middlesex 59 (R.Illingworth 5-26) & 143 (D.Wilson 7-36). *Won by an innings and 156 runs*
**Northampton**, June 22, 23, 24: Yorkshire 293-9dec, Northamptonshire 133-4. *Match drawn*
**Bradford**, June 26, 27, 28: Yorkshire 219 (J.B.Mortimore 5-30) & 1-0, Gloucestershire 143. *Match drawn*
**Sheffield**, July 6, 8, 9: Glamorgan 244 (R.Illingworth 6-81) & 55-5dec, Yorkshire 95-5dec & 101 (D.J.Shepherd 6-40). *Lost by 103 runs*
**Bradford**, July 10, 11, 12: Yorkshire 276 & 116-3dec, Kent 151-9dec & 83-4. *Match drawn*
**Cardiff**, July 13, 15, 16: Glamorgan 144 (G.A.Cope 7-42) & 146 (G.A.Cope 5-74), Yorkshire 254 (P.J.Sharpe 114) & 37-0. *Won by ten wickets*
**Sheffield**, July 17, 18, 19: Worcestershire 99 (R.Illingworth 6-42) & 105, Yorkshire 79 (N.Gifford 8-28) & 126-6. *Won by four wickets*
**The Oval**, July 20, 21, 22: Yorkshire 320 (P.J.Sharpe 125), Surrey 105 & 183. *Won by an innings and 32 runs*
**Westcliff-on-Sea**, July 24, 25, 26: Yorkshire 103 (K.D.Boyce 6-56) & 161 (K.D.Boyce 5-69), Essex 168 (A.G.Nicholson 5-59) & 99-5. *Lost by five wickets*
**Trent Bridge**, July 27, 28, 29: Nottinghamshire 238 & 182 (A.G.Nicholson 6-49), Yorkshire 245-6dec (P.J.Sharpe 143*) & 73-4. *Match drawn*
**Canterbury**, July 31, August 1, 2: Kent 81 (A.G.Nicholson 8-22) & 136-5dec, Yorkshire 93-9dec & 2-0. *Match drawn*
**Old Trafford**, August 3, 4, 5: Lancashire 162 (R.A.Hutton 5-53) & 151,

Yorkshire 61 (J.B.Statham 6-34) & 189-5. *Match drawn*
**Lord's**, August 10, 11, 12: Yorkshire 230 & 97-2dec, Middlesex 110 (D.Wilson 5-17) & 100. *Won by 117 runs*
**Scarborough**, August 14, 15, 16: Somerset 214 (R.A.Hutton 6-56) & 78, Yorkshire 321 (G.Burgess 5-74). *Won by an innings and 29 runs*
**Bradford**, August 17, 19, 20: Derbyshire 285-9dec, Yorkshire 1-0. *Match drawn*
**Worcester**, August 21, 22, 23: Worcestershire 101 & 163, Yorkshire 126 (B.M.Brain 5-37) & 137. *Lost by 1 run*
**Chesterfield**, August 24, 25, 26: Yorkshire 250-9dec (J.H.Hampshire 100) & 138-8dec, Derbyshire 137 (A.G.Nicholson 5-40) & 156-8. *Match drawn*
**Hull**, August 28, 29, 30: Yorkshire 327-9dec (R.D.Jackman 5-65) & 112-7dec (R.D.Jackman 6-58), Surrey 189 & 190 (D.Wilson 5-61).

## NOTES and HIGHLIGHTS

In what was the third-worst summer – weather-wise – of the entire century, more than half (123 games) of the complete programme of matches (238) ended in draws or were completely abandoned. A particularly wet May saw Yorkshire win two and draw five of the seven games scheduled. That other counties were suffering even more is shown by the fact that one more win – over Lancashire at the beginning of June – took the White Rose county to the top of the table. Not only that, by June 20th the lead had stretched to 32 points!

Inconsistency over the latter half of the season, however, meant that Yorkshire needed to win the final game of the campaign to clinch the title. At 186-7 with 40 minutes remaining, it looked as though Surrey might deny them but three wickets fell in two overs and Yorkshire had completed a hat-trick of Championships for the first time since 1946. Close had become the fourth Yorkshire skipper to achieve the feat, following in the footsteps of Lord Hawke, Geoffrey Wilson and Brian Sellers.

The disappointing month of May concluded with a nail-biting finish at Bristol. Thanks to Boycott's century the visitors gained a first innings lead of 103 and Gloucestershire's 238 set Yorkshire a target of only 136 for victory. This soon became a mountain as Mike Procter took the first four wickets and, with the score on 43-7, defeat was looming. However Illingworth (45 not out) steadied the ship and stumps were drawn with the visitors clinging on with the last pair at the crease.

One of many low-scoring matches produced a similar finale at Worcester but without the same result. This time Yorkshire's lead was 25 and the final target was 139. Although Hampshire and Binks both passed 30 no one could play the match-winning innings and despite a last wicket stand of 14, the visitors fell just two tantalising runs short of the target to leave Worcestershire the winners by one run.

Boycott came top of the national averages, a feat he was to achieve on a total of four occasions. He was approaching the peak of his youthful powers and, in scoring a century every three innings, showed outstanding form. The bowling averages were dominated by Yorkshire's spinners more than at any time since the 1920s. Cope (20 wickets at 10.55) came top with Wilson and Illingworth third and sixth, respectively. Binks, Hampshire and Padgett all played throughout the campaign.

The success of Cope (whose tally included figures of 12-116 against Glamorgan at Cardiff) was one of the factors that led to the unfortunate release of Illingworth. This decision would have far-reaching consequences for both county and player and, as if this were not enough, both Taylor and Trueman announced their retirements at the end of the season. In his 16-year career Taylor had often given the county a lively start to its innings and his tally of over 12,000 runs had been made with fluency and style. He will best be remembered, however, for being a brilliant fielder in the covers.

The loss of these three players signified the start of the break-up of the great 1960s side and it would be seen in due course as the clearly-defined end of an era.

# PLAYER of the SEASON

The leading run aggregate for the 1968 season was that of a utility batsman who had the ability to bat in any position. Phil Sharpe will, however, be best remembered for being the most brilliant English slip fielder of his generation. Born in Shipley in 1936 he was an outstanding all-round sportsman at Worksop College and made his county debut in 1958. It took him time to establish himself in the Yorkshire side but in 1962 he produced his best season both in terms of runs – 2252 – and catches – seventy, equalling the White Rose county's record. He was unlucky not to be chosen for the MCC tour of Australia but collected the first of his 12 Test caps in the following summer. Although never an England regular, his batting average of 46.23 showed that he was able to succeed at the highest level.

Despite his short and stocky build, his stillness and concentration meant that he was able to react in an agile manner whenever a chance came his way. He had the ability to delay the catch until the last possible moment and his 525 victims for Yorkshire were taken off the bowling of a great variety of practitioners. His 17,685 runs were made at an average of fewer than thirty and he duly left the county at the end of 1974 before enjoying two seasons with Derbyshire.

Sharpe has continued to give service to the county club as a member of various committees but those who were fortunate to watch him snaffle the most difficult of slip catches with the greatest of ease saw a true genius at work.

# Doldrums, Divisions, Disputes and Disillusion

*Geoff Boycott, who led Yorkshire for eight trophy-less seasons in the 1970s and was at the centre of the troubles in the early 1980s.*

# 1969-2000

# Doldrums, Divisions, Disputes and Disillusion

Having won 29 of the first 69 official County Championships, Yorkshire then proceeded to win precisely none of the next 32! Even more mystifying to the innocent observer is the fact that 19 of these campaigns concluded with the county in the bottom half of the table. The bare facts follow.

| | Champion County | Yorkshire's Position |
|---|---|---|
| 1969 | Glamorgan | 12th |
| 1970 | Kent | 4th |
| 1971 | Surrey | 13th |
| 1972 | Warwickshire | 10th |
| 1973 | Hampshire | 14th |
| 1974 | Worcestershire | 11th |
| 1975 | Leicestershire | 2nd |
| 1976 | Middlesex | 8th |
| 1977 | Kent and Middlesex | 12th |
| 1978 | Kent | 4th |
| 1979 | Essex | 7th |
| 1980 | Middlesex | 6th |
| 1981 | Nottinghamshire | 10th |
| 1982 | Middlesex | 10th |
| 1983 | Essex | 17th |
| 1984 | Essex | 14th |
| 1985 | Middlesex | 11th |
| 1986 | Essex | 10th |
| 1987 | Nottinghamshire | 8th |
| 1988 | Worcestershire | 13th |
| 1989 | Worcestershire | 16th |
| 1990 | Middlesex | 10th |
| 1991 | Essex | 14th |
| 1992 | Essex | 16th |
| 1993 | Middlesex | 12th |
| 1994 | Warwickshire | 13th |
| 1995 | Warwickshire | 8th |
| 1996 | Leicestershire | 6th |
| 1997 | Glamorgan | 6th |
| 1998 | Leicestershire | 3rd |
| 1999 | Surrey | 6th |
| 2000 | Surrey | 3rd |

The reasons for this barren period are not simple, nor are they confined to one single factor. As has already been mentioned, 1968 concluded with the departure of three significant players. The following year was the last for Binks and, after the 1970 season, Close was sacked, with Padgett retiring at the end of 1971. The sacking of Close was as badly handled as had been the departure of Illingworth. Given ten minutes to resign or face the consequences, Close chose the latter and, just as his lieutenant was to do with Leicestershire, gave new life to a previously unsuccessful county. Somerset was his destination and, although silverware was not forthcoming during his six-year tenure of the captaincy he laid the foundations of their subsequent period of five first-ever trophies in five seasons.

So a young side was placed under the wing of Boycott, who succeeded to the captaincy over the heads of the more senior Sharpe and Wilson. His immediate response was to become the third batsman to average over 100 in a Championship season but, more significantly, to lead the team to a fall of nine places in the table. In more than one way that combination of personal success and team failure epitomised the eight years for which Boycott was in charge. He was accused of batting selfishly but saw himself as being the only quality batsman in the team – the one who must succeed if the team were to threaten for honours. One of the consequences was that he often appeared to bat slowly, not wanting to give his wicket away, and this left the side with not enough time to bowl out the opposition.

However, the 1975 season – Boycott's fourth in charge - was extremely promising. Hutton, Sharpe and Wilson had all departed at the end of 1974 and so all the players who were current internationals in the 1960s title-winning sides had gone, excepting Boycott. The most successful bowlers, unexpectedly, were Phil Carrick, a left-arm spinner, and Cope, who between them took 47% of the county's wickets in that season.

Another important factor in this solitary campaign of relative success (runners-up spot) was the fact that the World Cup was taking place in England and several counties were deprived of the services of their overseas stars. Although foreign-based players had often been a feature of English cricket in the past the authorities decided to lift registration restrictions from 1968 and the result was a vigorous infiltration of Test stars seeking off-season employment. Many counties were not content with a token single signing and when Warwickshire won the title in 1972 their team contained no fewer than four West Indian stars in Lance Gibbs, Rohan Kanhai, Alvin Kallicharran and Deryck Murray.

Although around thirty non-Yorkshire-born players have represented the county, including, most famously, Lord Hawke, the official policy was not to accept such players. With the comprehensive influx of quality overseas cricketers now taking place Yorkshire could not really be expected to compete on an equal footing. However the White Rose county's characteristics of single-mindedness and stubbornness ensured that the team continued to compete with a metaphorical hand tied behind its back.

Eventually it was realised that the involvement of so many overseas players in the Championship was restricting the opportunities and holding back the development of England's own players. This resulted, from 1982, in a restriction of one foreign player per county. However it was a further ten years before Yorkshire bowed to the inevitable and, in 1992, Sachin Tendulkar, a young Indian destined to become the world's best batsman, became the county's first official overseas player. Not only that, the Yorkshire committee decided to welcome cricketers born in other counties and the prime benefactor of this complete about-turn was an elegant Manchester-born batsman named Michael Vaughan.

Meanwhile, despite the near-success of 1975, it was gradually being realised that Boycott's lack of man-management skills was doing more harm than good. After eight trophy-less seasons (a Yorkshire record for one captain) he was sacked – tactlessly between the death and funeral of his mother. Boycott, to his great credit, and unlike Illingworth and Close, remained with the county and responded immediately as only he could, by yet again averaging over 100 in a season.

The new skipper was Hampshire and he endured a miserable time staying the course for only two years before moving on to Derbyshire. The main problem seemed to be that Boycott had a huge personal following amongst the Yorkshire public and there was much bitterness at his losing the leadership and the way in which it had been handled. To add insult to injury Illingworth had come back from Leicestershire to become Yorkshire's first-ever manager. This was a post that other counties had been introducing, with some success, and the White Rose county was following suit.

Illingworth had been a great captain for England and his adopted county but the managerial role did not suit him, this being proved again much later with England. He clashed publicly with Boycott but his dictatorial approach encouraged him to take over the captaincy during the 1982 season from Old, who had drunk from the poisoned chalice from the beginning of 1981. Old left for Warwickshire and Illingworth led Yorkshire to the very bottom of the table, in 1983, for the only time in the White Rose county's entire history.

This was also the period during which the divisions that almost brought the county to breaking point were at their worst. A 'Reform Group' had been formed to support Boycott at the end of the 1970s but this was small fry compared with the vehemence with which the administration was attacked at the 1984 AGM. The Committee had attempted to pacify both sides of the conflict by not renewing Boycott's contract but yet at the same time giving him a testimonial. Far from being seen as a compromise solution the idea was viewed as smacking of double standards and both the General Committee and Cricket Committee were ousted. Boycott's supporters were triumphantly installed, Illingworth was sacked and the captaincy passed to David Bairstow, an enthusiastic and popular wicket-keeper-batsman.

All the while, a variety of counties was benefiting at Yorkshire's expense. As previously mentioned, Leicestershire won the Championship for the first time and Essex was another new name added to the list - in 1979. By now there were even more one-day trophies for which to compete: the Sunday League had been added to the schedule in 1969 and the Benson & Hedges Cup three years later. The latter began as a tournament based on a 55-overs per side format that combined both league and knock-out concepts. The former was a competition in which each county played each of the others once per season in a 40-over single innings match. It soon became derided as a form of the game which compromised techniques but was popular with crowds who seemed to appreciate watching a form of cricket meant for amateurs and which could be seen every week-end anyway.

*Skipper Phil Carrick poses with the Benson & Hedges Cup at Scarborough on July 12th, 1987. The trophy had been won at Lord's on the previous day with a narrow victory over Northamptonshire.*

Yorkshire had some success in some of these competitions. The 1965 Gillette Cup victory was repeated in 1969 but the 1970s was the county's first trophy-less decade since the Championship's inauguration. 1983 brought victory in the Sunday League (the same season as Yorkshire were bottom of the Championship) and 1987 saw an ecstatic Phil Carrick (in his first season as captain) lift the Benson and Hedges Cup at Lord's. However, although the in-fighting settled down (Boycott left quietly at the end of 1986) these were false dawns and the 1990s was another decade without any of the four competitions being won.

The pace of change hardly abated throughout this period. In 1969 the Championship programme was reduced to 24 games per team and to 20 three years later, both decisions resulting from the introduction of one-day competitions. There was an increase to 22 in 1977 and back again to 24 six years later. The authorities, all the while, were concerned with England's reduced standing amongst the Test-playing nations and were rightly anxious to confirm the Championship as the bedrock of the county game and the type of cricket which needed to be learnt in order to produce Test cricketers.

The crowds did not support this view, however, and the one-day tournaments remained. From 1988, therefore, four-day Championship cricket was introduced and each county would play six of its (now) 22 games over the longer period. The fact that these games were scheduled for the start and end of the season, when pitches and weather conditions were at their worst, meant that batsmen still did not have the opportunity to learn how to build a long innings – one of the advantages of four-day cricket.

This mixture lasted for five seasons and from 1993, a year after Durham had brought the total of counties up to 18, each county played 17 four-day games, one against every other county and this made for the first-ever equal league system, 103 years on from the Championship's instigation. All of this, along with the much-earlier decision to abandon uncovered pitches, was instigated for the supposed benefit of the national side. The decision to keep pitches covered still rankles with many old-stagers who, probably correctly, believe that batting on drying pitches was a true test and good training of a batsman's technique and temperament. However the practice had been abandoned in Test cricket and the first-class game was bringing itself in line.

It may be noted from the table at the start of this chapter that Yorkshire, since 1994, has not finished below eighth in the Championship. The single most important factor in this change was the arrival of the county's first overseas player to make a significant contribution. At the start of 1995 Michael Bevan was a promising batsman, certainly a typical confident young Australian, but by the end of the decade he had become the best one-day batsman in the world.

*Michael Bevan batting for Yorkshire in 1995 in a Sunday League match. The Australian batsman was the catalyst for the county's improved performances in the latter part of the 1990s.*

He seemed to imbue the Yorkshire side with that extra flair, panache and spirit which it had been lacking for so long. He was used to his state (New South Wales) winning trophies and wanted Yorkshire to do the same. Their new captain (from 1990) Martyn Moxon was an excellent cricketer from a technical point of view both as an opening batsman of quality pedigree and one who understood the game overall. The coaching set-up was a different matter, though, and had been concerning the membership, at the very least, for some time.

The one man involved more than anyone else with coaching at Yorkshire CCC over the last thirty years of the twentieth century was Padgett; he had been joined on the staff by Steve Oldham in 1984. Oldham had played for Yorkshire in the 1970s before moving on to Derbyshire but was only given his cap on his return in a move which astonished many of the players.

Bevan, like many members, saw Padgett and Oldham as having the necessary qualities to spot talent and develop young players but not to turn them into winners. There had been several instances of very talented and promising players such as batsmen Bill Athey, Jim Love and Kevin Sharp neither fulfilling their potential nor helping to bring the county the much-desired Championship.

However a meeting between this 24-year-old Australian and suitable members of the hierarchy set the wheels in motion to appoint a coach of international standing with a proven track record of winning trophies. That was easier said than done and such a person could not be found with immediate effect. Moxon, in the Yorkshire tradition of keeping its own, was appointed Director of Coaching on giving up the captaincy but when he left early in 2001 he had held a senior position with the county for eleven years during which Yorkshire had won precisely nothing. Six out of seven semi-final appearances in seven years from 1995 were lost and the one that was won led to a Lord's humiliation against Gloucestershire in the Benson and Hedges Cup final of 1999. The West country team scored faster than any other side in the 69 finals to date and the White Rose county, even on Yorkshire Day, had no answer.

Another factor in Yorkshire's improvement over the latter part of the 1990s was the establishment of the county's own Academy. This was the brainchild of Bob Appleyard, started in 1991, and usually a total of 15 players are now on two-year contracts, the main purpose being to prepare them for life as a first-class Yorkshire cricketer. Inevitably some do not make the grade but are helped to find a life outside the game, some end up with other counties, but graduates now include England internationals in Darren Gough, Vaughan and Mathew Hoggard. In terms of providing material to take Yorkshire to the title, it has certainly succeeded and it will no doubt continue to provide a production line of future stars.

So 1995 – Bevan's first season - may be seen as a turning point and every season since that year promised much – usually until around the beginning of August. It became typical during this period that Yorkshire would be in the running to win at least one of the four competitions on offer well into the season but to usually fail almost at the last gasp. The 2000 season sustained interest better than its predecessors in that Yorkshire finished runners-up in the National League (the 45-overs successor to the Sunday League) and came third in the Championship. The latter position was a bone of contention as it would have been second place had not Yorkshire been fined eight points for a 'poor pitch' at Scarborough for the vital game against Surrey, the eventual champions. This decision, by one of a group of inspectors whose visits were organised on a random basis, cost the Club £50,000 in prize money.

Yes, prize money, yet another innovation, because it seemed quite impossible by even the 1970s to organise a competition without a sponsor and monetary reward. By the end of the century the County Championship had been sponsored by Schweppes (1977-1983), Britannic Assurance (1984-1998) and PPP Healthcare (1999-2000). For the 2001 competition it would be in the convenient hands of Cricinfo, the internet cricket service.

Another revolutionary departure came in the year 2000 when the counties involved in the Championship were split, according to their final 1999 positions, into two divisions. Each team would play the other eight teams in the same division twice, on a home and away basis, and there would be promotion and relegation (three teams each way) between the two divisions. This also applied for the following season.

The points system for 2001, after many changes in the intervening period, would award twelve for a win and four for a draw. Bonus points would be awarded in the first 130 overs of the first innings for up to 400 runs and/or nine wickets. The fact that five points were available for batting and three for bowling was meant to encourage counties to prepare quality pitches. Another on-going concern was over-rates and this was reflected in a new method of deducing points for dilatoriness over this.

# Pride Restored

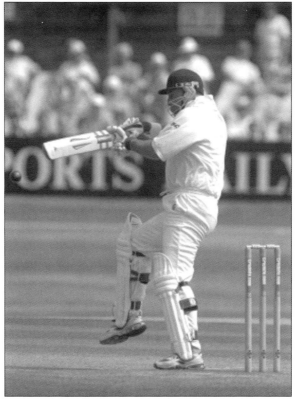

*Darren Lehmann in action during the 2001 season, when he topped the Division 1 averages with 1416 runs at 83.29. The Australian was appointed captain for 2002. Photo courtesy: Liz Sutcliffe (Yorkshire CCC)*

# 2001

# Pride Restored

## FIRST DIVISION FINAL TABLE

|  | Pld | W | L | D | Btt | Bwl | Pts |
|---|---|---|---|---|---|---|---|
| Yorkshire | 16 | 9 | 3 | 4 | 50 | 45 | 219.0 |
| Somerset | 16 | 6 | 2 | 8 | 55 | 44 | 203.0 |
| Kent | 16 | 4 | 3 | 9 | 48 | 44 | 176.0 |
| Surrey | 16 | 3 | 1 | 11 | 43 | 43 | 169.5 |
| Leicestershire | 16 | 5 | 6 | 5 | 38 | 47 | 165.0 |
| Lancashire | 16 | 4 | 5 | 5 | 38 | 39 | 153.0 |
| Northamptonshire | 16 | 2 | 5 | 9 | 52 | 36 | 148.0 |
| Glamorgan | 16 | 2 | 5 | 8 | 36 | 37 | 133.0 |
| Essex | 16 | 2 | 7 | 7 | 28 | 36 | 116.0 |

Yorkshire's victory was much more comprehensive than the 16-point margin suggests. Two of the county's three defeats were in their last two games when the destiny of the title had already been decided. Before these last two matches, at the point at which the Championship was won, Yorkshire had a massive 51-point lead and had won more than twice as many games as anyone else.

## LEADING YORKSHIRE AVERAGES

### BATTING

|  | M | I | NO | Runs | HS | Avge | 100 | 50 |
|---|---|---|---|---|---|---|---|---|
| D.S.Lehmann | 13 | 19 | 2 | 1416 | 252 | 83.29 | 5 | 5 |
| M.P.Vaughan | 7 | 13 | 0 | 673 | 133 | 51.76 | 2 | 4 |
| M.J.Wood | 14 | 23 | 1 | 1060 | 124 | 48.18 | 4 | 6 |
| D.Byas | 16 | 24 | 5 | 853 | 110* | 44.89 | 4 | 2 |
| C.White | 9 | 15 | 1 | 567 | 186 | 40.50 | 2 | - |
| A.McGrath | 9 | 15 | 2 | 417 | 116* | 32.07 | 1 | 2 |
| G.M.Fellows | 12 | 17 | 1 | 455 | 63 | 28.43 | - | 3 |
| R.J.Blakey | 15 | 21 | 6 | 405 | 78* | 27.00 | - | 3 |

The batsmen were the main successes behind the Championship victory. They scored big totals, quickly, so that the bowlers had enough runs in hand and time in which to demolish the opposition. Darren Lehmann scored almost 20% of Yorkshire's total number of runs made by batsmen throughout the campaign. He topped the Division 1 averages with a figure that was the best for Yorkshire since 1979 (Boycott, 116.00). However, the county did not always need to rely on him. In seven matches the first innings score was over 400 (thus gaining maximum bonus points) and on three of these occasions Lehmann's scores were 7, 26 and 1. On the only occasion he was absent before the title was claimed, his team-mates scored 374 and the match ended in victory. The total number of centuries (19) was the highest for Yorkshire since 1952.

## BOWLING

|  | O | M | R | W | Avge | 5WI | 10WM | BB |
|---|---|---|---|---|---|---|---|---|
| C.E.W.Silverwood | 209.1 | 42 | 644 | 33 | 19.51 | 3 | - | 5-20 |
| S.P.Kirby | 280.3 | 60 | 980 | 47 | 20.85 | 3 | 1 | 7-50 |
| M.J.Hoggard | 192 | 50 | 561 | 26 | 21.57 | 2 | - | 6-51 |
| R.J.Sidebottom | 258.2 | 73 | 646 | 27 | 23.92 | - | - | 4-49 |
| G.M.Hamilton | 211.2 | 43 | 672 | 26 | 25.84 | 1 | - | 5-27 |
| R.K.J.Dawson | 315.5 | 69 | 1014 | 30 | 33.80 | 2 | - | 6-82 |

Chris Silverwood (3rd), Steve Kirby (4th) and Matthew Hoggard (6th) all came in the top ten of the Division 1 averages. The bowlers all worked as part of a team and in the eleven matches where 20 wickets were taken the workload and successes were both shared out.

## FIELDING and WICKET-KEEPING

54 (49 ct, 5 st) R.J.Blakey
38 D Byas
10 M.J.Wood

David Byas held some magnificent catches at first slip and was the country's leading fielder by some distance, taking ten catches more than his nearest rival. His total of 38 was the best for Yorkshire by a fielder for six years.

# RESULTS

**Canterbury**, April 25, 26, 27, 28: Kent 142 (C.E.W.Silverwood 5-45) & 318 (E.T.Smith 103*), Yorkshire 285 & 176-6. *Won by four wickets*

The foundation of victory was laid on the first day when Chris Silverwood took his first five-for since the end of the 1999 season. Vaughan (71) and Lehmann (68) both scored freely in the visitors' first innings but Yorkshire were held up in their victory quest by Robert Key (98) and then Ed Smith, who manipulated the tail skillfully. Kent's seventh wicket fell with the score on 204 but a further 114 runs were added before the tenth wicket fell. Yorkshire's victory target was 176 in 38 overs and was accomplished in pulsating fashion with just two balls to spare. A rapid 41 from Lehmann set them on their way and Gary Fellows (43 not out) saw them home.

**Headingley**, May 9, 10, 11, 12: Somerset 257 & 327-8dec, Yorkshire 231 (A.R.Caddick 5-81) & 192 (A.R.Caddick 5-92). *Lost by 169 runs*

With both Gough and Andy Caddick having completed their period of rest after the end of the winter tours the outcome of the game hinged on the very different performances displayed by the pair. Gough's match analysis of 3-114 paled besides Caddick's 10-173 and he was undeniably the match-winner. Vaughan (79) received very little support in the first innings although Fellows achieved a career-best 63. It was a similar story second time around - despite Lehmann's 77 the last five wickets fell for 45 runs and the game finished after 90 minutes of the last day. Somerset's second innings was built around a second wicket partnership of 102 between Piran Holloway (85) and Jamie Cox (80). Vaughan's 4-47 was the best analysis for the home side.

**Chelmsford**, May 16, 17, 18, 19: Yorkshire 403-9dec, Essex 249. *Match drawn*

With the first two days lost to rain there was very little chance of a result and the acquisition of bonus points became the main aim. At 238-7 the visitors were a long way short of the 400 required but an eighth-wicket stand of 126 between James Middlebrook (84) and Silverwood (70) brought the total much closer. Stuart Law's wicket was going to be vital and when he fell for 53 Yorkshire always had a good chance of bowling Essex out. That they did so was a team effort, three wickets each falling to Fellows and Middlebrook.

**Headingley**, May 25, 26, 27: Yorkshire 374 (M.P.Vaughan 133, D.M.Cousins 8-102) & 77-6, Northamptonshire 195 (C.E.W.Silverwood 5-58) & 255 (M.J.Hoggard 5-82). *Won by four wickets*

Yorkshire's second win of the season took them to the top of the table – a position which they would never reliquish. The tone was set on the first day when Vaughan responded to the visitors winning the toss with an elegant century and a 143 second-wicket stand with Matthew Wood. Silverwood's hostility ensured that, despite Russell Warren's 65, Northamptonshire would follow on and Matthew Hoggard made certain that Yorkshire's target would be minimal. 43-4 was not the ideal platform, however, but David Byas (26 not out) and 27 extras steered Yorkshire to victory and a seven-point gap over Surrey.

**Swansea**, May 30, 31, June 1: Yorkshire 280 (A.G.Wharf 5-63) & 277-7dec (D.Byas 105*), Glamorgan 104 (C.E.W.Silverwood 5-20) & 125 (G.M.Hamilton 5-27). *Won by 328 runs*

Skipper Byas's decision not to enforce the follow-on caused much concern in some quarters in view of the very unsettled weather throughout the country. However, his policy of batting the Welshmen out of the game allied to Yorkshire's efficient battery of pace bowlers made sure that there was no escape. Byas scored his first century for three years and shared a fourth wicket stand of 120 with Fellows (61). Earlier on Yorkshire reject Alex Wharf completed career-best figures despite Lehmann's 75. The White Rose county's fourth-largest victory by a runs margin opened up a 15-point gap over second-placed Kent, their next opponents.

**Headingley**, June 6, 7, 8, 9: Kent 212 & 250 (S.P.Kirby 7-50), Yorkshire 413 & 53-1. *Won by nine wickets*

Leicestershire discard but Lancashire-born Kirby destroyed Kent with the best bowling performance by a Yorkshire debutant since Wilfred Rhodes's 7-24 in 1898. The fairy-tale scene developed when Hoggard, after taking four for 48 in Kent's first innings, was withdrawn from the match to join the England one-day squad as replacement for Caddick. Kent, 92-1 at lunch on day one, put doubt on the wisdom of Byas's insertion on winning the toss but the last nine wickets fell for 116. Yorkshire's reply began with a 152-run partnership between Scott Richardson (69) and Wood (90), the latter making the same score as Lehmann. Wicket-keeper Richard Blakey (59) held the lower-order together in making his best score since 1999. The relatively-unknown Kirby was unleashed on the third day and immediately created an impression of aggression, hostility and a career that would be full of incident. His first spell ended with him showing figures of 8-3-12-2 and, when Kent looked as though they would bat out for a draw on the final day, he returned to take the last five wickets for nine runs in 29 balls as the visitors collapsed from the apparent security of 237-5. Yorkshire's maximum 20 points gave them a 24-point lead over Surrey.

**Bath**, June 13, 14, 15, 16: Somerset 553-5dec (M.Burns 221), Yorkshire 589-5 (D.S.Lehmann 187*, M.J.Wood 124). *Match drawn*

Byas won the toss and could only watch as Somerset amassed 371-2 on the first day. Michael Burns shared in three century stands as he put together his career-best score in an innings lasting just over 13 hours. Somerset scored almost at will but Richardson and Wood responded with a second century opening stand (179) in consecutive matches and by the end of the third day the follow-on had been averted with only four wickets down. Lehmann's century was the 50th of his career and he shared in stands of 149 for the fourth wicket with Fellows (63, equalling his career-best) and 159, undefeated, for the fifth wicket with the rejuvenated Blakey (78 not out). Despite the result and Yorkshire gaining only one point over the first two days, the lead over Surrey was now extended to 27 points.

**Headingley**, June 29, 30, July 1: Yorkshire 500 (M.J.Lumb 122, D.S.Lehmann 104, M.J.Wood 102, D.E.Malcolm 5-123), Leicestershire 174 (S.P.Kirby 6-46) & 99 (S.P.Kirby 6-26). *Won by an innings and 227 runs*

Michael Lumb, in only his third championship match, scored his maiden century and shared a second-wicket stand of 227 with Wood. Lumb, whose father Richard was Boycott's most illustrious county partner, played an innings of class and it was also predictable that Lehmann would not miss out on one of the best pitches seen at Yorkshire's headquarters for years. Yorkshire passed 500 for the second time in consecutive innings – a feat last achieved in 1937. Unfortunately, Leicestershire could not take advantage of the conditions and their batting was a sorry spectacle especially on the third morning when the whole of their innings was completed before lunch, leaving Yorkshire winners with five sessions to spare. Kirby's match figures were the best for Yorkshire at Headingley since 1949 as his former county was swept aside. Yorkshire again gained maximum points and now had a 28-point lead over Lancashire, who had won four matches to Yorkshire's five. Surrey were in third place and so, at the half-way stage, the top three were the same counties as at the end of the 2000 campaign. The four games against these nearest rivals were expected to be the crucial ones in the second half of the season if Yorkshire were to maintain their challenge.

**Northampton**, July 4, 5, 6, 7: Northamptonshire 253 & 298 (M.E.Hussey 122), Yorkshire 309 (D.Byas 110*) & 10-1. *Match drawn*

Yorkshire went into this match with two novice off-spinners – Richard Dawson in his second game and Andy Gray in his first. The pair took five wickets between them on a turning track and showed some promise although they were tested when Graeme Swann (55) and Michael Hussey led a second innings recovery from 91-5. However the rain on the final day, the start of which co-incided with the beginning of Yorkshire's second innings, prevented a result. Yorkshire had required 243 for victory and the game was nicely poised. The lead was now 33 points and it was Somerset who were in second place.

**Headingley**, July 27, 28, 29, 30: Lancashire 373 & 314 (J.P.Crawley 113), Yorkshire 531 (D.S.Lehmann 252, G.Chapple 5-83) & 158-3. *Won by seven wickets*

A magnificent match played on an excellent pitch in glorious sunshine enthralled those lucky enough to witness it. The visitors, with Warren Hegg (76) and John Crawley (73) contributing most, were in a strong position on 348-6 as home spectators feared Yorkshire's usual late-season demise. Gough, in only his second championship game of the season, came back with three wickets in four balls, however, and the Red Rose county were soon dismissed on the second morning. Yorkshire's reply did not look promising at 45-2 but Lehmann and Wood (86) then put on 169 together before the former continued his brilliant and total domination of all that Lancashire could produce. He scored 112 runs between tea and the close on the second day, his second century taking just 86 balls, and the highest individual innings in the entire history of Roses matches was scored from a mere 288 balls and took just over six hours. No one else had quite the same disregard for the bowling, a stand of 86 with Blakey, for instance, saw the latter score a mere 18 runs. Gough took over and produced a scintillating cameo of 96 off only 101 balls, and found a valuable partner in Kirby to produce a last wicket stand of 83. Gough's most recent half-century had been 68 first-class innings previously. Kirby soon exultantly claimed Michael Atherton's wicket for the second time in the match and Lancashire were still in arrears with five wickets down. Crawley held things together with another beautiful innings but wickets fell at regular intervals and Yorkshire's eventual victory target was a formality on such a good pitch. Wood (51) again batted well and Lehmmann's 48 meant that he had scored exactly 300 runs in the match. Another 20 points gave Yorkshire a 14-point lead over Somerset, who had now played a game more than the leaders.

**Headingley**, August 1, 2, 3, 4: Surrey 278 & 281 (R.K.J.Dawson 6-98), Yorkshire 204 & 244-2 (D.S.Lehmann 106*). *Match drawn*

This was another vital game and Yorkshire, in fighting their way out of a tricky situation, showed considerable character. The visitors were pinned back to 152-7 on Yorkshire Day but a rescue act by Ian Salisbury (54) led them to respectability. Yorkshire's disappointing response centred around Lehmann's 52 and Surrey ended the second day 243 ahead with only four second innings wickets down. Yorkshire thus had an uphill task and although 64 overs were lost to rain on the last two days Surrey still had 68 overs in which to take the last remaining eight wickets. That they could not do so was entirely due to the skill and fighting qualities of Lehmann and Wood (85*) who shared an unbroken stand of 190. This not only thwarted the reigning champions but also made the crowd wonder if a target of 356 might not have been too many after all. Earlier Dawson had taken the first five-wicket haul of his career as Ben Hollioake (68) provided most resistance to his flight and variety of pace. Yorkshire's lead over Somerset was now only 13 points although there was still a game in hand. Lancashire (5th) and Surrey (6th) were looking increasingly out of the picture.

**Old Trafford**, August 7, 8, 9, 10: Yorkshire 467-9dec (C.White 186, M.J.Wood 115), Lancashire 242 & 188. *Won by an innings and 37 runs*

After a blank first day Craig White and Wood wasted no time in posting a 309-run opening stand. Crawley won the toss and paid for his mistake as White, in particular, tore the Lancashire attack to shreds to post the highest score of his career. His first century since 1998 came from only 94 balls and the stand was the second-highest for the first wicket in all Roses matches, being beaten only by Holmes and Sutcliffe at Sheffield 70 years previously. 358-2 was the overnight total, so rapidly did Yorkshire score, and on day three they got stuck into the Lancashire batting with similar relish. A real team-effort saw no bowler take more than three wickets and after the follow-on had been enforced the home side had already lost the vital wicket of Crawley by the time the stumps were pulled up. The Red Rose wilted even more pathetically on the final day as, on a blameless pitch, Dawson (4-29) and Hamilton (3-33) tempted their opponents into strokes of ineptness and sheer unwillingness to fight. At lunch and 172-5 Lancashire had reason for some optimism but the loss of the remaining wickets for only 16 runs immediately afterwards handed Yorkshire their first Roses Championship double since 1978.

This was the victory, and another maximum 20 points, that really established Yorkshire very firmly as hot favourites for the Championship. The poor weather that had reduced the Lancashire game to a three-day match had affected Yorkshire's rivals even more and the lead over Somerset was now 24 points. More relevantly, Yorkshire now needed a maximum total of only 36 points from their final four fixtures to secure the title.

**Leicester**, August 15, 16, 17, 18: Yorkshire 230 & 429-8dec (D.S.Lehmann 193, D.Byas 100, J.Ormond 5-146), Leicestershire 121 & 370 (V.J.Wells 133). *Won by 168 runs*

Although Yorkshire's first innings looked a meagre total it was soon put into perspective by another team effort to dismiss the home side for a much lower score. On the first day Vaughan, in his first Championship innings for almost three months, was back to his elegant best and the visitors had much to be thankful for in his innings of 82. When Yorkshire batted for a second time Lehmann made up for his first innings duck (his first-ever for his adopted county) as only he could. He shared a stand of 138 with Vaughan for the second wicket and enabled Yorkshire to be 376 ahead by the end of the second day, such was the speed of his scoring. Byas, with poor weather about, surprisingly delayed his declaration on the third day until after lunch, setting Leicestershire a target of 539 – one never achieved in county cricket. It enabled him to take his fourth-wicket stand with Lehmann to 186 and for him to complete his own century. With the home side on 132-7 a three-day win looked highly probable but Phil DeFreitas (97) dug in with Vince Wells not only to make the extra half-hour fruitless but also delay victory until well into the final morning. The last three wickets had added 238, the turning point occurring when Kirby took an outstanding boundary catch to remove DeFreitas. Although the wickets were shared amongst five bowlers, White had the best figures in each innings (3-11 and 3-28). Kent had overtaken Somerset but Yorkshire's lead was 33 points.

**Scarborough**, August 21, 22, 23, 24: Glamorgan 223 (R.K.J.Dawson 6-82) & 245, Yorkshire 580-9dec (C.White 183, M.J.Wood 124, D.Byas 104). *Won by an innings and 112 runs*

At 12.13 on the final day of this match Glamorgan's Simon Jones top-edged a ball from Lehmann high into the grey sky, Byas ran round from slip to backward point, held the ball safely as it eventually came down and was immediately surrounded by his ecstatic team-mates. Yorkshire had won the Championship for the first time for 33 years and it then started raining – another example of Byas's knack of timing his declarations to perfection and defeating the weather as well as his opponents. The first day had belonged to Dawson who posted the best figures of his short, but already impressive, career. The pace of his bowling, allied to his turn and bounce, gave the batsmen no chance to adjust if they should mis-judge the length. The second day was dominated by another quality innings from White, again in combination with Wood. Their second-wicket stand was worth 243, a record beaten only once by the county at Scarborough as both players took advantage of wayward bowling. Byas and Blakey (54) took over on the third day, put on 113 for the eighth wicket and turned the screw so tightly on the visitors that Yorkshire's total was their highest-ever against the Welsh county. The visitors began their uphill task with over four sessions remaining and, with wickets falling steadily, ended the day on 142-6. The highlight of the short amount of play on the final morning was a whirlwind innings of 46 from only 14 balls by Jones. Lehmann suffered most as six sixes came from his bowling but it could not last.

**The Oval**, September 5, 6, 7, 8: Yorkshire 235 (A.McGrath 116*) & 235 (Saqlain Mushtaq 7-58), Surrey 516-9dec (M.R.Ramprakash 131, B.C.Hollioake 118). *Lost by an innings and 46 runs*

With the title won Yorkshire rested several first-choice players with niggling injuries and a below-strength side fought well against the previous champions who were threatened with relegation. McGrath played much the best innings of his injury- and form-hit season but received little support except from Wood (51). Surrey's batting, in a line-up that consisted of eleven internationals, took advantage of an attack that consisted of only one capped bowler. Mark Butcher (90) and Ian Ward (63) led the way with 164 for the first wicket but Mark Ramprakash, scoring his customary century against Yorkshire, and Ben Hollioake, with his first-ever century in the Championship, made merry to the tune of a sixth-wicket stand of 215. Gray (4-128) had some success against the middle order but all of the bowlers suffered. Another fine innings by McGrath (73) with support from Vaughan (61) merely served to delay the inevitable on the last day as Saqlain weaved his magic to the tune of the new champions losing their last eight wickets for a mere 40 runs.

**Scarborough**, September 12, 13, 14, 15: Essex 250 (M.J.Hoggard 6-51) & 172-8dec, Yorkshire 104-5dec & 267 (M.P.Vaughan 113, A.P.Grayson 5-20). *Lost by 51 runs*

With little play possible on the first day and none on day two the half-way stage of the game had Essex on 99-3. However, Hoggard, in approaching his best form since returning from injury, demolished the rest of the visitors' batting and Yorkshire declared against the already-relegated southerners as soon as the follow-on had been avoided. Essex responded in kind and set up a thrilling finale to the season. With Vaughan and McGrath sharing a third-wicket stand of 204 a home victory looked to be on the cards. However Paul Grayson, bowling against his former county, put in a career-best performance in only ten overs and Yorkshire lost their last eight wickets for only 63 runs. The crowd had value for money but it was a disappointing conclusion to such a wonderful season.

## NOTES and HIGHLIGHTS

The final piece in the jig-saw that changed Yorkshire from being a nearly-side into champions was an Australian relatively unknown outside his own country. Wayne Clark had played for his country with limited success in a few Test matches during the Packer crisis of the late-1970s but a second career in the game, as a coach, had been much more successful. He had guided Western Australia to four trophies in five seasons and it was with this in mind that he was approached and appointed to possibly achieve the same with Yorkshire.

Clark maintained a relatively low profile with the press and the public during the campaign but it soon became obvious that he was working wonders with the players. He deliberately ignored the pressure to win the Championship and encouraged the squad to take each session as it came and turn the success-rate over a two-hour period into a victory. Gradually the victories accumulated and eventually Clark was able to bask in the credit that the players' performances had given him.

Byas was the only player to appear in every game of the campaign and he also played in all 26 of the county's limited-overs matches (a feat equalled by Blakey). Byas announced his retirement after the end of the season. He had led Yorkshire for six seasons and clearly felt that, at the age of 38, he had reached the climactic point of his career. His record for his county stood at over 14,000 runs at an average of more than 35 but most significantly his 351 catches were taken at a better rate per match (1.31) than any other fielder except Tunnicliffe, whose career had ended 94 years previously.

Yorkshire used no less than 25 players during the Championship season and this created a new record for a title-winning year for the White Rose county. The previous record had been set by the 24 players used in 1905.

Of players who made their debuts during the season, the greatest impact was made by Dawson and Kirby. They were the leading bowlers of the campaign, in terms of the number of overs bowled, and both were chosen to participate in England's winter activities. Dawson earned a place on the Test touring party to India and New Zealand while Kirby was selected to join the new Academy squad to train and play in Australia.

## PLAYER of the SEASON

There seems little doubt that Darren Lehmann was most probably at the peak of his powers during the 2001 season. His sheer ability to compile high scores and yet, at the same time, entertain all and sundry made him a highly popular player with team-mates and spectators alike.

Lehmann originated in Gawler, South Australia, in 1970, and first played for his state at the tender age of 17. The 1989/90 season saw him become the youngest player to score 1000 first-class runs in an Australian season. He played for Victoria for three seasons in the early 1990s but returned to his roots later and took over the captaincy of South Australia at the beginning of the 1998/99 season. During the early part of the 2001/02 season he became the highest run-maker of all-time in Australia's inter-state first-class competition - the Pura Milk Cup (formerly the Sheffield Shield).

Despite playing in sixty one-day internationals, including hitting the winning runs in the 1999 World Cup final, and his consistently heavy scoring in the longer form of the game, it is most surprising that he has represented his country in only five Tests. His feat of scoring more first-class runs than any other compatriot before making a Test debut shows how much he was neglected and it is possible that his rejection of a place at the Australian Academy when he was already established in his state side may have counted against him.

Lehmann's first season with Yorkshire was the 1997 campaign. He was a third choice behind Bevan and Michael Slater, both of whom were with the touring Australians but made an immediate impression by scoring over 1500 runs at an average of over 60 and this standard has remained with him since. He has now made over 5000 runs for the county in total at an average – 67.96 - that is at least ten runs higher than any other major player in the Club's history.

Lehmann is able to adapt to different pitches and conditions with incredible ease. He arrives from hot Australia to a cold spring, from hard pitches to soft pitches and yet scores runs as if everything was the same. He apparently bats with abandon, has two or three strokes for every ball and plays the same way whether on 0 or 252! His skilled improvisation entertains the crowds and a lengthy innings by Lehmann will contain strokes, several of them audacious, all round the wicket.

Unsurprisingly, after the resignation of Byas, he was rewarded with the captaincy of the county. This is a role he clearly will relish, at the same time as having one eye on the future. On the few occasions on which he has already deputised for Byas he has impressed with his positive attitude and ability to involve others in important on-the-field discussions. He clearly aims to continue where 2001 left off.

So what of the future? It was quite clear that Yorkshire's Academy was the envy of many counties and would continue to produce cricketers of first-class and international potential on a regular basis. With this in mind, predictions from former players and media experts that Yorkshire would once again win the Championship on a regular basis may not be too wide of the mark. Above all, however, it is to be hoped that the competition produces seasons of keen competitiveness and interest so that whichever county is victorious has had to gain its success by virtue of high-quality cricket.

# About the Author

*Photo courtesy: Tennant Brown, Harrogate*

Paul Dyson originated in Thurnscoe, a mining village in South Yorkshire, and attended Wath Grammar School. For the past thirty years he has lived in North Yorkshire and now lives with his wife in the beautiful town of Knaresborough.

This is his fifth book, following on from:-

*The Counties and Test Cricket 1877-1988*
*The Benson and Hedges Cup Record Book 1972-1995*
*A Century of Headingley Tests 1899-1999*
*100 Greats: Yorkshire CCC* (co-authored with Mick Pope)

He has also written for *The Cricketer* and *Wisden Cricket Monthly* as well as various other magazines and journals, and contributes regularly to *The White Rose*. He is responsible for the one-day records section in the Yorkshire Year Book.

After completing professional studies at Birmingham School of Music and Leeds University he began his teaching career in Harrogate in 1971 and has been Head of Music at Easingwold School since 1976. He has two grown-up children one of whom, Jonathan, has written many player profiles for wisden.com as well as several articles for other sectors of the media.

# BIBLIOGRAPHY

Philip Bailey, Philip Thorn, Peter Wynne-Thomas: *Who's Who of Cricketers*
Robert Brooke:     *The Collins Who's Who of English First-Class Cricket*
                   *A History of the County Cricket Championship*
John Callaghan:    *Yorkshire's Pride*
Derek Hodgson:   *The Official History of Yorkshire CCC*
Bill Frindall:      *England Test Cricketers, The Wisden Book of Cricket Records*
Peter Griffiths (Ed.): *Complete First-Class Match List Vol. 2 1914/15-1944/45*
Mick Pope:        The Archive Photograph Series - Yorkshire CCC
Mick Pope and Paul Dyson: *100 Greats – Yorkshire County Cricket Club*
Barry Rickson:    *Hedley Verity – His Record Innings-by-Innings*
E.L.Roberts:      *Yorkshire's 22 Championships 1893-1946*
Roy Webber:      *The County Cricket Championship*
Roy Wilkinson:   *Yorkshire County Cricket Club First-Class Records*
                   *1863-1996*
Tony Woodhouse: *A Who's Who of Yorkshire County Cricket Club*

Other ACS Publications including Counties Booklets.

Various editions of *Playfair Cricket Annual, Wisden Cricketers' Almanack, Yorkshire CCC Year Book*